The Ar
Scre
19

The Art of American Screen Acting, 1912–1960

DAN CALLAHAN

McFarland & Company, Inc., Publishers
Jefferson, North Carolina

ISBN (print) 978-1-4766-7405-6
ISBN (ebook) 978-1-4766-3252-0

Library of Congress cataloguing data are available

British Library cataloguing data are available

© 2018 Dan Callahan. All rights reserved

No part of this book may be reproduced or transmitted in any form or by any means, electronic or mechanical, including photocopying or recording, or by any information storage and retrieval system, without permission in writing from the publisher.

Front cover: Cary Grant and Katharine Hepburn, 1938; background photograph by Hal Bergman (iStock)

Printed in the United States of America

*McFarland & Company, Inc., Publishers
Box 611, Jefferson, North Carolina 28640
www.mcfarlandpub.com*

For my sister Tracy

Table of Contents

Introduction: "Pre-Brando" and Bernhardt and Duse	1
Lillian Gish: Blossom in the Wind	5
Gloria Swanson: Still Big	21
John Barrymore: Sweet Prince of Irony	29
Louise Brooks: Naked on Her Goat	35
Greta Garbo: Mademoiselle Hamlet	46
Marlene Dietrich: Illusions	58
Bette Davis: The Hard Way	76
Katharine Hepburn: Sadly Happy	93
Joan Crawford: A Woman's Face	112
Ingrid Bergman: You Must Change Your Life	127
James Cagney: Hard to Handle	137
Cary Grant: Just a Butterfly	144
Charles Laughton: Leaning and Birthing	157
Clark Gable: The King	170
Spencer Tracy: Still Waters	176
Humphrey Bogart: The Stuff That Dreams Are Made Of	184
Marlon Brando: Before and After	192
Montgomery Clift: Fallen Aristocrat	199
Kim Stanley: Private Moments	208
James Dean: Cause and Effect	215
Bibliography	223
Index	225

Introduction
"Pre-Brando" and Bernhardt and Duse

In the 50 years or so before Marlon Brando arrived on screen in *The Men* (1950) and *A Streetcar Named Desire* (1951), acting for film went through a variety of both convulsive and subtle changes, none more exciting than the early talkie period of the 1930s when actors like James Cagney, Bette Davis, Cary Grant, and Katharine Hepburn emerged. They didn't want realism. They wanted magic, and they tried to give that to people. They told what ought to be truth. These were the stars of classic Hollywood, the ones with the distinctive voices and manners, the ones who were imitated, dreamed of, and dreamed on.

They still insist on themselves all these years later in whatever way we can see and hear them—in clips from their best work, in whole films that we can rewind or fast forward, in revival houses where they still do what they did to audiences of their time but slightly differently, as part of history rather than as part of a moment. They do travel, these so-called stars of old Hollywood. Look and listen to them for the first time, then look and listen to them for the hundredth time in the same film or films, and they are alive again, in a way, beckoning and complete, precisely because they are somewhat distant. They are not "natural" a lot of the time but more than natural. They are heightened, an ideal of themselves offered up to us (though with the flinty Davis, that ideal could also be turned to an instructive nightmare).

Actors still sometimes speak about some of these old Hollywood players as "pre-Brando" or dismissively refer to them as "*so* pre-Brando." Occasionally there will be an article in a putatively reputable newspaper or magazine in which a writer attempts to encapsulate and dismiss these "pre-Brando" actors on strange and ignorant grounds having to do with perceived phoniness or posturing. These articles fall apart instantly when it becomes clear that the writer is basing this opinion on the viewing of a handful of classics on television or maybe not even full movies but scenes: a bit of Hepburn in *The Philadelphia Story* (1940) or Davis in *The Letter* (1940), taken out of context to show that "nobody talks and moves like that." No, nobody did, though

Hepburn came closest, most likely, to living up to the extremely unusual person she was trying to project.

Contemporary acting teachers have been known to wonder at these old Hollywood creatures, to discreetly put them down, to assert the dominance of Brando and the enshrinement of the Stanislavski Acting Method and all that came after that. Brando himself in the documentary *Listen to Me Marlon* (2015) contemptuously dismisses movie actors of the 1930s and 1940s as "breakfast cereals," obvious in their gestures and always the same. "And that kind of acting became absurd," Brando said. His point of view has become the dominant narrative about acting. It is deeply wrong, and it cannot be allowed to stand.

My hope in this book is to pay close enough attention to the major players from 1912 to 1960 or so to prove that what they were doing is both different from what the Method actors started doing in the 1950s and also similar, sometimes, at its core, and to also show that it is valid in its own quick, vital, often eccentric right. The artifice of some of their work is not a lie but a creation, and the best of these creations shine just as much light on human behavior as did the most doggedly naturalistic of the Method actors. In fact, they shed more light in certain ways. In some cases, the styles of the stars did also change over time (see particularly the way Davis adapted herself to the Method changeover, as detailed in the extensive piece on her to come).

When Jack Lemmon asked Rosalind Russell to define acting for him, she said, "Acting is standing up naked and turning around very slowly"—as solid a definition as any. That's what Greta Garbo did, at her best, and she is the ultimate old Hollywood film star, letting us fill in the blanks. Always there is the lure and the hope that we will see something private, something that Grant, Hepburn, Cagney or Davis didn't necessarily want us to see but is there if you keep looking and looking hard. I hope I have found some of these moments, and I hope they encourage you to do your own search for the times when these players are exposed in all their idiosyncrasy and glory, moving between their public and private selves.

Garbo is slow, as is Lillian Gish in her close-ups, whereas Grant, Hepburn, Cagney, and Davis are fast—as fast as Grant taking a pratfall when Hepburn drops her olive on the floor in *Bringing Up Baby* (1938). The movement of this book follows the slowness of Gish, Garbo and the silent era players, giving way to the speed of Cagney and Davis and then halting for the very different, labored-over slowness of Brando and Kim Stanley and their Method ilk of the 1950s.

The famed French stage star Sarah Bernhardt was one of the first name actors to be filmed. In 1900, she played Hamlet dueling Laertes in a two-minute movie. In 1908, Bernhardt did a 12-minute *Tosca* that so offended her she insisted the film be burned. With no sound and the camera so far away, Bernhardt felt that her work was not being represented accurately. She was happier with *Queen Elizabeth* (1912), a nearly hour-long film for producer Adolph Zukor, but that movie shows a kind of showboating, rag-doll woman constantly throwing her arms about for no reason. It's all arms, this performance. It does not add to Bernhardt's legend but diminishes it. Her powdered face and black currant eyes make no impact. "Monsieur, you have put me in pickle forever!" Bernhardt supposedly told Zukor, but that is not quite the case, unfortunately.

By comparison, Bernhardt's closest rival, the Italian actress Eleonora Duse, made one film in 1916 called *Cenere* (*Ashes*), a tale of mother love. She was unhappy with it, lamenting that movies needed a whole new approach she didn't have time to learn, but her work in *Cenere* is still outstanding, everything it was supposed to have been on stage: liquid, soulful, slow, and penetrating.

For the first 10 minutes of *Cenere*, Duse acts with her head fully covered, making fluid gestures to express her deep love for her son. When she is finally unveiled, we see an old woman with white hair (she was only 58 at the time). Febo Mari, the actor playing her son, makes fussy gestures with his hands, and his poor playing only throws the high quality of Duse's work into relief. She can express more with the back of her head for a moment here in silence and black and white than most actresses can from the front for two hours with color and sound. Her concentration is transfixing, and that's what all fine acting is based on—concentration. But Duse felt that an even deeper kind of concentration was needed for the camera. It would have to do, for a time, without voice and without words. This new concentration would be pioneered by Lillian Gish.

Lillian Gish
Blossom in the Wind

"I was never young, and if you were never young, how can you ever feel old?" Lillian Gish was fond of saying. She was ageless, timeless, above all that. So many of her emotions on screen were expressed through nothing but her large blue eyes in intimate close-up, and this made for a decisive break with theater acting, where no audience could possibly see so close.

When director Lindsay Anderson complimented a close-up Gish had done for him for *The Whales of August* (1987), her co-star Bette Davis snapped, "Of course! She *invented* close-ups!" Like Davis, Gish never cared about looking good on screen. If it was appropriate to the part and to what was being felt, she would make herself look grotesque, fevered, overcome, possessed. Emotions are like gales that sweep through her, leaving damage and destruction in their wake.

Though she acted with her whole body, and very poetically, too, Gish was the first actor to take advantage of what a close-up could see. In her big scenes, Gish can get so deeply involved in what she's doing that sometimes she seems to surprise and frighten herself. And us. There is a danger to the way she immerses herself in emotions. She might not come out the other end of them unscathed, and there is that same risk for us in observing and feeling them with her. Her gift is in summoning emotional extremes that might be untidy, difficult to control, and finding a container for them that keeps a powerful hold over them. The joy, the enrichment, of watching Gish do this comes from the triumph of her art over the artless chaos of human feelings.

Her work was based on her concentration. Here's how she described building this concentration, her own Zen acting Method, in her 1969 autobiography, *The Movies, Mr. Griffith, and Me:*

> At the start of my career, when we were on location or even on the set, I was often painfully self-conscious, particularly in love scenes. I found it impossible to shut out completely the presence of outsiders. So I devised a method of improving my concentration. I would put a salt cellar on the mantel, stare at it, and then, shutting my eyes, call up a picture of it in my mind. If other thoughts intruded, I blocked them out. At

first, a minute seemed a long time to hold only that image in my mind, but gradually I increased it to two minutes and longer. Eventually, I could blot out the noise around me.

It was a mystic sort of thing, what Gish was trying to do, and this also ties her to the example of Eleonora Duse, whose work was based on nearly supernatural focus and intuition.

Gish was the first actor who intuited what the camera needs. At her best, her feelings pour out of her and assume the most unusually expressive shapes when she acts in long shot with her full body, and all of these shapes are illuminated by her urge to communicate. She saw acting as a high calling, divorced from her own needs or emotions, yet in her preparation and hardcore willingness to do what it takes to get results she sometimes prefigures the mid-century Method actors to come.

Gish deals in pure emotion and you never feel her formidable technique because her pure emotion is so radiant that it seems to burn her technique away from our view. That's what the highest acting talent is, maybe. Her standards are those of the late nineteenth century, and some of her movements can seem outdated, like something left over from the Delsarte method, a stage proscription for indicating various emotions that was widely taught in the America of her day, but her very finest work inaugurates screen acting for the twentieth century: rapt, instinctive, exhibitionistic yet sheltered, both open and closed-up, sealed off just enough so that the best of her feelings can never spoil or fade. There was a self-satisfied quality that marked so much of her work, wise and all seeing, or so it would seem. In a film career that spanned 75 years, Gish was a girl of 19 who seemed like she was 90 and at 90 she seemed like a girl of 19. Lillian Gish was eternal—then, now, and forever.

Her childhood was filled with cold, hunger, and material deprivation. Her mother put Lillian and her sister Dorothy on the road as child actresses, but the family was never able to make ends meet for long. Gish thought of becoming a nun, and she is in many ways a religious artist, always in a dialogue with God. When she and Dorothy went over to the Biograph studios in New York to see their friend Mary Pickford, another child actress who was working for D. W. Griffith, Lillian fell into the world of filmmaking.

Griffith was the love of her life and she was the love of his life. Whether their relationship was ever sexual is open to debate, but I'd guess no. They consummated their love in work, and in an uncomfortable sadomasochistic push and pull on film that left Griffith drained and Gish stronger than ever. They created a Victorian *Story of O* based on emotional and physical suffering as a replacement for Griffith's sublimated sexual desire for the holier-than-thou Miss Lillian.

In her first film, *The Unseen Enemy* (1912), Gish seems relaxed, secret, and sly, with listlessly sad eyes and formidably lyrical arms and hands with marvelously expressive fingers. She suffers her first Griffith ordeal in that movie, locked in a room with her sister as a gun is waved at them through a hole in a door. The next year, in *The Mothering Heart* (1913), Gish gave her first major performance. As a frumpy wife in a floppy hat, she seems much older than the 20 she was at the time; her face is almost elderly in spirit. Walter Miller, who plays her husband, uses his hands like a theater actor of the period, making clear points, sawing at the air. By contrast, all of the things Gish feels run directly out to her hands, which make fluid dance-like patterns for the camera.

In her first scene in *The Mothering Heart*, Gish throws her arms up in sheer happiness, as if she is so filled with joy that she has to fling some of the surplus out to us (it radiates out of her eyes, too). Her character is a homebody, out of place when her husband takes her to a nightclub. When she discovers he has been unfaithful to her, Gish gets woozy, as if she's swimming in her own emotions, and she even lets out two desperate little laughs, an unconventional thing to do in such a moment.

Then her baby dies. Her eyes go blank, which is especially upsetting since they have been so filled with quicksilver life. A doctor puts a hand on her shoulder, and she tugs it away gently but firmly. Breathing heavily, she walks out into her garden like a zombie. Suddenly, all at once, she grabs an axe and starts hacking apart her rose bushes. In extreme long shot, her explosion seems slightly overdone, but perhaps Gish was overcompensating because she knew how far away the camera was. She was learning what worked and what didn't on film, and her audience learned along with her.

In *The Musketeers of Pig Alley* (1912), she's a tough, haughty street kid, bending her fingers into claws. In other Griffith shorts of the period, she's little more than an extra, but in *The Battle of Elderbush Gulch* (1913), Gish has her first chance to go all-out crazy when her baby goes missing. Her hands play in the air, she cradles an imaginary infant, she bugs her eyes, and it's all too much too fast. Her emotions clearly come from a pure source, but their expression is too insistent and hokey in *The Battle of Elderbush Gulch*.

Gish then maneuvered herself into the female lead for Griffith's epic *The Birth of a Nation* (1915), both a landmark in the history of the film medium and a story of the Civil War predicated on unexamined, remorseless racism and an odious falsification of history. Gish only disgraces herself in this regard in one scene; when "mulatto" Silas Lynch (George Siegmann) appears from behind her, she reacts as if she's just smelled something bad and flinches at shaking his hand. As a whole, Gish's performance in *Birth* is filled with a coy sexuality and an unattractive calculation that Griffith might not have noticed. Her shyness and frailty seem like an elaborate put-on, and she's very campy when petting a portentous white pussycat.

But Gish has one outstanding scene in *Birth* where she sees her brothers off to war. She keeps herself furiously busy, checking to see that they have this and that, putting a brave face on her emotions, pretending she has a gun, as if she's saying, "You shoot 'em, and come on home!" When her brothers are gone, she immediately puts her hand to her mouth in despair and runs off, throwing herself on a woman's lap to be comforted. It's the *speed* with which Gish drops her bravado here that makes the scene touching. In the film's particularly objectionable second half, she spends a great deal of time bugging her eyes and throwing her arms around as Silas threatens her interminably with a "forced marriage." You can divorce what Gish is doing here from its context (her flailing arms are used for dancer-like effects), but it takes a lot of work.

After rocking the cradle for interludes between the stories in Griffith's epic *Intolerance* (1916), Gish took the lead in his World War I propaganda film, *Hearts of the World* (1918), where the rapacious blacks in *Birth* are replaced by rapacious Germans. In *Hearts*, Gish starts out as a fresh ingénue with her hair in curls who plants a half dozen little kisses on her mother's face. Griffith always wanted his virgins to express their sexual energy with little squirrel-like jumps, and Gish got so tired of doing this that she actually complained to Griffith, but when he said he wanted her to contrast with the older and slower actors she accepted his explanation. He films her so that she's prettier and dewier here and given the full star treatment.

When her father dies during a German attack in *Hearts,* Gish screams up to heaven and then suddenly gets calm, and then she shifts her eyes around. These are bold choices, but the transitions between such extremes come slightly too fast here (she might have gotten away with them if she had just smoothed them out a bit and made them less staccato). When she goes to sit outside and her mind starts to unravel, however, her slow sense of exhaustion is very simply expressed and moving.

She drags her wedding dress through the ravaged town like a wasted Mary Tyrone and comes upon a corpse that she thinks is her fiancé, approaching him gently and then placing her head slowly on his chest. This is an extremely touching scene for Gish, and Griffith's decision to keep this moment in long shot kills any possible corniness, giving her a proper privacy for her grief. For the rest of the film, though, we watch hulking Germans threaten Gish's virginity and whip her mercilessly, Griffith's sadism coming to the fore. Gish's mother was horrified when she found welts on her daughter's back from these scenes, but Gish was willing to give anything for a performance, and Griffith took advantage of that.

And he was not happy that she was getting so much attention. "That should be my picture, not yours," he told Gish, when he saw an advertisement with a large photo of Gish for their lost film *The Greatest Thing in Life* (1918). At first she thought Griffith was joking, but when she looked at his face, he wasn't smiling. He was very serious.

Film directors from Griffith onward would feel neglected in relation to their actors, especially when they had a longtime collaboration with one star. So few audiences even now bother to suss out the finer points of such artistic alliances, but it is no mistake that a performer is almost always best, or best remembered, in films by directors who loved them, understood them, brought them out, and then settled back, disgruntled or quietly proud, as the performer was showered with nearly all the accolades.

"Ever since the beginning of films, writers and directors have been jealous of the actor's glory, trying to find some way of wiping them off the screen with words," wrote silent screen icon Louise Brooks, a woman who was well aware that one well-chosen close-up can cancel out the most airtight aesthetic argument in favor of the director, the auteur. Yet the director is often so key to a performer's success, in ways that we can often only guess at.

Griffith next made two smaller, gentler films with Gish. As "Forgetful Jenny" in *A Romance of Happy Valley* (1919), Gish stares into the camera with homely longing, trying to keep Bobby Harron from leaving their Kentucky home and seeming like the clinging, oddball girl you *shouldn't* stay home for. Gish refined this character in *True Heart Susie* (1919), a rural romance. As Susie, a plain girl in love with a country boy named William (Bobby Harron), Gish holds herself proudly, primly, stealing furtive glances at her beloved during a spelling bee. Ideally, an actor needs to be believable as either plain or beautiful, and Gish could transform herself for either fate.

For once, a Gish character actually wants a kiss, but Harron's William won't give it, and so she walks with him down a road after school, loping along faithfully, ploddingly, expectantly, in a way that is nearly comic but not quite, for Gish shies away from the laughs her sister Dorothy liked to get on screen and in life. To give William a college education, Gish's Susie sells her family's cow, all without his knowledge. He sends her a letter from school, and Gish slowly and intensely kisses the paper, but then she plants a bunch of frenetic "girlish" kisses on it. I would guess that the slow first kiss came from Gish and the fast girly kisses, a big mistake, were Griffith's idea, and this is a key to understanding how different they were from each other as artists. Griffith favors the obvious. Gish always wants to go deeper.

William returns and tells Susie that men usually marry plain and simple girls, and Gish briefly touches her face and gives it a little stroke, a very touching, subtle detail, but the bare ankle of bad girl Bettina (Clarine Seymour) changes William's mind. When Susie sees them together, Gish takes a moment to compose herself outside a door, going deep down into the mess of emotions Susie is feeling in that slow, unsparing, scary, precise way that she expressed herself in close-up.

Her distress after William and Bettina announce their engagement is painful and acutely real and just discernible in her eyes, very much a young girl's bottomless despair, but Susie holds herself together in a kind of semi-smiling mask for everyone around her. Gish knew that giving in to grief on screen would not win her the sympathy of her audience. It is in the fighting against her own feelings and bravely putting on a front for others that she wins our hearts and our respect for Susie.

After staying out too long at a party, the now-married Bettina goes to Susie and asks to stay over so that her husband won't be suspicious. At first, Gish's Susie tries to blink her rival away (again, this is almost a comic choice but not quite). After giving in and letting Bettina stay, Susie gives her sleeping rival some hateful looks and makes a fist as if she wants to punch her, but her feelings soften during the night, and Susie eventually embraces her. This touching image sweetly expresses the high Christian charity of loving your enemy, a deep urge in Gish on screen. *True Heart Susie* is one of the few Gish vehicles with no scene of hysteria and no scene where she is physically battered, a little oasis that displays her at the height of her skill and her empathy.

If *Susie* is too little known, *Broken Blossoms* (1919) is as famous as *Birth*, but this small-scale chamber piece is sado-masochistic in a way that can feel nearly gaudy now, uneasily virtuosic. Griffith imagines Gish here as Lucy, a little girl constantly beaten by her boxer father, Battling Burrows (Donald Crisp). *Broken Blossoms* is filled with

The clear and penetrating eyes of Lillian Gish could express any emotion.

memorable Gish inventions, like Lucy's pitiful attempt at a smile where she pushes the ends of her mouth up with her fingers and her frantic whirling around and around in a closet as her father tries to break in and get at her, both of which she thought up herself as Griffith stood back in awe. For Gish, this is a part that calls for many different ways of cowering in wide-eyed terror, and she does find substantial variety in this limited mode, reaching for effects that push her imaginative talent to its very outer limits. Her Lucy is not numb to violence. Every time she is threatened, her fear is childishly fresh.

When Richard Barthelmess's adoring Chinese shopkeeper takes her in, Gish's Lucy looks at her benefactor with naked love and relief, and it is clearly her *character* who is naked here, not Gish herself—an important distinction. Lucy seems very servile in a nearly smug, lower class English kind of way. There seems to be no point where this little English girl resembles Gish in any of her other films, or interviews. She is a creation for the camera, imagined with consummate skill.

Gish makes the scene in the closet where Lucy whirls in place a sort of universal plea for all abused children, so that from an acting standpoint it is similar in its size to the outrage over suffering children in the Grand Inquisitor section of Dostoyevsky's *The Brothers Karamazov*. In her exceptional death scene, she does one more fake smile for the road and then her eyes roll up into her head, and she really does seem to die. Gish had a freakishly realistic gift for playing death, for leaving her body and letting us look at a seemingly empty envelope.

More suffering was ahead. As Little Miss Yes'm in *The Greatest Question* (1919), Gish is an open-mouthed, dim victim who covers her doll's eyes before she undresses. Her purity incites the base lust of a hulking older man and she gets whipped by his evil sister, but not before pleading with her to have mercy, ad nauseam.

In *Way Down East* (1920), a lengthy melodrama, Gish has two big moments: the death of her illegitimate baby and the famous long sequence where she is stranded on an ice floe. The first scene is classic exploratory Gish, moving from despair mixed with a daring bit of anger at God (her eyes up, her hand cupped in an extended "why?" claw) to a totally emptied-out face, as if she too has died, and then ending on a silent scream, her mouth wide open in an uncanny, almost singer-like fashion that suggests that it might stay that way forever.

The ice sequence displays Gish's extreme masochistic devotion to her art, and to Griffith. To put it in crude S&M terms, she was topping from the bottom and intimidating the supposedly dominant Griffith with her recklessly inventive submission. She decided to trail her arm in the icy water and suffered physical consequences for that later (whenever she was out in the cold as an older woman, that arm would ache). When icicles formed on her eyelashes and snow covered her face, Griffith went in for a close-up, and this shot of her snow-encrusted face emphasizes that beguiling mix of old woman and little girl in Gish. She was very disappointed in Griffith when he insisted she get made up and pretty for the scene after the rescue in the storm. Gish wanted always to be realistic, but Griffith felt the audience needed to see that she was not only all right after her ordeal but looking lovely, too.

Her last film with Griffith, *Orphans of the Storm* (1921), throws Gish and her sister Dorothy into the maelstrom of the French Revolution. She runs a gamut of emotion as she gets separated from Dorothy's Louise, who is blind and dependent on her, and at this late date Gish is still playing the genteel tease with her suitors and coyly denying kisses. Griffith delights in bringing her sleeping virgin body into a French orgy so that she has her usual rough time and delays her sexual ravishment over and over again with all the force she possesses. When Gish has an important close-up here, Griffith blacks out all background of the room she's in just so that we can focus more intensively on what she's doing, which he had started to do in *Way Down East*. She might look frail, but the size of her will is so large that it admits no physical boundaries, and this is a key part of the excitement of Gish, the contrast between her soft looks and her iron constitution.

In the famous scene where she thinks she hears her kidnapped sister outside a window, Gish's intensity is Wagnerian in its size and duration, and she's able to build this sequence up as high as it can possibly go, using her whole body and practically flinging herself off a balcony to scream to her sister; she finds the exact physical correlative for the emotional response and goes wonderfully, even cathartically all-out with it. Surely she uses her own real feeling for her sister in this movie, especially in close-ups where she looks at Dorothy with tender love, but such borrowings from her own life are appropriate to the part.

About to be guillotined in the fraught climax, where Griffith does his patented cross cutting between the imperiled Gish and her galloping rescuers to create suspense, she screams to heaven for help, and she is saved in the nick of time, of course. Gish's performances saved Griffith's films again and again, and her unquestioned integrity still shines reflected glory on his work.

Gish took full control of her next two movies. In her first production, *The White Sister* (1923), fetching location shots of Italy bolster her performance as Angela, a girl cheated out of her inheritance. Angela is viewed in a title card as "an unattainable ideal—a woman too holy for mere man to possess," and that's most likely the way Gish viewed herself. Colleen Moore remembered at Gish's American Film Institute Life Achievement Award ceremony in 1984 that all of her directors and co-stars fell in love with her and wanted to marry her. Why? Because "she is unobtainable," MGM producer Irving Thalberg told Moore.

Gish's depiction of love for fiancé Ronald Colman in *The White Sister* is surpassingly delicate. She looks like she might faint in his mere presence, but it is clear that she has the will to cling to him forever. She kisses him gently as if she's kissing a cross, for her love is not worldly or bodily, and in one of Gish's most lyrical moments she kisses her hand and gently presses this kiss on Colman's bent head. She seems free and unfettered here, erring only when she goes way over the top on hearing of Colman's supposed death: bulging her eyes, covering her ears, whirling around, and finally falling into glazed catatonia.

Her next film, *Romola* (1924), is a handsome but inert version of George Eliot's novel in which Gish falls back on mannerisms from her earlier work. She often hung a mirror by the camera so that she could check what she was doing, as if she were a dancer working at a barre, fully conscious of what she wanted to express and shape.

Signing with Metro-Goldwyn-Mayer studios proved to be a fruitful decision at first, and she made her three finest films for them: *La Bohème* (1926), *The Scarlet Letter* (1926), and *The Wind* (1928). Each movie upped the ante for Gish's artistry, and she had artistic control over all of them. She knew enough to pick talented collaborators, and on *La Bohème* she chose King Vidor as her director and John Gilbert as her leading man because she had been impressed with their work on *The Big Parade* (1925).

Gish's beauty is at its most translucent in *La Bohème*. When she goes to a pawnshop, Gish's Mimi is proud and fastidious as she says goodbye to treasured belongings in order to survive, a girl out of her time. After Gilbert and his Bohemian friends help her out with food, Vidor lingers on her grateful/embarrassed reaction to their kindness as she weighs each of her feelings, jumping from one to the other as if they're hot potatoes, and then finally settling them by drinking a glass of wine.

Gish seems to enjoy dealing with overzealous Gilbert's romantic attentions and still plays the Griffith tease, but Vidor has the healthy emotional sophistication to meet her halfway and create with her and match her vitality, so that their *La Bohème* is glowing with purpose. The distinctly Vidor-ian scene where Gish's ill Mimi allows herself to be dragged home through the streets works so vividly because it is the exact opposite of Gish's ordeal on the ice in *Way Down East*, an active clinging to life rather than a passive buffeting by fate and nature.

Gish's death scene in *La Bohème* is like something out of a horror movie, a real face of death. To prepare herself, Gish supposedly went without food and dried her mouth out with cotton pads. This exemplifies the dedication to realism of Method acting years before the Actors Studio, a masochistic or religious denial that Bette Davis or Katharine Hepburn would never have submitted to just to make a performance more convincing. Her eyes are black and sunken, and life struggles to come to the surface of her face but keeps getting yanked back down to oblivion. This scene is just as impressive as her death in *Broken Blossoms*, but in a much cleaner movie, a love story that Vidor treats with focused intensity and sincerity.

It was Swedish director Victor Sjöström, however, who helped Gish attain the pinnacle of her art as an actress. In *The Scarlet Letter*, a diminishment of Nathaniel Hawthorne's novel that has merits of its own, Gish's mock-shy Griffith teasing has been supplanted by a full-blooded, two-faced sexuality. Her Hester Prynne has more than a touch of the coquette about her, and to highlight this, Sjöström focuses on one of Gish's best props, her long, luxurious, waist-length hair. When she looks for her pet bird and her hair tumbles down, it's a visual marker of Hester's lust for life, something that will not be tolerated in her Puritan village.

Gish's Hester is locked up in the stocks as punishment for her light-hearted behavior on the Sabbath, and the Reverend Dimmesdale (Lars Hanson) gives her water and touches her arms. She looks up at him with sad eyes, and it's obvious that he is dangerously aroused by her. This scene is pure S&M, but it's erotic S&M, not the pure abuse porn of Griffith.

When Dimmesdale forces her to show him her underwear, she has no shame when she says, "It would be pleasant, sir, to walk beside thee and hear thee condemn me for my sins." A married woman, she gets pregnant with Dimmesdale's child and is branded with the scarlet A. Gish's pride and control is at its zenith in the scene where Hester is condemned. She says so much with just her eyes as the townspeople pass judgment on her.

Gish's mastery reaches new levels here. When Dimmesdale asks Hester with his eyes to confess that he is her fellow sinner, she dares to sustain this sequence with almost no movement of her facial muscles through 11 reaction shots. This is far beyond the semi-smiling through grief she did in *True Heart Susie* and closer to the Zen control she was always striving for, which is so akin to the spirit of Victorian repression. In despair when Hester's husband (Henry B. Walthall) comes home, Gish expresses this emotion by blocking out parts of her face with her hands, denying us access to her main creative and interpretative tool because she knows that this denial suggests the depths of Hester's panic, as if she would like to disappear.

In the end, as she cradles a dead Dimmesdale, Gish's Hester looks up at God with anger, defiance, and sorrow. When she looked up at God for Griffith, it was a cry for help, a plea, complete supplication. For Sjöström, Gish looks up with formidable intellect, emotion, and scorn. She stares up there as if she wants answers. Griffith had dubious answers. Gish, now a liberated artist, has mature and searching questions.

Sjöström and sex held sway for her best film, *The Wind*, an audacious, intuitive investigation of Gish's narcissism, female sex fantasies, and the brute power of Mother Nature as expressed, and reflected, by checked and unchecked male libidos. In the first scene on a train, as she travels through prairie country, Gish's frail, knowing Letty smiles when she notices she has the carnal attention of Wirt Roddy (Montagu Love), and she is instantly hit by sand from her open window. Later, at a barn dance, she looks at herself in a proffered mirror and obviously likes what she sees, and this bit of confirmed vanity is immediately followed by a cyclone.

The Wind prefigures Hitchcock's *The Birds* (1963) in its depiction of a pampered woman who is gradually undone by forces larger than herself, with the constantly howling wind serving as a metaphor for Letty's repressed sexuality. When a jealous wife calls her "Miss Sly Boots," we understand just what she means. Sjöström sees and makes use of the nearly smarmy calculatedness in Gish when it comes to sex in a way that Griffith never could. He calls her on her hypocritical Griffith sexuality and strips her bare of it. To her credit, Gish is more than ready for this revelation of her inner nature.

Forced into a marriage with shy, handsome Lige (Lars Hanson), Gish's Letty reacts in horror when he tries to consummate their union. He kisses her roughly and she pushes him away, wiping her mouth, saying she hates him. Sjöström highlights Hanson's good-natured blondness, filming him in tight, high pants that outline his butt. Letty is disturbed by his obvious sexual appeal and she puts off his sexual desire indefinitely. She wants the attention of men, but her real love object is herself, the girl she sees in the mirror. Gish's Letty needs to be desired, even abused, but she is petrified of desiring a man, which would leave her exposed to real pain. All of her power lies in her control of a man's gaze, and as she starts to feel something for her husband, Letty begins to come apart.

When Lige gives shelter to Wirt Roddy, who has ceaselessly tried to seduce her and has become her nemesis, Gish's Letty desperately imagines him looking at her lewdly, even though his hands are covering his face. Unraveling, she says, "I'm not afraid of the wind. I—I like it!" She's *afraid* that she likes it (sex), or will like it. Sjöström builds the tension to a nearly intolerable height, with Gish's fabled virginity waiting like a time bomb to explode into sexual and romantic abandon. Her eyes get huge and blank, her pupils fixed on one distant point. Finally, Wirt Roddy takes her by force, carrying her to bed as if Letty is a prairie Blanche DuBois who has met her Stanley Kowalski, and real rape is felt as a release from Griffith's endlessly smutty threats of rape.

But does the rape actually happen? When Letty shoots Roddy (or *penetrates* him) the next morning and then buries him and freaks out when the sand uncovers his dead face—couldn't this be seen as just a detailed hallucination from a woman who is working through her issues about sex? If so, the happy ending, which Gish lied about being forced to film later on, is not a tacked-on conclusion but a purifying catharsis where she accepts her sexuality and decides to stay with her loyal, sexy husband. It's as if she's killed Griffith's sick male gaze once and for all. The ending to *The Wind* is too abrupt, but it's the climax to Gish's career in silent cinema. No matter how outsized her performances were in this vanished, still undervalued medium, they were always emotionally connected and truthful. When Gish made a gesture, it stayed made.

Gish's sound debut, *One Romantic Night* (1930), definitely hurt her chances in the new medium. Though she's transfixing in some of the film's silent close-ups, when she opens her mouth to speak the Gish mystery evaporates and we're left with a slightly stilted performer, too cautious, too retiring, a little laborious. The girl was gone and the old lady was taking hold of her.

Other factors were also in play. The public was tired of Gish. It felt like she had been around forever, and her material, if not her playing of it, was quite repetitive. In King Vidor's MGM comedy *The Patsy* (1928), Marion Davies does an elaborately accurate parody of Gish's acting style, putting a *Scarlet Letter* cap on her head and then drawing her mouth into a tiny Gish dot, which makes her face look wizened and prim. She mimics Gish's hand gestures, especially her tendency to throw her fingers around, and to complete the Gish effect, Davies raises her sad eyes up to heaven beseechingly. It's all very unfair, really, but so punishingly detailed and funny that I was unable to watch Gish seriously for some time after I saw it. Such mockery helped to end her starring career on film.

Gish returned to the theater with some success and in an adventurous repertoire. She played in Chekhov, Sean O'Casey, and Shakespeare. She played axe murderer Lizzie Borden. Photos of her Marguerite Gautier in *Camille* reveal a juicily sexual middle-aged courtesan, and her Ophelia, opposite John Gielgud's definitive Hamlet, was said to be a "lewd" young lady (Sjöström had had his tonic effect). John Houseman called it "one of the most convincingly *lunatic* Ophelia's I've ever seen" at her AFI ceremony.

The movies of this time could find no place for one of its finest artists.

In her only other 1930s film, *His Double Life* (1933), Gish's voice is high and thin and she seems like a more genteel ZaSu Pitts in the thankless part of Roland Young's placid wife. In the late 1930s, Gish floated a suggestion in the press that she might come back to Hollywood, but only if she could star in a silent movie. Perhaps her exile was partly self-created.

In any event, when Gish did come back to films in the 1940s, she couldn't even secure solid character parts. "Before I had been responsible for my films," Gish wrote in her memoirs. "I had involved myself in various facets of production. Now acting in films was largely a matter of doing as you were told and collecting your salary." She barely has a role in *Commandos Strike at Dawn* (1942), and in her few other 1940s movies she looks wan and has little to do. Only producer David Selznick gave her a sizable part in King Vidor's flamboyant *Duel in the Sun* (1946), so that Gish presided over another embarrassing epic about sex and miscegenation 30 years after *The Birth of a Nation*.

She seems a more severe Billie Burke in *Duel in the Sun*, and her lavender paleness is visually contrasted with Jennifer Jones's dusky, full-blooded sexuality. In most of her scenes, she reacts silently, fading into the woodwork, but Vidor knows that nobody dies like Gish, and he gives her time to expire with Isadora Duncan–like dramatic impact. With her long hair down, she crawls to her husband (Lionel Barrymore) and caresses him, closes her eyes, and then falls out of the frame to the floor, a shockingly fast movement. This death scene showed Gish's undiminished skill, but Selznick next put her in *Portrait of Jennie* (1948) for one scene as a nun, a sort of thankless Our Lady of Exposition.

Gish continued to play on the stage and entered the era of television wholeheartedly, most notably in Horton Foote's poignant play *The Trip to Bountiful* (1953). As Carrie Watts, an unhappy old lady who wants to see her birthplace again, Gish has a breathless flirtatiousness in her first scenes. She goes a bit too fast and stumbles sometimes, for this is early live TV, but gradually her focus and specificity intensifies.

Gish doesn't wallow in her own emotions here, as Method doyenne Geraldine Page did in the later 1985 movie version of *Trip to Bountiful*, because this woman she's playing just doesn't have time. From the moment she hears that an old friend died and then one obstacle after another gets in the way of her trip, Gish is desolate and joyful by turns, hitting every note in her scale, from the frightened little Griffith girl to the imperious Hester Prynne. This virtuoso performance shows what Gish could do in a talkie, with those words that she didn't particularly need. Luckily, she soon made her last major film, Charles Laughton's *The Night of the Hunter* (1955), which capped her career.

As Rachel Cooper, an elderly woman who takes in two children and protects them from Robert Mitchum's evil preacher Harry Powell, Gish effortlessly embodies qualities of pure goodness tempered by earthy wisdom. Powell's sexuality is diseased, perverted by hate and repression, and he seems like Mr. Griffith to a T, especially when he watches a stripper gyrate and a stickknife bursts out of his pants in response. Gish, whose sexuality was liberated by King Vidor and Victor Sjöström, is his ultimate opponent, and it's payback time.

Laughton admired Griffith and wanted to make a Griffith-style movie, but instead he instinctively made a film that repudiates Griffith, utilizing Griffith's ace-in-the-hole artist to put him in his place and vanquish him. Gish's eyes glisten here as she speaks toughly of her strength. "Women are fools, all," she says enigmatically at one point, when her oldest adopted girl starts having trouble with boys.

Gish never married. Did she ever sleep with anyone at all? In her autobiography, she quotes Griffith on females and sex: "Women aren't made for promiscuity," he told her. "If you're going to be promiscuous, you'll end up having some disease." In the mid–1920s, after putting up with the ceaselessly litigious attentions of a dastardly former business manager named Charles Duell, Gish said, "I wish I never had to see another man." Her only other involvement seems to have been with sharp-tongued drama critic George Jean Nathan, who looked down on movies and advised her to return to the theater in the 1930s. But the evidence of her Sjöström films would suggest that she came to terms with her Griffith-bred fears of sex in one way or another.

In *The Night of the Hunter*'s best scene, a deep and inexplicable moment of balance between good and evil, Mitchum's preacher sings, "Leaning, leaning, leaning on the everlasting arms," in his low, creepy, hypocritical voice. As she listens to his singing, guarding her brood from him with a shotgun in her lap, Gish's Rachel has a look of rueful vulnerability. But she can top him.

"Lean on Jesus, leaning on Jesus," she sings, trumping his baritone with her high, sweet voice. They sing together for a few goose-pimply moments, and then she looks on as an owl kills a rabbit. "It's a hard world for little things," she says, a former broken blossom who survived countless whippings from her chosen master Griffith and continued to make her artistic case for the weak and unprotected after he had exhausted himself, so that you might be led to believe that the supposedly meek will indeed inherit the earth. Gish's career is an unbroken line from Lucy's whirling in the closet in *Broken Blossoms* to Rachel's melancholy but strong and centered conclusion on life's

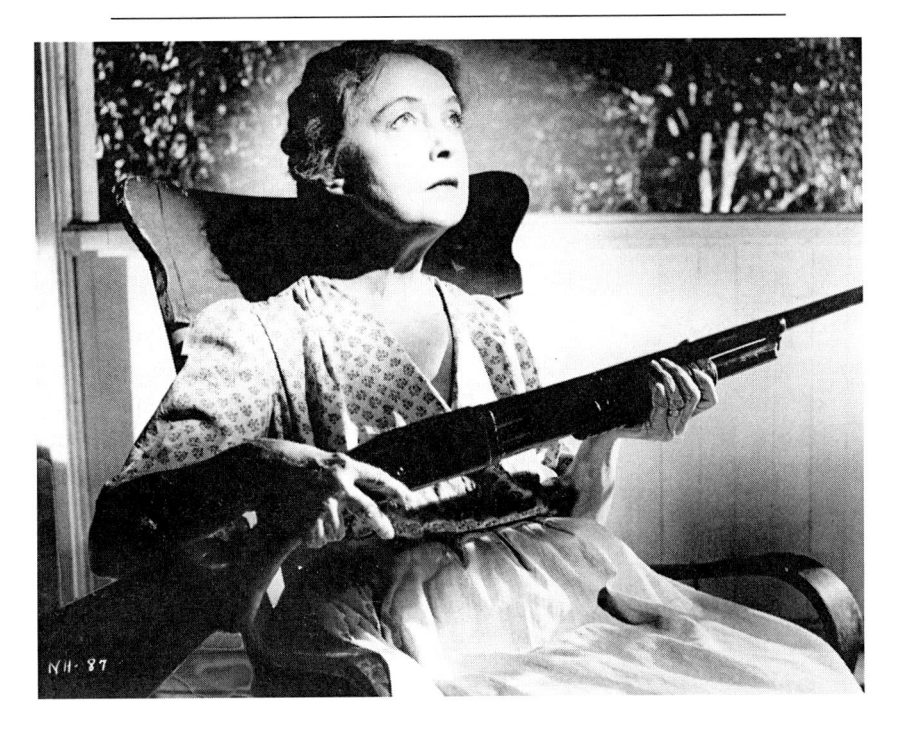

Lillian Gish guards children from evil in *The Night of the Hunter*.

injustices, mediated and transcended in between by her rebellious, unforgiving Hester Prynne.

Gish's artistry was ill served by most of her subsequent films, though she was vividly and quite atypically bitchy in Vincente Minnelli's *The Cobweb* (1955), an all-star movie set in a sanatorium. As manic spinster administrator Victoria Inch, Gish overplays, but she dominates a movie peopled by Charles Boyer, Gloria Grahame, Lauren Bacall, Richard Widmark, and Oscar Levant, and her caricature of Miss Inch is funny, something Gish seldom allowed herself to be. In *The Unforgiven* (1960), a coarse, unpalatable racial western, John Huston used her tremulous emotionalism contemptuously, and by the time of Robert Altman's *A Wedding* (1978), Gish is beatific and world-weary, yet she says, "Thank you, God," before expiring, positively and charitably summing up her career-long inquiry with the almighty.

At age 94, she took her last starring role, *The Whales of August*, an uneventful account of old age that paired her with the intransigent Bette Davis. It's an undemanding part, but Gish's participation underlined her eerie timelessness. In her best scene, where she drinks a glass of wine and salutes the memory of her dead husband, her eyes are as expressive as ever.

Gish's project in the second half of her long life was promoting D. W. Griffith, and she did so continuously, giving interviews and appearing gamely at many events honoring their work together. On film she freed herself of him, but in life, alas, she never did. He was her God on earth, but she never asked questions of him, unfortunately. Her autobiography does everything it can to convince us that Griffith was a lovable, inspired, if often misguided man, piling on detail after detail of his wisdom, excusing all of his missteps. It's wholly convincing, until you see their movies.

Griffith once suggested that Gish should look at animals to inform her body movements on film, a reasonable, even advanced bit of acting advice. But then he said, "Look at that dog, jumping up and down, turning in circles, barking for his master. If only my actors could be so expressive." This speaks ominous volumes about his work with Gish, as does one revealing mid-1940s photo in her book: Gish looks lovingly at Griffith, who is staring flirtatiously into the camera. Wedged between them is Griffith's young bride, a girl he met when she was a teenager.

La Bohème and *The Scarlet Letter* are too seldom seen, and *The Wind* has been treated as an impressive but simple tale of breakdown when it is really a complex and moving treatment of a very specific kind of self-regarding sexuality. *The Night of the Hunter* is a classic and is doubly impressive in relation to Gish's work with Griffith. The famous moments from her Griffith films should be extracted and collected by connoisseurs of the art of acting, just as the few precious later fragments from her talkies should be added to her monument. Four major films burnish her legacy, and her work taken as a whole is awesome and needs few alibis. Gish proved that you didn't need to talk to communicate to an audience, and she also proved how far you could go with emotions on screen as long as you kept as strong a focus as possible.

Gloria Swanson
Still Big

"I can say anything I want with my eyes," insists Gloria Swanson in her most famous role, faded silent film star Norma Desmond in Billy Wilder's *Sunset Boulevard* (1950). Norma murmurs to Joe Gillis (William Holden) about how they had faces then, in her day. "There just aren't any faces like that anymore," she says. No, there certainly aren't, not like Norma, or Swanson. Those staring eyes, those chomping teeth, that defiant chin, that blade of a nose! And yet Swanson's Norma is quite a talker, even if her thunderous monologues tend to be against talking, against words.

Sunset Boulevard is basically a hard-edged, nasty-rude comedy that treats Swanson herself harshly, but Swanson was always a harsh presence on screen, so she is perfectly suited to its tone. She gives an exuberantly comic performance, so outrageously over the top that it set a standard for imperious drag femininity. Norma is the sort of person who attempts suicide for attention. She is almost a pure monster with very little human left. The public made her an idol and then smashed her. The remains of her ego are not a pretty sight.

"Comeback, I hate that word!" Norma storms, in her plummy, knife-like voice. "It's *return*! Return to the millions of people who have never forgiven me for deserting the screen!" The deluded has-been Norma might be a very sad case for anyone else but Wilder, to whom she is a hoot. Then again, if you were to treat her story with its full pathos, it would probably be too much to take, so Wilder's cynical, moving-right-along touch is not the worst way to deal with it. The only thing to do with failure of this magnitude, maybe, is to laugh and shudder.

Norma's eyelids are drawn back as if she's had plastic surgery (one of many prescient touches here about aging actresses), and when Swanson wants Norma to be particularly grotesque she draws the eyelids even further back until she seems to be staring down into an abyss, with a challenging-diva "Well?" look in her eyes. Stand back! When Carol Burnett did her send-up of Norma on her TV show in the 1970s (which Swanson loved), she didn't have to exaggerate Swanson's performance at all; she just had to copy it.

Swanson had been away from movies so long by 1950 that to a new generation it was thought that she was playing herself. Not really, or not quite, though Swanson referenced the lifelike, doubling Pirandello qualities of *Sunset Boulevard* when she wrote about it in her memoirs. It is her movie in more ways than one, for she herself suggested that Norma visit Cecil B. DeMille, who had directed Swanson's own star-making vehicles in the early 1920s. "You know, a dozen press agents working overtime can do terrible things to the human spirit," DeMille says here. He puts in a good word for Norma, telling us that she had wit and heart as a girl of 17 and only became a terror to work with towards the end of her career.

Norma had been in Mack Sennett movies, just as Swanson had been, and she has been waiting 20 years for Paramount studio to call, so presumably her first talkie was a flop. Swanson's own first talkie, *The Trespasser* (1929), was a success, but the films she made after that were not. *Sunset Boulevard* was something new, Hollywood raking over its old coals, and one of its biggest stars "of yesteryear" raking over her own. Swanson plays Wilder's bad taste jokes full out, with gusto even. But she made sure DeMille was there as a spokesperson for Norma and for people like her, stars like her. For people and stars like Swanson herself.

The pint-sized (4'11") Swanson got her start as a teenager in Sennett shorts like *The Danger Girl* (1916), where she dresses in male drag. She had a vivid face even then, with big eyes and flashing teeth to light up the screen, or slash it. In *Teddy at the Throttle* (1917) she is feisty and strong-willed before being tied to the railroad tracks by villainous Wallace Beery, the man who would be her first husband (and not that less villainous in real life, according to her autobiography). There is never anything passive about Swanson. She is always active on screen in these early days—reckless, fighting, flouncing, making things happen. A pip of a gal, she will uninhibitedly grab people by the ear and shove them and laugh lustily.

But she didn't want to be one of Sennett's "hyperactive giggly girls." Swanson disdained the low comedy she was working in, though this doesn't show on screen. She wanted to do something serious, something dignified, and she got her wish, at least relatively, when she starred in DeMille's *Don't Change Your Husband* (1919). That movie made her a star the likes of which had yet to be seen. She was beloved by her female fans, who lived for the fantasies of luxury she presented them, particularly in the area of elaborately beaded dresses. Swanson wore new frocks for practically every new scene.

In 1922, she said, "I have gone through a long apprenticeship. I have gone through enough of being nobody. I have decided that when I am a star, I will be every inch and every moment the star! Everybody from the studio gateman to the highest executive will know it." And she gave out quotes to fan magazines like, "I not only believe in divorce. I sometimes think I don't believe in marriage at all." Swanson embarked on a series of films for DeMille in which she was always a wife who decides to test her marriage and at the end go back to it, in typical DeMille "I'll have my cake and eat it too" style.

Swanson was the first aspirational film star for women, someone to try to emulate. The very slow Swanson-DeMille films periodically stop for "visions," fantasy scenarios in which her character works out her issues in lavish settings, with peacock feathers, jewels, and more jewels at the ready. Swanson herself is like a peacock in these films: huffy and proud, and very decorative.

There was a curious emphasis in her DeMille movies on expensive bathrooms with sunken marble tubs, too, as if the space and wherewithal to make up were the ultimate fantasy for women. "Why shouldn't the Bath Room express as much Art and Beauty as the Drawing Room?" asks a title in *Male and Female* (1919), a film in which Swanson is pawed on the back by a lion in one of DeMille's visions. The impressed DeMille offered Swanson a choice of jewels in return for her bravery in this lion scene, and she happily chose a gold mesh handbag with a sapphire clasp.

She got increasingly grand and ponderous—a process exactly parodied by Marion Davies in King Vidor's comedy *Show People* (1928), where Davies's Peggy Pepper goes from Keystone antics to costume snobbery. By the time Davies got done skewering the major silent stars in her last few films, there was no one left standing; she makes particular hay out of the way Swanson would haughtily expose her teeth to her co-players.

It is difficult now, unfortunately, to give a rounded picture of Swanson's stardom in the 1920s because a full 15 of her starring vehicles are lost. Many of them were directed by Sam Wood, a leaden director if ever there was one, but that doesn't mean that Swanson might not have been intriguing in them. Then again, when one of the lost was found, *Beyond the Rocks* (1922), her film opposite Rudolph Valentino, it turned out to be a slow and timid dud where the stars barely struck a spark against each other.

In the 1920s Swanson was favoring deathly white make-up and pitch-dark mascara and heavy dark lipstick with a heart-shape at the top of the upper lip, not a look that has traveled well. Stills from her lost features suggest that high dungeon was a favorite attitude along with disgust and alarm. And her dresses, wraps, and headdresses get more elaborate with the years. Excess in everything was what she represented.

The only Swanson film of this time that didn't make money was the now lost *Under the Lash* (1921), where her waifish character wore simple frocks.

The profits from her movies made Paramount, but their vision of wealth looks a bit threadbare when placed next to what was to come in the area of art direction at that studio in the 1930s. Romance novelist Elinor Glyn often supplied Swanson's scenarios, as in the lost *The Great Moment* (1921), in which she is bitten on the shoulder and must have the poison sexily sucked out by her leading man Milton Sills (in Glyn's original idea, the heroine has been bitten on the breast, but we can't have everything).

In comedies like Allan Dwan's *Manhandled* (1924) and *Stage Struck* (1925), Swanson hardly has a light touch. Her hoydens and working girls are usually a little monstrous, like a queen deigning to imitate a commoner for the entertainment of the commoners. Her instinct is to bite and snap at other people with her large teeth like some jewel-encrusted, exotic animal that you need to be careful with. Swanson's pictures usually were pretty small, but she transfigures them with the enormity of her self-belief. She needs to be seen on the biggest possible screen as a giant head issuing imperious signals to her fans.

Swanson lived to pose, to thunder, to suffer, because suffering looked so fetching as a contrast to her gowns. She was happiest when she was allowed to go as big as possible, her ice-cold blue eyes dazzling, as she does in Dwan's *Zaza* (1923), where her full-bodied performance is filled with all kinds of scintillating detail and larger-than-life mannerism, as if she were a living and breathing powder puff.

"Watching the rushes, I could see that the energy level of *Zaza* was higher than in any other film I'd made in years," Swanson wrote in her memoirs. "Allan had found some mysterious way of unleashing me." Her reviews for her Dwan films, several of which are lost, were far better than for her Sam Wood work, and it was felt that she was learning and advancing. She was particularly proud of her performance in Dwan's lost *The Coast of Folly* (1925), where she played the duel role of a fusty old dowager mother and the dowager's athletic daughter.

In silent films, the actors use their whole bodies a lot more than anyone ever does in talking pictures because they have to get their points across without the aid of words. It was expected of Swanson, from her Sennett days onward, that she do everything on an enormous scale. Try communicating with someone just through pantomime and it becomes clear just how large you have to go to be understood. Swanson was understood by anyone who watched her. It may seem fussy now, but that's what was needed in the teens and early 1920s, when cameras usually captured players at full length.

Swanson is far cruder than Gish or Mary Pickford, but she got her points across. She does not draw you in, as they do, but demands that you attend to her every emotion, every one of which is underlined several times before it is sent out to us. In spite of the largeness of her head, Swanson actually seems as short as she was in life on screen, and perhaps that smallness led her to over-compensate in other areas. As with Joan Crawford later, it was as important what she represented off screen and in fan magazines and publicity as what she actually did on screen. The fan magazine image and the image on screen could not be separated out from each other (director Edmund Goulding told Swanson in the late 1920s that Crawford considered her an idol, someone to emulate).

In her extreme close-ups in *Fine Manners* (1926), her last film on her Paramount contract, it's as if Swanson is demanding some special sort of awe and worship from us. She has a kind of savage power in close-ups, with banks of light putting particular focus on those eyes that can say anything but choose most often to say, "Bow down and worship!" There isn't a trace of vulnerability in her work, in spite of all the crises she acted out. Maybe that's what her fans most enjoyed.

Swanson began producing her own movies, playing it safe at first with an elaborate melodrama called *The Love of Sunya* (1927), which is filled with heavy breathing, elaborate turbans, and DeMille-style "visions" of the past and future. And then she took on a real challenge, fighting censorship restrictions to play *Sadie Thompson* (1928), a role that had made Jeanne Eagels a star on stage. Swanson does not have the same nervous intensity that Eagels reportedly brought to the role in the theater and which Eagels brings to *The Letter* (1929), her only surviving talking film. But suddenly Swanson does seem like an actress in this film, and a good one.

Her Sadie is dreamy and hard, armored and decent, leading with her rump, which she sashays all over the rainy island of Pago Pago. Swanson's physical effects here are remarkably spare and focused after all the posing and errant nonsense of the films that had come before. She's a believable chippie with a nasty streak, not just a movie queen deigning to pretend to be one. Partly that must have to do with her director and co-star Raoul Walsh, but partly it had to do with the challenge of the part itself, which she responds to with all her ambition backing her.

The role and Walsh's fluid direction bring out something fetchingly roughneck and profane in Swanson, a genuine and very magnetic toughness. At a peak of frustration with the hypocritical preacher Davidson (Lionel Barrymore), Swanson chooses to put her whole forearm over her eyes to hide her tears, like a little kid would, and this is just one of many apt, sure touches in her work here. *Sadie Thompson* is Swanson's best silent film and performance. Unhappily, even this achievement is touched by her persistent bad luck with print survival; the last reel of the film is missing.

To top *Sadie*, her lover Joseph Kennedy bought her director Erich von Stroheim and his epic scenario for a film to be called *Queen Kelly* (1929). It shot for three months until Swanson, fed up with Stroheim's perverse love of detail and details of perversion, fired him and shut the whole thing down after he demonstrated how he wanted infernal character actor Tully Marshall to dribble tobacco juice onto her hand.

What's left is one tantalizing third of the story, in which Swanson, a very worldly-looking convent girl, is seduced by a prince (Walter Byron) and then sent packing to run a brothel. Alas, the remaining footage is all of Swanson as Kelly before her metamorphosis, and all of her effort cannot convince us that she is an innocent girl at this point. The film was released in a truncated version while Swanson prepared to make her first talking picture.

"In silent pictures you had to convey everything in the first few words of a line and still have something left for the end," Swanson wrote in her capacious 1980 autobiography *Swanson on Swanson,* which takes you through practically every day of her life (no shopping spree is left undescribed). "You had to know where the titles were going to be. Listening and reacting had to be delayed, controlled. What seemed unnatural on the set became natural on the screen."

This is a very clear explanation of why so many silent stars faltered in talkies. Though her talkie debut *The Trespasser* (1929) was a hit, it showed that she suffered from the habits that afflicted veteran silent performers—she begins an emotion and then freezes it slightly, as if a title card is about to come on, and then she goes into the next emotion. Swanson's inability to make behavior flow together with dialogue stranded her, and the devil-may-care flamboyance of her 1920s roles could no longer find a place with the onset of the Great Depression. Like Pickford in *Coquette* (1929), Swanson does too much in *The Trespasser,* and it looks very odd. Their laborious miming was not fluid and quick enough for the talkies. They were stylized now in the wrong way.

A series of poor films brought her first career to a close, things like *Indiscreet* (1931), the very unpleasant *Tonight or Never* (1931), where the plot contrives to punish her at every turn, a misbegotten film in England that she paid for herself called *A Perfect Understanding* (1933), with a miserable-looking young Laurence Olivier, and a shrill musical called *Music in the Air* (1934), which was co-written by Billy Wilder. She then spent 16 years in the wilderness, broken only by *Father Takes a Wife* (1941), a mild comedy programmer for RKO where she looked very stranded and out of place.

And then she was summoned to do a screen test for Norma Desmond. A screen test! For Paramount, the studio she had made millions for. Uncertain at first, Swanson asked several friends if she should test, including director George Cukor, and they all told her to go for it. Montgomery Clift was supposed to play Joe Gillis, but he turned it down at the last moment (he is unthinkable in the part, too blocked and overly sensitive for the wise-ass narration that William Holden does to perfection).

There is exactly one moment of naked vulnerability in Swanson's very game performance in *Sunset Boulevard*, when Norma lies back during one of her beauty treatments and a magnifying glass is brought up to her right eye as composer Franz Waxman's violin player goes nuts on the soundtrack. If Swanson had played the entire part like that moment under the magnifying glass, she would have killed the audience dead with pathos. Instead, she shot the works as Wilder wanted her to, so that Norma's failure can be enjoyed as horror, as comedy, as spectacle.

Gloria Swanson around the time of her return in Billy Wilder's *Sunset Boulevard*.

When Norma's drama queen antics fall back again to the threat of attempted suicide, this time with a gun, Holden's Joe brutally tells her, "You'd be killing yourself to an empty house." And then he advises her, "There's nothing tragic about being 50—not unless you try to be 25!" But she isn't listening. She's off the deep end now, for good, like a dedicated movie fan who refuses to live in reality anymore. "The stars are ageless, aren't they?" she asks herself. Spoken like a press agent.

The famous scene where Norma comes down the stairs to Waxman's Richard Strauss-inspired music never fails to raise the goose pimples, particularly when Swanson slowly lifts her arms up and starts to undulate them slightly. Her work in this last scene, where she addresses an imaginary crew, is beyond exaggeration, in some other realm Swanson has discovered. It's campy, of course, but unbearably sad, too, just below the surface glitter.

She was at her best when she got to play a performer, a diva, though her best part was always Gloria Swanson, Movie Star, Big Spender. She set the template for so many others. Swanson was much married, making small comebacks periodically after *Sunset Boulevard*. She would carry a single red carnation and be elaborately hatted and gloved and veiled to give interview after interview with great style and attack, as when she would come on TV in the 1950s and '60s and swear that, "Sugar is poison!"

Swanson played herself in *Airport 1975* (1974), loopily reminiscing about DeMille and others and finally dumping her jewels out of a case in order to save her memoirs, which she dictates to a recorder periodically. She played occasionally on TV, most memorably when Curtis Harrington covered her in *Killer Bees* (1974), though he did not offer her jewelry in return.

John Barrymore
Sweet Prince of Irony

For a long while, the influence of John Barrymore on the art of acting has seemed more archeological than actual. During his theatrical heyday in the early 1920s, his name was synonymous with serious thespian, much as the name Laurence Olivier became shorthand for "great actor" in the 1940s and beyond. Olivier and John Gielgud both spoke admiringly about seeing Barrymore's performance as Hamlet in London, and surely he laid the cornerstone for a more modern Shakespearean performance, but modernity is a relative term.

In 1924, Barrymore's Hamlet might very well have seemed modern compared to earlier tragedians like Edwin Booth, Henry Irving, and Richard Mansfield, and there is persuasive testimony to the subtleties of Barrymore's melancholy Dane. The critic Stark Young thought that Barrymore made you feel that Polonius's dithering represented the corrupt world that had taken Ophelia away from him, while Helen Hayes was moved by the pained way he reacted to Rosencrantz and Guildenstern, who had once been his close friends and were now set against him.

"When he was on stage, the sun came out," Olivier proclaimed. But the man himself was defeatist. "Isn't it extraordinary that the most popular character ever written should apparently be defeated by life instead of transcending it?" Barrymore said, speaking of Hamlet. He was also suspicious of the camera. "If you stay in front of that camera long enough, it will show you not only what you had for breakfast but who your ancestors were," he reflected. A sobering thought.

Barrymore left behind a few scraps of his Shakespearean past on film and radio. In *The Show of Shows* (1929), a Warner Brothers revue, Barrymore does a Richard III soliloquy from the third *Henry VI,* and it must be said that he's fairly hopeless here from a contemporary perspective. He sings the verse, prolonging vowels for no clear reason, and he can't stop moving his eyebrows. On radio, he did bits of Hamlet, and this too is hopeless, even just to listen to, but he recorded his Dane when he was well past his prime, so it's entirely possible that the whinnying "pear-shaped tones" of these recordings are not representative of his original work.

As Mercutio in *Romeo and Juliet* (1936), Barrymore brings a blast of buffoonish fun to a stately film, giving a rip-snorting performance where he belches during the Queen Mab speech. Overweight and clearly ill by this point, Barrymore still manages to offer a wildly over the top but colorful and valid reading of the role. In his later years, he was often called a ham, but this isn't necessarily a bad thing. His Mercutio is good ham acting, meaning that it's emotionally connected but unafraid to gild the lily to the nth degree, whereas his Richard III looks like bad ham acting, mugging with too little emotion and thought underneath.

Watching Barrymore on screen, we are always waiting to see whether he will engage with his material. If he does, he's capable of large-spirited magic, and if he doesn't, he merely moves his face and pops his eyes, wearily, as if he's trying to be amused. Though he provided inspiration to the hardworking Olivier and Gielgud, Barrymore was the first in a line of outsized American talents who wound up trapped in self-parody.

On Broadway in the late 1990s, Christopher Plummer did a one-man show as Barrymore, and he had an indelible moment towards the end where he stopped short during a raucous Shakespeare recitation, and in that pause, which lasted only a few seconds, Plummer gave you the full impact of Barrymore's ghastly self-knowledge. He knows he's a slacker, a shirker, and that he's pissed away his promise with drinking and whoring and easy money. On film, the real Barrymore could be indulging in cringe-worthy horseplay, and then, like all drunks, he could suddenly turn totally serious, the corrupting years and the liquor barnacles falling away and his young face emerging, with its poetic, flashing eyes and its fabled Great Profile.

It was a face made for greasepaint, and The Profile held a carnal promise that he cashed in so often that he wound up in debt. It doesn't much matter what woman The Profile looks at, for even Garbo loses some of her individuality when confronted with it in *Grand Hotel* (1932). His body was made for doublet, hose, and sword, and he walks stiffly, grandly, until this natural grandeur inevitably gives way to a self-mocking parody of sexual prowess.

It was his blessing and his curse that Barrymore couldn't take anything seriously as he got older, and this quality infuses his greatest triumph on screen, in Howard Hawks's *Twentieth Century* (1934), where his theatrical impresario Oscar Jaffe runs the physical and vocal gamut yet remains resolutely clear-eyed, even cynical, under the rococo frills and furbelows of his own vain delusions. To evade his creditors, Jaffe dresses as a Colonel Sanders type, and when he takes off his costume, Barrymore saves his false nose for last, pulling on it until The Profile turns into a version of Cyrano de Bergerac, a romantic role that would have suited him in his prime. As if aware of this fact, he blithely starts to *pick* his Cyrano nose, a revelation of The Profile's refusal of meaning and romantic love for a bracing "who cares?" laugh.

But Barrymore also offered ample display of the opposite side of that coin or impulse, for self-pity was his specialty on screen, and on him it was never unattractive because it was as if he'd earned the right to luxuriate in it. Few actors are moved to diamond-like tears as often as The Profile, especially in his late silent movies like *Don Juan* (1926), *The Beloved Rogue* (1927), *When a Man Loves* (1927), and *Eternal Love* (1929). The left coast intelligentsia was scornful of these lucrative efforts after they had acclaimed his Richard III and his Hamlet, and they were right to be, for these Barrymore vehicles are exactly the kind of silent costume romances so mercilessly parodied in *Singin' in the Rain* (1952).

In his forties, Barrymore can still get away with wearing tights and could Douglas Fairbanks it up to a fare thee well, but he can't muster much interest in the claptrap plots. "One must sorrow that a man of such genius should be a drunken clown," reads an intertitle in *The Beloved Rogue,* and this isn't the last of such meta-commentary in Barrymore's films. In *The Great Profile* (1940), Anne Baxter calls him "a great artist who destroyed himself with drink." Offended by this carping yet also reveling in it, the late Barrymore lays it on so thick in his last movies that his facial acrobatics might make Marie Dressler blush. He was often drunk on set, and you can tell because he has jerky spurts of energy and then falls back into a sort of glazed, pickled brooding.

But his innate talent will sometimes be activated fully and intensely. In *Tempest* (1928), a sumptuously designed satin pillow of a movie, subtle ideas and feelings flicker across Barrymore's face in close-up until it seems as if he is capable of raising silent film acting to a crest of private pantomime and fulfilled dreams. He takes a framed photograph of his beloved (Camilla Horn) and caresses it sensually, and when he is alone in her room, he takes her pillow and passionately kisses it.

A moment like this feels completely private, and we can trace a direct line from this desperate kiss to Marlon Brando's embarrassing scenes in front of the mirror in *Reflections in a Golden Eye* (1967), where he exposes a wretched man's buried fantasies. The most seductive acting, from Barrymore to Brando, is a private thing, either an opening of windows on finer feelings (Barrymore) or an airing of dirty laundry (Brando). It can also be pure id, pure fantasy, which Barrymore proved with *Dr. Jekyll and Mr. Hyde* (1920), an early film undertaken during his most creative period on stage.

As Dr. Jekyll in the first scenes, Barrymore's movements are contained and a bit staccato, as if the doctor feels he needs to control his worst impulses (surely The Profile could relate). When he drinks the potion that will unleash his dark side, in one shot, without aid of lighting or make-up, Barrymore transforms his classically beautiful face and body with a German expressionist contortion of his hands and facial muscles.

This image is so outré that it could conceivably get a laugh, but it doesn't because Barrymore is reaching as low as he can for the most full-blooded malignancy, and he achieves it visually by tapping into an extreme ugly interior to go with the extreme ugly exterior, amplified in the next shot by some helpful make-up, which includes a pointy head and snake-like fingers. Like Olivier, he'll throw his entire body around the space to get the effect he wants, but the sardonic humor Barrymore brings to his roles is entirely his own. When Hyde casts off a girl (Nita Naldi) he has used up and abused, he indulges in a very funny little shrug of indifference. You won't find a better, more physically daring performance from the silent era than Barrymore's Jekyll and Hyde.

In the sound era, Barrymore was at his best when under the direction of George Cukor, who must have known just how to handle him. In the melodrama *A Bill of Divorcement* (1932), Barrymore proves his range by creating a hesitant, damaged man, gentle and confused, his eyes shining with fear as he describes the "black hand" of madness that sometimes overtakes him. Cukor harnesses and focuses Barrymore and Katharine Hepburn, in her debut, and the two of them make the hoary plot work through sheer star power.

Look at the way Barrymore nervously shakes the hand of the asylum director who's come to check up on him, as if he's a fearful little boy in a ruined, middle-aged man's body; at his best, this was an actor who could pump gestures like this full of the largest kind of imaginative empathy. (His hands are his most expressive tools, though the gestures he makes with them are sometimes slightly stiff and old-fashioned, whereas James Cagney's hand gestures in this period are as stylized as Barrymore's but feel more fluid and immediate—more modern.)

John Barrymore opens himself up to emotion in *A Bill of Divorcement* (1932)

In the perilous role of a fallen movie star in Cukor's *Dinner at Eight* (1933), Barrymore builds a believable has-been gesture by gesture, hilariously misquoting Ibsen, feeling his lower face as if to say, "I'm still handsome!" and sneering the word "love" as if he still desperately wants to believe in it. What could be akin to the self-exploitation of his last films is instead closer to a mini *Last Tango in Paris* (1972), an all-cards-on-the-table movement towards death.

When his agent (Lee Tracy) calls him a corpse and says that he "sags like an old woman," Barrymore hardly flinches. Left alone, he trips over an ottoman, and his body lands on the carpet with a horrible thud, yet the asymmetrical posture of his body on the floor has a kind of dancer-like élan and expressive power. A trouper to the end, he picks himself up, turns on the gas in his room, and makes sure that he'll look good when he's found dead. Cukor moves his camera in and contemplates The Profile in winter, the perfect finish to this small, honest portrait of reaching the end of your tether.

Barrymore was too cutesy as the schoolteacher in *Topaze* (1933), putting quotation marks around the character's unlikely innocence, but he's a hoot in the first scenes of *Svengali* (1931), a sort of Gothic horror movie where Barrymore chooses to make us laugh at his mesmerist for the first two reels so that he can catch us off guard as he reveals the man's evil powers.

When cast with his older brother, the dread Lionel, who ruins just about any movie he's in, Barrymore takes it easy, smiling indulgently at his sibling's gruesome hamming. Attempting to strangle Lionel's Rasputin at the end of *Rasputin and the Empress* (1932), Barrymore seems to know that you can't really kill a performance this bad. Off to the sidelines in that movie, sister Ethel looks at both of her brothers impatiently, as if she thinks that the movies are beneath her. John, Ethel, and Lionel were the most famous fruit of a theatrical dynasty that went back several generations, and all that's left of it nowadays is John's granddaughter, the amiable Drew Barrymore, in whom glimpses of her grandmother Dolores Costello can be seen but little of the Barrymore fire and temperament.

Barrymore was a romantic up to a point. You can see it in the all-out expression of love he showers on Mary Astor in *Beau Brummel* (1924) and Costello in *The Sea Beast* (1926). By the 1930s, though, his belief in practically every finer emotion has been extinguished, so that he looks at Greta Garbo, Hepburn, Myrna Loy and many other delectable leading ladies with a kind of exhausted, disinterested sympathy. Even a Joan Crawford at her most self-loving and sexed-up in *Grand Hotel* can barely stir the embers of his once ardent and now merely courtly attention.

And his heavy drinking brought a major problem. Filming a retake on the set of *Counsellor at Law* (1933), an adaptation of an Elmer Rice play filled with reams of rat-a-tat-tat dialogue, Barrymore found that he couldn't remember his lines even after trying all day long. Henceforward, he would come to rely heavily on cue cards, and this explains the often-absent quality of some of his later performances. You can't really act in any focused way when you're reading your lines off camera, though Marlon Brando later attempted to do just that, with uneven results.

His last years brought a series of catastrophes that Barrymore embraced with unseemly relish. Beset by a designing fourth wife and failing health, he made a fool of himself regularly on radio programs and finally succumbed to a series of films that made mock of his once high reputation. "Some things are too low for even me to stoop to!" he roars in his last film, *Playmates* (1941), which features him as "John Barrymore," a tired old ham who "reacts" spasmodically before anyone says or does anything. Lupe Velez actually threatens to *cut off* his profile here, and he is made to show off padding that he supposedly wore to fill out his tights when he played Hamlet. At the end, he is unable to play Shakespeare and a large audience laughs at him.

In the middle of this nightmare, Barrymore sits down and recites the beginning of the "to be or not to be" soliloquy from *Hamlet*, in all seriousness. As he intones the well-known words, his face collapses and his nose droops while his bleary eyes stare upwards, begging for relief, for death, which would come shortly after filming was concluded. "He inspired love," said his sister Ethel. The work he left us on screen was a mixed bag, but when he cared about what he was doing, you can see why he inspired love, and why he influenced all the actors that came after him.

Louise Brooks
Naked on Her Goat

When she made her films in the roaring 1920s, Louise Brooks was at best a second-tier star, at worst a nonentity. Yet she is better known today than Mary Pickford, Lillian Gish, Gloria Swanson, and many other silent heavyweights, and her supposed failure has lasted much longer than their success. The Brooks cult has spurred many articles, including the famed Kenneth Tynan profile for *The New Yorker* in 1979, a coffee table book by Peter Cowie in 2006, and an extremely seductive, definitive biography by Barry Paris first published in 1989. Her image remains as biting, sensual, and provoking as ever.

At a book signing for his third bio, on Audrey Hepburn, Paris all but confessed that there was not much to write about Audrey. When I brought my Brooks book to be signed, his face lit up. "Ah, Louise," he sighed, like a man who has never gotten over his first love. Paris inscribed my book with his favorite Brooksie quote: "If I ever bore you, it'll be with a knife."

Born in Cherryvale, Kansas, in 1906, Brooks was molested by an older man at the age of nine. She called her molester "Mr. Flowers" and sometimes "Mr. Feathers," and he increasingly pre-occupied her as an adult. When she told her mother Myra Brooks what had happened, Myra told her daughter that she must have done something to lead Mr. Flowers or Feathers on, a reaction that Brooks reported to friends with exuberant disbelief when she was an older woman. After this traumatic sexual encounter, Brooks always looked for some sort of domination in her personal relationships that she could fight against as hard as possible.

She started out as a dancer with Ruth St. Denis and Ted Shawn, became a Ziegfeld chorus girl on Broadway, and then made 14 silent films at Paramount. She flitted to Europe, where she made two silent films for G. W. Pabst and one French sound movie, and when she returned Brooks was reduced to a two-reel comedy, small parts in two early talkies, and two leads in bottom-of-the-barrel westerns. Her most significant film, Pabst's *Pandora's Box* (1929), where she incarnated Franz Wedekind's Lulu, was not appreciated until nearly 30 years after its release. When her image she was resurrected, Brooks wrote a series of articles about her Hollywood experience, and her writing helped to cement her legend.

Brooks seemed to have known or at least met just about everybody in Hollywood (who else can claim to have slept with Chaplin *and* Garbo?), and in her writing she somehow managed to make her own stubborn masochism invigorating. She is seemingly easy in that you really only have to watch one, perhaps two films at most and then glide across the sparing, highly controlled pages of her 1982 book of essays, *Lulu in Hollywood*, and you are left with the heady impression that she was so modern, so ahead of her time, a self-styled intellectual who read Schopenhauer on sets. Brooks was a beautiful loser. She pioneered the marketing of a special kind of superior loserdom and won everlasting cult love in the process.

Most of her American silents are lost. Of the remaining few, William Wellman's *Beggars of Life* (1928) contains her most personal work, particularly in its opening half-hour. Brooks plays a girl who has killed her lecherous benefactor, and when we first see her she stumbles into the frame explosively, which makes clear that no one moves more freely on screen than she does (by contrast, her leading man, Richard Arlen, moves self-consciously). A flashback of the murder plays over her face as she confesses to Arlen, and in Brooks's wet, black-as-sin, bad seed eyes we see an abused kid whose purity is still visible but shot through with the first pangs of disillusionment.

As late as 1974, when she filmed the one-hour interview *Lulu in Berlin*, Brooks still has that quality of having been somehow ruined or stained. She booms flutily, with zesty morbid amusement rippling through her rapid storytelling, and she is impatient or tipsily internal when interviewer Richard Leacock speaks. Her face is unwrinkled, but her mouth has collapsed into a perpetual frown. In repose, her eyes are narrowed, sunken, and sad.

During that confession scene in *Beggars*, Brooks is starkly demanding and convincing and touching. But she tells Leacock, "I was never an actress, I was never in love with myself ... to be a great actress, you must know what you're doing ... when I acted, I hadn't the slightest idea what I was doing." On camera, she was simply *being*, a very different thing from acting on stage, say. She was being and caught for the camera, observed and circumscribed, unobtainable yet helplessly, sexually *there*, too, fighting, in flux, simultaneously offering herself up and holding herself back, and she proved that there is nothing more erotic than that particular push-and-pull. The camera can't get enough of the stiletto-like Brooks, who rarely "acts." She stares the camera eye down, slicing it and us with her gaze, the sharpest cut, all at once, before a kind of contemplation sets in.

In *Beggars of Life*, Arlen takes her abused girl on the road with him, where she dresses as a young boy and walks like a swaggering stud. This masquerade gives Brooks the opportunity to indulge her spikiest behavior, the idea of herself as a bitch that she so loved. For *Beggars*, she gets to be a bastard. "The men I liked most were the worst in bed, and the men I liked least were the best," she admitted. "I liked the bastards."

Brooks's article on the making of *Beggars*, "On Location with William Wellman," makes Richard Arlen into an all-around jerk and kiss-ass who told her that she couldn't act and wasn't even pretty. At this crucial time in her development, Brooks needed the people around her to support what she was doing, but she got no help from anyone. Her *Beggars* piece paints a grim picture of how little she was valued on sets. Worse than her intellectualism was her sexual freedom, which branded her a whore as well as a snob.

The other extant films from America include *Love 'Em and Leave 'Em* (1926), a sweet and sour comedy with sexy Brooks, encased in gleaming black satin, employing expertly stylized gestures as she vamps all the men in the cast, at one point putting water on her face from a nearby goldfish bowl to simulate tears. Speaking about acting to film historian Kevin Brownlow, Brooks said, "You don't have to feel anything ... it was timing—because emotion means nothing."

It's the Old Army Game (1926) is a W. C. Fields comedy where Brooksie laughs appreciatively at the Great Man. In one memorable moment, after losing boyfriend William Gaxton, Brooks poses against a tree, throwing her head back and digging up an arresting mixture of laughter and tears. A scene like this shows what a fine dancer Brooks was, and it also lets us see her debt to Martha Graham, a great dancer she knew and worked with when she performed with the Denishawn troupe.

Even in her lighter scenes in *Army Game*, Brooks's flippant, bird-like movements are deeply charming, yet Walter Wanger, an important Paramount producer and one of her many lovers, made fun of her acting and put her down, which destroyed some of her natural superiority and left her lacking in confidence in what she was doing, which was original, clean, un-obvious. Brooks, who had wanted to be a major dancer, was made to feel that she was inadequate, "beautiful but dumb."

In *The Show-Off* (1926), Brooks eyes the overbaked cast with alarm, and even does a nasty parody of star Ford Sterling's acting in one sequence. "I was supposed to flirt with Ford, and laugh ostensibly at his jokes, in order to satisfy his insatiable ego," Brooks reported. "I couldn't play that part." For Howard Hawks, she was a teasing vamp in *A Girl In Every Port* (1928), a hot girl who does as she pleases, cool and modern. This is the film that got her noticed by director G.W. Pabst. He saw the qualities that others around her did not.

Before going to Berlin and Pabst, she made her kiss-off to Hollywood, *The Canary Murder Case* (1929), where her character is killed after the first 15 minutes. When Paramount head B.P. Schulberg offered to keep her on at the same salary without a raise, which she was due, she walked out on her contract. Her rich lover George Marshall, who was advising her, told her about an offer from Pabst to make a film in Berlin. Thus she sealed her fate of poignant squandered potential and grabbed, unknowingly, at her morbid legend in Lulu.

Pandora's Box is a film as volatile in its way as another movie shot in Berlin around that time, Josef von Sternberg's *The Blue Angel* (1930). While Marlene Dietrich's Lola Lola, named by Sternberg as a double-sexy homage to Wedekind's Lulu, is a self-aware seductress and ambiguous destroyer, Brooks's Lulu is a portrait of unthinking, instinctual, Jamesian innocence. A happy hooker, her calculations feel as natural as breathing, and the pleasure she takes in her life might still be shocking to some. This is a movie that, like Brooks herself, is unconcerned with conventional morality.

If on film black and white proved to be somehow more realistic than color, then *Pandora* somehow seems more realistic because of its silence. There is no glib talk to smooth anything away or blur what Brooks is conveying through movement. This is not realistic material, and the silence keeps it that way, keeps it archetypal, symbolic.

Brooks's Lulu enters the film smiling seductively, like a little girl who has learned how to please. Mr. Flowers/Feathers turns up in the person of Schigolch (Carl Goetz), who is her pimp, and perhaps her father. Lulu tips over in excitement on seeing him, clutching at her breasts in a childishly unaware, tactile fashion. You can catch bits of Brooks in Lulu sometimes, in stray close-ups here and there that look sharp, intelligently appraising, agitated. There is a mingling of performer and role in *Pandora's Box* in which they start out separate, and then they are in exchange, and then they are at one.

When Lulu's big meal ticket Schön (Fritz Kortner) tells her that he's getting married and they need to break things off, she lies on her back submissively and they eventually kiss heatedly, Lulu giving herself up completely to the moment at hand. She is the object of desire in the center of a storm of people, coming and going, and she juggles them all with cheerful high spirits.

"Strong!" she says, in English, when she shakes the hand of acrobat Rodrigo Quast (Krafft-Raschig) and then feels his muscles. The famed Brooks hedonism is visible as she starts swinging on Quast's arm, pulling herself up on his bicep and letting go with a face-squinched-up laugh, like the silvery

"A-HA-HA-HA!" Brooks unleashes for Leacock in *Lulu in Berlin*. This is truly a woman who, as they used to say, knows no law but her own desires. All the men in *Pandora's Box* are primarily concerned with sexual gratification, and Brooks saw this as Pabst's keenest insight. She painted herself as a whore who gives her body but not her soul, which is precisely what Lulu does, with pleasure, most of the time.

In the film's most vivid sequence, Lulu performs on stage dressed in a mod space-age outfit as chorus girls come out from behind her with swords. Brooks's impression of innocence shines like a beacon as Pabst's cut-cut-cutting feels like an editing orgy, the rhythm of the editing intensifying under the wavering lights. Lulu's scanty costume gives us a direct view of Brooks's weapon, glory, and downfall: her upper body, with its strong, straight back, its graceful shoulders and arms.

When Lulu sees Schön's fiancée Charlotte (Daisy D'Ora), her eyes tear up and she refuses to go back on stage. Schön waves a phallic finger at her, but she rejects his machismo, Brooks infusing the childlike Lulu with her own indignation at male chauvinism and sexual hypocrisy. Schön takes Lulu to her dressing room to bully her into going on (Brooks reported she had 10 black and blue marks from Kortner's fingers after the scene was finished), but she will not give in.

Lulu flings herself down to the floor and cuts at the air by kicking out her shapely legs, and then Pabst transitions, via a viciously hard cut, to Lulu biting Schön's hand, which leads to them kissing intensely, his hand trembling with desire as he clutches her head. Then comes the money shot of Brooks's career: Lulu is caught with Schön on the floor by Charlotte, and she looks up at her with an expression of smeared satisfaction, an indelible come-on and an outright gloating admission of female sexual power.

And that power had few limits. The most touching thread in the film is Lulu's relationship with the lesbian Countess Geschwitz (Alice Roberts), a Sapphic study that remains unlike anything else in the cinema of this time. Geschwitz loves Lulu obsessively. At Lulu's wedding to Schön, the women dance together and Geschwitz closes her eyes in ecstasy over holding her beloved. During this dance scene, Lulu goes through a series of ambivalent emotions that testify to Brooks's nearly tender, sexy openness as well as her worldly knowledge of many still-unspoken feelings.

Brooks intimated that she had a few lesbian encounters, one with Garbo, out of "vanity," and it is this vanity in a straight woman that she puts on the screen in *Pandora's Box* wholly and without flinching. Lulu looks amused, shy, exploratory, alarmed but game, as her hands intertwine with her besotted Countess. Later, when Geschwitz hugs Lulu tightly, Brooks does a perfect reaction of smiling vagueness at this affection, as if it came from an unexpected source but was not unwelcome, for Lulu is all instinct, no intellect, unlike her creator.

The humiliated Schön confronts Lulu and gives her a gun to kill herself, but she shoots him, seemingly by accident, and we only see the merest puff of smoke. Lulu looks bewildered when he slumps down dead, clutching at her body, of course, before dying. In court, Lulu's lawyer proclaims, "She is innocent!" and damned if she isn't just that, sitting in the witness box in her widow's weeds, looking downright mythological, inscrutable, as she smiles at the assembly. Geschwitz furiously defends her Lulu, explaining that the crime was caused by a bad upbringing, just as Brooks might be explained by her encounter with Mr. Flowers/Feathers.

Lulu is sentenced to prison for manslaughter, but Schigolch and Quast make sure a fire alarm is pulled, and in the ensuing panic she drifts casually from the court. After her escape from town with her admirers in tow, Lulu eventually winds up walking the streets of London, as Brooks later landed in New York, though not quite on the streets. (When Lulu gulps liquor and shudders, we can see proof that Brooks had some imaginative talent, for her own fondness for gin was chronic.)

Lulu actually finds some real affection with one john, but he turns out to be Jack the Ripper (Gustav Diessl). He doesn't even have any money, but she tells him to come up anyway because she likes the look of him. When he stabs her, all we see is her hand stiffen and then fall like a flower. "It is Christmas Eve, and she is about to receive the gift that has been her dream since childhood," Brooks wrote. "Death by a sexual maniac."

Pandora's Box was a flop in Germany, and she received uncomprehending reviews. "Louise Brooks cannot act," wrote the critic Auberon Waugh as late as 1982. "She does not suffer. She does nothing." This and other earlier notices entirely missed the point and drift of her amoral interpretation and Pabst's clear-eyed point of view. In America, Pabst's film was cut to pieces by censors and an ending was tacked-on where it was said that Lulu had reformed and joined the Salvation Army.

The critics didn't know how to handle the subtlety of Brooks's performance in movement in *Pandora's Box*, her shameless appearance, as if she doesn't know she's being watched, the fact that she doesn't "act," but she achieved the highest level to be attained in screen acting, what Brooks later called, "the movement of thought and soul transmitted in a kind of intense isolation." Paradoxically, her admitted lack of control and knowledge of what she was doing in films makes her *look* like she is in total control, as if her abandon and freedom from any kind of self-consciousness were so extreme that it left her seeming all-knowing and alive and consummately truthful moment to moment.

In the capricious decision that ruined her career ever after, Brooks refused to come back to Hollywood to dub in her own voice for the sound conversion of *The Canary Murder Case*, which was poorly dubbed by another actress, Margaret Livingston. At the same time, she slept with Pabst once in Paris and found the experience so exciting that she didn't want to risk a repeat performance. This would prove very frustrating for him off screen, but very fertile for one more film collaboration.

In her second communion with Pabst, *Diary of a Lost Girl* (1929), one of the most erotic films ever made, Brooks is glowingly convincing as a wholly pure girl ready to be corrupted, arching her neck in radiant submission as she surrenders herself at a whorehouse. Her Thymian does what she is told and is constantly taken advantage of, but she finally finds freedom in prostitution, like Catherine Deneuve's *Belle de Jour* (1967) for Luis Buñuel.

In her handful of films, Louise Brooks proved that the camera was hers to command.

"I was simply playing myself," she told Leacock. "Which is the hardest thing in the world to do. You can give most actors any part in the world to do and they can play it, but if you say, 'Be yourself,' they get terribly self-conscious. But because I never learned to act, I never had any trouble playing myself." Brooks was like someone up on a tightrope walking across with no net, and no one ever made her aware of that or shouted "Look down!"

In a scene where Thymian is supposed to be drunk at a club, Pabst gave Brooks some champagne so that she could really be tipsy. No "acting" is allowed to get in the way of her *being* on screen here. Few people responded to this at the time. "Louise, if I ever write a part for a cigar store Indian, you will get it," screenwriter Anita Loos told her. But it is that very lack of effort, that cleanness of line and effect, that made her seem so modern when she was rediscovered.

Brooks isn't expressive in the way that, say, Gish or Bette Davis is, but no one before or since on screen has ever been more purely *there* than she is. Her gaze is challengingly direct, and it matches the rare sexual honesty of her two films for Pabst. She moves lyrically in *Diary of a Lost Girl*, instinctually, like the dancer she was. In every way that counts, she is naked up there on screen, and turning around as slowly as possible, with no defenses, no technique, nothing to shield her from our scrutiny.

Brooks played one more lead in *Prix de Beauté* (1930), directed by Augusto Genina after René Clair prepared it and then bailed out. Filmed as a silent but then partially converted to sound with some inexpertly dubbed French dialogue, *Prix de Beauté* is something of a rough mish-mosh, but its theme is unusual and pointed and it has a stylistic lightness that makes for a refreshing contrast to conclude her holy trinity of feminist movies.

Office drone Lucienne (Brooks) has a jealous boyfriend (Georges Charlia) whom she keeps reassuring, but this is clearly not a woman made for reassurances. She's filled with restless gaiety, her armored face exploding into frequent smiles, but her sexy hints of submission are nothing but sensual playacting, and her childish abandon often gives way to angry, adult glares.

Brooks was drunk most of the time while she acted in *Prix de Beauté*, according to her director Genina, who kept asking her to smile, smile, smile. Yet she still has that rare, jolting camera charisma. Such is her physical authority and gleaming patent leather singularity that she's an enslaving presence, and she needs no accouterments, no pretexts, nothing. If she hits you the right way, you want to do nothing else but look at her, doing anything, doing nothing.

Lucienne wins a beauty contest and is given the title Miss Europe, but her boyfriend makes her give up on pageants for marriage. Languishing in a kitchen, Lucienne looks at a canary in a cage and clearly identifies with it. When deciding to leave her marriage in *Prix de Beauté*, Brooks's face is drenched in anguish, which makes her more beautiful. Giving in to tears, she is very touching because she never loses her hauteur, or her pride.

In the final sequence, which was entirely written and conceived by René Clair, Lucienne goes to see a screen test of herself singing a song about jealousy. She watches her own image with childish enthusiasm. Her vengeful husband lurches into the screening room and shoots her, and we see the impact of the shot on her face. She falls forward, and then Genina cuts to a prescient composition: Lucienne's corpse is in the foreground but her image continues to sing on the screen in the background. And then there's a cut to her deathly white face in close-up, the light from the projector still flickering on it.

She really does seem dead, just as Gish does in *La Bohème*, but in a radically different way, because everything about Brooks seems to have some kind of sexual connotation. There's almost something supernatural or vampirish about the appearance of her corpse here, something cold and luscious still. This brief series of shots is an almost too perfect metaphor for her life and career. Brooks would never star in another film.

When she got back to Hollywood, there was nothing waiting for her. Silent film stars needed to cross that sound divide quickly, and Brooks had stayed in Europe too long. She claimed that Paramount blacklisted her, and a contract at Columbia didn't work out when she turned down the sexual advances of boss Harry Cohn. Even though she was at the height of her beauty and only 25, she was reduced to a poor two-reel comedy, *Windy Reilly Goes Hollywood* (1931), in which she doesn't seem to know what she's doing but tries her best, and thereafter she played only four small parts.

Brooks has a brief, piquant scene at the beginning of *It Pays to Advertise* (1931), but then she disappears from the film. She's tenth-billed in a Frank Fay vehicle, *God's Gift to Women* (1931), and for most of the movie she merely sips drinks and disappears into crowds and is little more than a pretty extra. But there are two shots that leave no doubt that the camera is hers to command. One is a long shot as she fixes her stockings in Fay's bathroom, with her long-stemmed legs accentuated in the light. The second shot is a gasp-inducing close-up. It's a close-up meant to shake or even stop the world.

William Wellman offered her a role in *The Public Enemy* (1931), which would have put her right at the center of the talkies opposite James Cagney. She accepted but then changed her mind in order to visit her lover George Marshall in New York. The part went to Jean Harlow. It was Brooks's last promising film opportunity.

She made her living dancing in nightclubs for a few years and then took a chorus girl job that was cut from Columbia's *When You're in Love* (1937) after Harry Cohn publicized her comeback in insulting terms. Brooks then took a thankless role in a fly-by-night western, *Empty Saddles* (1936), and her last film part was in another cheap western called *Overland Stage Raiders* (1938), opposite a young, green John Wayne.

In her two westerns, Brooks is just a moody journeyman player with a soured face and an affected voice (she was uncomfortable with dialogue and never got the proper direction to ease her anxiety). Incapable of strategic moves sexually, socially or financially, unlike just about every other figure in this book, Brooks didn't play the game with powerful men because the game offended her and also because there was enough perversity in her to really finish her off.

Finally, in 1940, she went home to Kansas in the role of a disgrace, scrubbing kitchen floors for penance. In the mid-1940s, Brooks went to Manhattan, and her humiliation of herself sunk to its lowest and scariest level, leading to stints as salesgirl and call girl, until she was an overweight, alcoholic middle-aged near-recluse who "started to flirt with fancies related to little bottles filled with yellow pills." Luckily, CBS founder William Paley, an old friend and lover, came to her rescue and began to give her a monthly allowance, which she lived on for the rest of her solitary days.

Around the mid-1950s, the miracle happened. Due to the help of film preservationist James Card at Eastman House Museum and others, she was acclaimed, chiefly for *Pandora's Box,* as a neglected and essential film player. "There is no Garbo, there is no Dietrich, there is only Louise Brooks!" cried Cinémathèque Française head Henri Langlois when asked why he put a blow-up photo of Brooks in the lobby of his theater. At last, everything fell into place for her. Brooks looked back at her 20 years of nothing and her long-neglected sense of superiority finally seemed confirmed.

She wrote her memoirs and then destroyed them, taking the title *Naked on My Goat,* an allusion to a section of Goethe's *Faust.* "Powder becomes, like petticoat, a grey and wrinkling noddy," says a young witch to an old one. "So I sit naked on my goat, and show my fine young body." The old witch replies that the young girl will soon be sagging and rotting. Yet it was only as an older woman that Brooks really came into her own. When she was young, her gleaming snarly sexy exterior did not match the intellectual and cultural yearning of her interior, and so the men and women around her never realized who she was and wanted to be.

If Brooks had died in the early 1930s, her film work would likely still have been re-discovered and celebrated, but she would not be as suggestive and attractive a figure if she had not lived to become a writer and a mainly merry recluse. Her full essays and her various wisecracks in interviews can still be quoted and they still retain their shapely F. Scott Fitzgerald-like perfection. It is easy to respond to her Lulu and her Thymian, but the real test is if you respond to Brooks's self-styled intellectual persona as an older woman in Rochester, New York. In many ways, the Rochester version of Brooks is her most seductive and most provocative achievement.

In 1960, when Brooks was in Manhattan to introduce a screening of *Prix de Beauté,* she had lunch with Lillian Gish and got very drunk. "Goddammit!" she cried, out of nowhere, as they were saying goodbye. The patient Gish took her by the shoulders and said, "Louise, God *bless* it." Brooks joked that Gish then gave her "an encouraging hug and damn near broke [her] rib cage."

She saw herself as a victim of Hollywood and men, and she began to say she had left Hollywood to escape from motion picture slavery. Yet others saw her differently. When she sat for artist Don Bachardy, he described Brooks as "a dipsomaniac for sure, probably a nymphomaniac, and certainly a destructomaniac, she is driven to excess and helpless to resist." She was caught up in what her friend Roddy McDowall called "some personal vendetta against herself, which short-circuited a lot of things for her … in the hands of the unsympathetic, she would fragment."

Rarely leaving her apartment in Rochester, where Card set her up near Eastman House, Brooks gleefully went about constructing her latter-day image in a handful of hard, precise, sometimes evasive essays. The best is a consideration of her friend Pepi Lederer, Marion Davies's cousin, which is an unsparing look at a failed life that ends with Lederer's suicide and tragicomic funeral, where actress Katherine Menjou, in a white dress with black polka dots, was "waving to everyone as if she were greeting friends at a garden party. She quite stole the scene from poor old Pepi, lying there in her bronze casket." Brooks, too, committed suicide and then had the joy of seeing reactions to it while she was still legally alive, knowing that the love and pity for Lulu and her creator would only increase after her actual death.

Brooks embodied America in the 1920s, and she was also the emblem of decadent Weimar Germany. To quote Stephen Sondheim, in the Depression she was depressed. She is Edna St. Vincent Millay's candle that burned at both ends, and when the lovely light of the 1920s was extinguished, Brooks was also snuffed out before rising again as a writer. Past 1955 or so, her self-loathing coupled with a growing self-admiration turned her into a very magnetic older woman in solitary who spent the rest of her life in bed with books and gin. Many people would like to link failure to integrity, and she managed that quite righteously well.

Brooks never lost that first disillusionment in adolescence that seems bottomless because there is nothing to compare it to. Frozen in mortification, her face a lasting monument to outraged purity, she learned not to expect anything from life. Pabst, her erstwhile Josef von Sternberg and mentor, finally gave up on her childish fury and aimlessness. "Your life is exactly like Lulu's," he concluded, "and you will end the same way."

Greta Garbo
Mademoiselle Hamlet

The legend of Greta Garbo has started to fade a bit with time, though she still has a coterie of fans who can't get enough of her. Her image used to exist in an atmosphere of incense and acres of prose from intellectuals like Roland Barthes and Kenneth Tynan right on down the line to the old movie magazines. After she retired from acting in 1941, her solitary, threadbare life was an object of intense curiosity for 50 years, and in 1995, five years after her death, Barry Paris published his definitive biography of Garbo, presenting the real person as found in letters and interviews with her friends. What emerged was not displeasing. There were rumors that Garbo had been dull, even stupid. But that was not true at all. From the evidence of Paris's book, Garbo was a genuinely offbeat person with an eccentric personality to match her one-of-a-kind face.

Garbo was once voted the most beautiful woman who ever lived by the Guinness Book of World Records. Is she? There's no way of judging such things, of course, but let's say for a moment that she is, or was. What made her beautiful? Technically speaking, it has to be the large velveteen gap between her eyelids and her eyebrows. This area was emphasized with make-up as her career progressed, so that her eyes looked like the excessive, nearly gaudy invention of an inspired painter. Her nose was rather large, her mouth thin, with barely a hard line for her upper lip.

Her body was gangly and she moved awkwardly, tipping over to the right and to the left like a ship on a stormy sea, her shoulders constantly hunched up around her ears. She designed to display her swan-like neck by throwing her head back in submission, joy, despair, and everything else in between. Garbo's expressive hands had long tapering fingers, and these extremities were matched by her large and frequently hidden feet. Her breasts, usually sans brassiere, sagged and pointed stylishly in sweaters and in some of the screen's most outlandish costumes. She preferred her hair to hang lank to her shoulders, and she walked with a determined stride.

Just looking at her is transfixing, hypnotic. Was Garbo a great actress?

She hardly needed to be. During her relatively short movie career, she worked in several drastically different performance modes, and her films, taken chronologically, show her somewhat tardy development as a performer. As late as 1932, in one of her most famous movies, *Grand Hotel*, she was capable of giving a very poor performance, but after that she gave several performances that place her in the small pantheon of major screen actors. And in her silent and early talkie programmers, she was never less than an extraordinarily vibrant and autoerotic screen presence.

She was born into a lower-class family in Sweden in 1905, and she wasn't a beauty from the start; early photographs reveal a large girl with frizzy hair and bad teeth. She went to drama school and picked up some stagy technical tricks that would mar her early films in Hollywood (closing her eyes slowly to register despair and clutching her head in a crisis were the worst of them).

Garbo cavorted in a bathing suit in her first film, *Peter the Tramp* (1922), a comedy short that is the *ne plus ultra* of undistinguished debuts. As is so often the case with stars of the first rank, she was discovered and mentored by a fine director, Mauritz Stiller, and he cast her in his lengthy ensemble piece *The Saga of Gosta Berling* (1924). She turns up about 40 minutes into the film, disappears for most of the second hour, and then steals the whole thing completely in the last 15 minutes.

As an Italian Countess in love with Lars Hanson's sexy defrocked priest, Garbo is a bit tentative physically and seems apprehensive when asked to interact with others, but she has several close-ups that stop the movie cold (she asked for champagne before her important scenes, and the resulting tipsiness in her eyes reads as voluptuous sensual abandon). In the movie's most famous sequence, a sleigh ride chase across icy tundra, Hanson and Garbo create a real erotic excitement based on the contrast between his assurance and her tingly, nervous submission.

Stiller then brought her over to Germany to make G.W. Pabst's gritty, ambitious *The Joyless Street* (1925), where her character nearly becomes a prostitute. In these early European films, Garbo is still in an unfocused, woozy, embryonic state. She sometimes indicates emotions in *Joyless Street*, but in a highly unusual, minimalist way, her face twitching ever so slightly to show what she is thinking without enough smoothing out to make a full or believable transition from thought to thought.

In close-up in *Joyless Street*, the camera seems sure that Garbo has *something*, but just what it is isn't clear yet. Is she a sexpot? Is she ill? Just what is going on with her? Pabst knew what he had: "Such a face you see once in a century," he told the film's lead, the formidable Asta Nielsen. *The Joyless Street* isn't a Garbo movie but a movie, and a fine one, that Garbo is in. This would soon be rectified. In her subsequent work, there would be nothing but vehicles for her, all of which become Garbo Movies.

Louis B. Mayer, head of MGM, saw *Gosta Berling* and brought Stiller and Garbo to Hollywood. Stiller did not direct her debut, *Torrent* (1926), a melodrama that was laid in Spain, so to speak, where Garbo's character becomes a famous opera singer called La Brunna. At this point it was clear that she was bringing an unprecedentedly heated, liquid quality to the screen, a simmering, complex, loaded and weighted down sensibility that periodically took off into flights of ironic mockery, as when she laughs at her leading man, Ricardo Cortez. Sometimes her movements were clunky, galumphing, but she swoons in her love scenes with Cortez, already taking the top position in horizontal romantic duets, bearing down on him to kiss him.

Stiller was supposed to guide her sophomore effort, *The Temptress* (1926), but he was fired and all his footage was re-shot by Fred Niblo. During the filming of the movie, Garbo was informed that her sister Alva had died at the age of 23. When she heard of Garbo's loss, Lillian Gish sent her flowers, and Garbo came to thank her. "Tears came to her eyes," Gish said. "I couldn't speak Swedish so I put my arms around her and we both cried." As Gish and Garbo so often proved on screen, sometimes you don't need words to communicate.

The opening of *The Temptress* is very sexy. Garbo appears at a party wearing a mask. Already wanting to be alone, she rushes through the crowd and can't seem to lose them, but then The Man comes into her life. The Man in Garbo movies is of little importance. He can be feminine and overwrought (John Gilbert, Ramon Novarro), masculine and indifferent (John Barrymore, Fredric March), pretty and lively (Lew Ayres, Robert Taylor), or even a great actor like herself (Charles Boyer). But Garbo works alone.

The Man in *The Temptress* is Antonio Moreno, and he asks Garbo to take off her mask. Her head bobbing back, her mouth opening submissively, she slowly removes the mask and the camera lingers on Moreno as he reacts before we see her face in all its nakedness, as if she has taken off her panties for him. They share a love scene, and then *The Temptress* goes dead until it lands in Argentina, where a vampy, down-and-out Garbo taunts Moreno at length and seems relieved to be free of feminine clothes and affectations. Suddenly she's riveting: drunk, wasted, whispering lewd suggestions to Moreno. The actress displaces the sex star, but only momentarily.

Garbo in her Hollywood silents is selling sex, sometimes to the exclusion of all else. But she has a spiritually magnetic quality as early as *The Temptress* because of one essential paradox: her need to be alone, her resistance to society at large, and her helpless, immense response to love in the abstract for one person. When she first kisses Moreno, her hand trembles a bit as she clutches at his head, and her love scenes are still erotic today because her sexuality is so rough, so filled with nervous energy. She always subjugates her leading men, grabbing them bodily and getting on top, and this was just natural to Garbo, a large part of her subversive quality. Her sublime lesbian authoritativeness worked best, of course, with slightly nelly men.

Garbo's next film, *Flesh and the Devil* (1926), paired her with randy John Gilbert. Most of the movie is buddy stuff with Gilbert and Lars Hanson, who are flanked by a young ingénue with Mary Pickford curls, but Garbo wipes such D. W. Griffith antiques aside when she gets Gilbert in a clinch. She has charm, danger, and irony, putting bug-eyed Gilbert in his place on bearskin rugs and making him love it, just as he loved it in real life, too. About their much-publicized off-screen coupling, Louise Brooks was blunt: "She went out with him and gave him a casual lay from time to time for the sake of her career. On safe ground, she gave him a fast broom."

Flesh and the Devil made her a star in America, but Garbo is less an actress in that movie and more of a sex goddess, playing her famous love bouts with Gilbert as if she's in some kind of sex coma. In a naughty scene set in church, Garbo takes a communion chalice and moves it so that she can press her lips to where Gilbert's lips just touched, a cartoonish, high camp blasphemy. Towards the end of the film, when Garbo tries to emote, she betrays her inexperience, throwing an extremely atypical hissy fit as the ingénue prays. She is so hot here that the story has to end with her falling into a crack in an iced-over lake.

Garbo still had much chemistry with Gilbert in *Love* (1927), where she practically French kisses her pretty young son, but she went over the top in some of her more extravagant reactions (a scene at a racetrack where she reacts with fear to Gilbert's dangerous riding is especially overdone). In *The Mysterious Lady* (1928), however, she has become the Garbo of legend, her hair longer and straighter,

Greta Garbo offers a come-hither glance as she devours John Gilbert in *Flesh and the Devil*.

her eyes carefully made up, her mask-like visage able to suggest old age and extreme youth in flashes. Her face has become more austere here, more masculine, and it is this masculinity that completed her beauty. In life, Garbo habitually referred to herself with masculine pronouns, exhibiting an unusual sort of camp lesbianism.

The Mysterious Lady contains a memorable entrance for Garbo. She sits in a box at the opera and looks transported by the music, but when it is over she cries out and seems to laugh at herself a little for being so deeply moved, which shows her instinct for self-parody, at times as acute as that of her future *Grand Hotel* co-star John Barrymore. She's a spy with flashes of conscience in *The Mysterious Lady*, a fantasy woman, her manner nearly swaggering.

In *A Woman of Affairs* (1928), smoothly directed by Clarence Brown, Garbo perfected her image of haunted, tender, sometimes disdainful discrimination, slowly arching one eyebrow or furrowing her brow so that it looks like artfully wrinkled silk. Her best work is usually very minimal. As Charles Affron puts it in his 1977 book *Star Acting*, "Garbo clearly knows the degree of expression that will convey the situation without seriously jeopardizing the arrangement of her face, which we always perceive in its formal repeatability."

But she was still capable of missteps that did indeed jeopardize that contemplative arrangement, like the open-mouthed "scream!" she does when Johnny Mack Brown jumps out of a window in *A Woman of Affairs* and a similar scream when she wakes from a nightmare in *Wild Orchids* (1929). Her overall impression of soulfulness got her over any and all hurdles like this, though occasionally this soulful thing of hers resembled dyspepsia more than anything else.

In *The Kiss* (1929), she stares directly into the camera in screen-filling close-up, the ultimate in come-hither movie goddessdom. Garbo went through the motions of despair over love again and again in her movies, clutching her head and collapsing, though no one has ever claimed or verified that she ever did so in life, where her focus was almost entirely on herself.

The dream woman of her silents had to make way for sound, and she finally spoke in a movie of Eugene O'Neill's play *Anna Christie* (1930). The American version, helmed by Garbo's most frequent director, Clarence Brown, is an early talkie with all the defects of its tentative time period. Shots are held for no reason when people have exited the frame, as if no one is behind the camera, and the sound is very muffled.

Garbo's deep voice wowed audiences at the time, and her short staccato laugh is distinctive, but she's trying too hard here, especially when she talks tough. Her Anna, an embittered prostitute, is filled with unappealing self-pity. As an imperious drunk, Marie Dressler steals the film. Watch the way Dressler puts her hand to her face when she realizes she's blown Garbo's cover with her new lover. That's focused, imaginative acting, like Gish shyly touching her plain face in *True Heart Susie*, and it is something Garbo herself was incapable of at this point.

A second version of *Anna Christie* was shot in German immediately after the Hollywood film, and Garbo is much more at ease in this language because the dialogue seems more to the point. The German Anna has been to jail, and she's much believably tougher than her Hollywood counterpart, less sorry for herself. Garbo's Hollywood Anna seems like a movie star impersonating a hooker, and it's hard to imagine her turning a trick. Garbo's German Anna seems like a pro, and though she loathes men, she's obviously fond of sex.

In the American version, her lover, Charles Bickford, is a harsh-voiced Irishman who talks to her paternally, and he stokes her strenuous anger. Her German lover, Theo Shall, is smaller and prettier, a sensual child, and she reacts to him as if she's both touched and turned on (the obscure Shall is one of her best leading men). The two versions of *Anna Christie* are fairly untenable for a modern audience, but the German version is far superior.

Established in talkies, Garbo then made a series of films where she was typecast again as a sexually promiscuous woman swayed by love for a more innocent man, among them *Romance* (1930), *Inspiration* (1931), *Susan Lenox: Her Fall and Rise* (1931) and *As You Desire Me* (1932), an awkward stab at Pirandello where she plays her first scenes with bleached blond hair and delivers most of her lines with heavily underlined irony.

Her emotional transitions have become as smooth as silk in this period, all liquid like Eleonora Duse, and yet she also specializes in very unusual kinds of in-between feelings and mixed states of mind all her own. You cannot put some of what she is trying for facially into words, at least not in English. Perhaps she was still *thinking* in Swedish? So many of Garbo's best close-ups tell us that words are not enough for all she is feeling. She is a tuning fork in these pictures, almost absurdly receptive.

"I'm just a nice young woman. Not too young, not so nice—I hope," she says campily in *Inspiration*. She had her moments in all of these rushed early talkies, moments of charm and bubbly gaiety, of sophisticated humor, of very heightened sensitivity, both vocally and physically. Her low voice completed her screen persona and made her more direct, more understandable. There are some things she cannot do, though, such as slap a female rival in *Inspiration*; she looks very uncomfortable doing so. But within a focused range of romantic intensity, no one could touch her commitment or belief, even if she herself looked down on these first sound movies. She charmingly tries to be "Italian" sometimes in *Romance*, a faded antique based on an Edward Sheldon play, and sometimes she poses a bit too much in despair, but such defects are like the accumulated dust or dirt on a beautiful old painting, understandable and easy to overlook.

Mata Hari (1931) seems to have been made solely so MGM's costume designer Adrian could put Garbo in some of the most outlandish outfits he could think of. Her tongue firmly in her cheek, she tries and fails to do an exotic dance, romances Ramon Novarro, wears a succession of jeweled skullcaps, kills Lionel Barrymore, and marches off to the firing squad. "This is absurd," she says, early on, as if she wants to walk off the set.

At the peak of her popularity in spite of these cheap little movies, which did big business for MGM, she was then placed as the figurehead of the first all-star production, *Grand Hotel*. Again, one of Garbo's key early films is stolen by someone else: Joan Crawford, who was born to play the role of Flaemmchen, a stenographer on the make. As a weary ballerina, Garbo is very miscalculated, making errant, staccato, unconvincing choices. Her first "tired" close-up is the purest camp, and she lingers on the bad dialogue so cluelessly that it finally becomes obvious how lost she is with the English language.

Her body language in *Grand Hotel* is equally off pitch as she tries to be a dancer and throws herself around her hotel room. Garbo postures, declaims, and overacts, even when she says her most famous line, "I want to be alone." She's easier to take when the character is awakened by love, but she descends into camp again when she talks melodramatically to a telephone. It's a cringeworthy performance, but her best work was just around the corner.

Garbo took some time off, and when she returned under a new contract at MGM, she had more control over her films. Gradually, the biggest movie star in the world and the most beautiful woman began to gain the confidence necessary to become a major actress. This process began with *Queen Christina* (1933), a spectacle about the Swedish queen directed by Rouben Mamoulian and saddled with John Gilbert in his penultimate movie. Garbo insisted that her ruined former lover have the part, and she doesn't let his awkwardness get in her way even once. She never needed partners. She is a solitary creator.

It's clear that English is still an obstacle course for her in *Queen Christina*, especially during long verbose speeches, which she plows through in a determined, forceful manner, but the Sapphic flavor of the film is quite fetching, and Garbo obviously loves striding around in velvet trousers and soul kissing her favorite lady in waiting. In some ways, this is a movie more for her enjoyment than for ours, but her work here is strong and varied. Watch the symphonic series of grimaces she does when her Christina, dressed as a boy, is forced to share a room with Gilbert, or the many gestures with her hands that are the very essence of queenly authority. Thoughts seem to be tumbling behind her eyes and we only see the ends of them, so that her emotional registers are curiously both fluid and static.

Queen Christina comes to life in a long scene at an inn where Garbo spends the night with Gilbert and then memorizes the contents of the room where they have shared their tryst, a risky set piece that was choreographed like a dance by Mamoulian. It showed her poignant attachment to the physical world, her sensualizing of it, before it was time to go and be alone. Age was smoothing out Garbo's features, and her Helen of Troy aspect was becoming more mask-like.

When she lifts herself off of Gilbert's dead body at the end of *Queen Christina*, there are two tracks of tears coming out of her left eye, one to the left, one to the right, and the visual effect of this is unaccountably moving (there is a slight trail of a tear coming from her right eye, too, but it is relatively insignificant next to the two-from-one next door). The famous final close-up of her impassive face in *Queen Christina* is one of those movie things that you never get over, an always-renewable subject for contemplation. It has the inscrutability of life, of creation itself. What does it mean? Whatever you want it to. And Garbo makes that concept seem filled with limitless possibility rather than just empty. It's a religious moment, really, a Zen revelation. There, for however long you can feel it, is God, beauty, emptiness, the void.

Reviewing her career, the real surprise is *Anna Karenina* (1935), which features a superlatively concentrated, minimal performance by Garbo. It is directed in a pedestrian fashion by Clarence Brown, indifferently acted by the rest of the cast, truncated, unenthusiastic, a dead thing as a film. But Garbo is in her element. Gone is the absurd posturing of *Grand Hotel*. Gone is the need to try too hard, as in *Anna Christie*. Here she is in complete command.

Her face first emerges in *Anna Karenina* from a gust of smoke, haughty, remote, tired of being looked at, and behind her slumberous, captivating eyes is a Niagara Falls of quicksilver thought. She is able to fill any line of dialogue here with the deepest emotion, and she accomplishes this without strain, as if she's in a trance, which she has to be in order to create in this MGM vacuum. When her cuckolded husband (Basil Rathbone) shouts her out of the house, her walk down the stairs is thrilling because of its steady focus and near impassivity; she just keeps moving with a weary, somewhat bewildered look on her face.

When Anna's brother (Reginald Owen) reminds her that mores must be upheld for the benefit of the public, she says, "Yes, they're very important," in a piercingly rich, insincere, distracted voice. Garbo's late performances are filled with these large jolts of meaning, as if she is capable of joining together any opposing ideas in an instant, a living, breathing, beautiful dialectic. She makes Anna's suicide look like the product of grave and intelligent reflection.

At this point, Garbo was in the zone artistically speaking, and she serendipitously got herself into a film that did her mature talent full justice, George Cukor's *Camille* (1936), a Balzacian study of suffocating, vulgar nineteenth century Parisian life. "I'm afraid of nothing except being bored," says Garbo's Marguerite Gautier, a consumptive courtesan impelled by her heartless milieu, and impending death, into a life of flip bitchery and frivolity.

Garbo's light touch in *Camille* is as rarified as her beauty, and her new-found sense of living and acting dangerously and without a net informs every bold, contrary choice she makes. That Marguerite is physically ill allows Garbo to be ultra-liquid in *Camille*, with split-second but legible emotional nuances glimmering all over her face like light on a body of water. This is work that is still as advanced as acting can possibly get, and almost beyond behavior sometimes and on to something else, something impatiently beyond even her responses and our perceptions.

She kills all sentimentality in this material with her masculine severity, and even with hints of anger, but only hints, as when she stares up at the censorious father (Lionel Barrymore) of her lover Armand (Robert Taylor). She goes as far as she can with her own wooziness in this picture, with just a touch of madness flickering ever-so-gently sometimes behind those quicksilver eyes of hers. Garbo in *Camille* makes feeling and thinking too much seem very erotic. No one else ever kicked over the traces and burned candles at both ends quite like this on screen.

Producer Irving Thalberg was very excited after he saw the early rushes of *Camille*, and Cukor asked

Garbo looks up in anger in *Camille*.

him why. "Don't you understand?" Thalberg asked, "She is completely *unguarded*." She is naked on her goat. Garbo is in such control here that she has no visible control whatever, no visible technique, like Lillian Gish at her best, and this is a substantial change from her self-consciousness in *Grand Hotel*. Her sexuality is even more brazen than it was in her 1920s kissathons. In her first love scene with Robert Taylor, she plants a half-dozen hungry kisses all over his face without using her hands and then bites into his mouth as if she's sinking her teeth into a particularly luscious éclair.

Maybe the finest scene Garbo ever played is a brief bit of dialogue in *Camille* that she shares with Henry Daniell, who plays Marguerite's rich lover the Baron de Varville. As the Baron plays a driving piano melody, he smiles ominously at the thought of Marguerite's new lover Armand ringing her bell outside. When the Baron asks who is ringing, Garbo's Marguerite intones, "I might say it was someone at the wrong door, or the great romance of my life!" She makes a heady emotional leap in between these phrases, as if she's hurling herself off a cliff, and Daniell stays right with her. "The great romance of your life!" he howls, "Charming!" She leaps right back in: "It might have been," she says quickly, and he starts to play the melody louder and faster on the piano. Garbo throws her head back to laugh but no sound comes out. All we hear is the pounding piano melody as the camera draws close to her agony.

This scene is a perfect synthesis of actors, material, music, and direction. We must give Cukor credit here, for surely he is responsible for some of the daring give and take between Garbo and Daniell. The scene leaves an exquisite wound. And so does Garbo's death scene in that moment when her eyes roll up into her head and life leaves her body, which is enough to rival Gish's death in *La Bohème*, but from a far more sensual, sophisticated, knowing sensibility, less realistic, maybe, but memorably delicate and perverse. The film as a whole is filled with the impulse to joke about tragedy, and that's the subversive charm of *Camille* and also the essence of what Garbo was capable of at the peak of her inventiveness.

Jokes about tragedy are also the essence of Garbo's first American comedy, *Ninotchka* (1939), a smooth romantic farce and a satire on Soviet Russia that features one-liners about the secret police and even the Moscow show trials of the late 1930s: "There are going to be fewer but better Russians," insists Garbo's Ninotchka, a dour commissar who is soon bewitched by capitalistic Paris. The joke in the first half of *Ninotchka* is that Garbo totally shuts down her famous responsiveness for Isabelle Huppert–like, stone-faced disapproval, but then another side of Ninotchka slowly comes alive.

Garbo does a visually unflattering and amusingly peasant-gauche reaction when Ninotchka first drinks champagne that is very Eastern European and perhaps close to her own character, or the character of people she knew back in Sweden. This was a totally different sort of performance from her and a change of pace in every way, and the triumph Garbo has in *Ninotchka* is singular because it is based around a serio-comic characterization that uses and re-activates only parts of the dazed persona that had started to seem tired in her previous costume picture *Conquest* (1937).

Her performance in *Ninotchka* is almost entirely deadpan, and she performs the foolproof script with graceful economy, her slow timing just droll enough to get her laughs. Somehow she is both believable as someone who was a ruthless army sergeant during a war and also as an adorably ungainly woman opening herself to hedonistic pleasure for the first time. "I'm so happy!" she says during her enchanting drunk scene, but Garbo has seen enough of her own movies to know better: "No one can be so happy without being punished!" she concludes.

When we hear Garbo's voice in our head, she is always saying lines like that. "I knew I was too happy," she moans in *Camille*. Garbo was always dying or being killed. So obviously doomed by fate, she clutched at people and even at things around her for reassurance. She made love to so many inanimate objects: John Gilbert's flowers amidst the Art Deco rapture of *A Woman of Affairs*, her ballet slipper in *Grand Hotel*, so that everything she touched was eroticized and heightened, and some might laugh at uninhibited impulses like that now. Audiences of the time took pleasure in watching this exotic woman die, seeing her beauty fade into nothingness slowly but surely.

Modern audiences coming across Garbo cold are usually suspicious of her and unimpressed by her grandstanding and her severe beauty. She has lost her status as a cultural event, and a lot of her work has dated. Garbo is pre-modern and then briefly modernist while Marlene Dietrich is already post-modern. Dietrich's cool plays better today than Garbo's mannered heat, but both women are essential film experiences.

It is still popularly accepted that Garbo retired after her last movie, the crass comedy *Two-Faced Woman* (1941), because its failure hurt her pride. This is true, but she was willing to return several times in the late 1940s, most tantalizingly for a version of Balzac's *Duchesse de Langeais* to be directed by Max Ophuls with James Mason as her co-star. Garbo submitted to a screen test for that prospective film, and she is even more beautiful in that test with a bit of age on her. But this dream project ran out of money, and this humiliated her.

She never seriously considered returning again. Garbo lived out her life as a "hermit about town," doing nearly nothing for decades on end. Mainly she walked around Manhattan, carrying a St. Jude statue in her purse. "The best thing is not to think, just trot," she told a friend, after they had done 120 blocks together. She kept a group of troll dolls under one of her couches, moving them into different formations every now and then. Sometimes she had difficulty deciding whether or not to move from one room to another in her spacious, spare apartment in midtown Manhattan. "I am the image of living inertia," she said sadly. "I am a lonely man circling the earth."

Even her most dramatic urges were related matter-of-factly. "Mr. Hitler was big on me," she told her friend Sam Green at dinner one night. "He kept writing and inviting me to come to Germany, and if the war hadn't started when it did, I would have gone and I would have taken a gun out of my purse and shot him, because I'm the only person who would not have been searched."

There was TV to stare at. "I watch the dreck," she said. Garbo "just looked," said her maid, at *Matlock* or *Wheel of Fortune*, or, sometimes, some of her own movies. She had two drinks—usually whiskey—every afternoon. Her life followed a rigid routine, usually, and she went in for health food. She once told a friend:

> I always buy fresh vegetables. They're everywhere and it doesn't take brains to fix them. They don't taste like anything and they just sit there, but I'll tell you a little secret: buy sour cream. They sell it in buckets. All you do is take a great big heap of sour cream and put it on a vegetable with salt and it's delicious ... more fun than with margarine. So get your sour cream, and get going.

Once someone mistook her for Marlene Dietrich in an antique shop: "She obviously didn't get a look at my legs," Garbo quipped. Even her perpetual gloom often had a kind of mordant, camp charm, as if she were some J.K. Huysmans dandy in retreat. When fans would recognize her and approach her (she called them "customers," as in, "Here comes another customer"), she had ways of holding them back. Once a man realized he was seeing Garbo as she was crossing the street, and when she noticed the recognition on his face she simply held a single finger to her mouth to tell him, "Shh," as if her identity could be their momentary, intoxicating secret. Her legend was created by her withdrawal and its resultant publicity. Now that this is behind us and we can look at her films for themselves, Garbo's early shortcomings as an actress and her later achievements stand in stark, still-heady relief.

Marlene Dietrich
Illusions

Marlene Dietrich the person has been revealed to us, it would seem. She has been magnified and amusingly glorified in an extensive 1992 biography by Steven Bach and exposed in a lengthy memoir by her own daughter, Maria Riva, which was also published in 1992. The ambiguities she conveyed on screen, however, will never quite be fully explored or explained.

Can she act, or "act"? Well, she might have purred, does she need to? To her, acting was a magic act, a shell game, a joke, but also an occasion for some tenderness, mock or otherwise. Dietrich is the least naked of all stars, the most hidden, the most artificial, so much so that Louise Brooks called her "that contraption." She is maybe the least truly creative person in this book, and also the most artful.

She seems hip, sometimes, but that might be a mirage. She could suggest many things, but she rarely fully commits to any idea or emotion. She relies on "mystery" and glamour and externals to see her through, the right hat, a new lover. She has faith only in the superficial, in what she can see, in what we can see. She thought of herself as ageless, and she was, in the right light and with the right support, and she was funny and nasty and inappropriate in life, romantically promiscuous, a conqueror who might offer succor or might laugh in your face. "Dietrich's ridicule could have reduced Casanova into nonperformance," Riva wrote.

Some writers think that her collaboration with director Josef von Sternberg on seven films in the early-to-mid 1930s contains the essential Dietrich and that the rest of her film career was a failure to recreate what he saw in her. But Dietrich still made an impact after she left Sternberg's obsessive tutelage. On several occasions she even rose up to the absurdity and corrosiveness of those not-to-be-believed seven fantasies she made with her Svengali.

Without question, though, the most important Dietrich, the one that has lasted, is the Dietrich of the Sternberg films. They are dense works that convey ideas about sexuality and adoration that are still too potent and complex for easy consumption. They deserve continual retrospectives, for there is nothing like them in film history, and certainly no collaboration between an actress and a director that is so private and intense. The haughty Sternberg fell in love with the equally haughty Dietrich, and the only way he could possess her was through the way he cast light on her face. Studded throughout his work with her is his curiosity at her romantic carnivorousness as well as hatred at the way she has enslaved him, mixed with his own self-loathing and lots of camp humor.

If we are to believe her daughter's book, Dietrich was an unrelentingly critical person who put down everyone and everything except her own product and creation, Marlene Dietrich. She was born Marie Magdalene Dietrich in 1901 and started calling herself Marlene as a child. Her childhood diary entries, as quoted in Riva's memoir, reveal an attention-seeking little girl consumed with the idea of romance, and Dietrich would remain this excited exhibitionist and emotional glutton her entire life. Dietrich's mother told her to mask her feelings, told her that showing emotions was bad manners, and this always was stuck in the back of her head.

By the time of her film breakthrough in Sternberg's *The Blue Angel* in 1930, Dietrich was close to 30 and had been around for years in Berlin. She took pains to hide her sequence of German silent films, and she had reason to. In her first movie, *The Little Napoleon* (1923), Dietrich is chubby and full of gross natural energy (after seeing the film she rightly called herself "a potato with hair"). She was an ingénue in William Dieterle's first credit as a director, *Man by the Roadside* (1923), and she often wore a monocle to play a series of frantic trollops in films like *Love Tragedy* (1923), where she met the man who would be her husband and confidante for life, Rudi Sieber.

While appearing on stage at night and winning much favorable comment, Dietrich was reduced to being a dance extra in several mid–1920s films. When she did get real parts in movies they were in crude comedies like *His Greatest Bluff* (1927), which is probably her lowest point as a performer, and she practically gets humped on the dance floor while doing the Black Bottom in *Café Electric* (1927). On stage in the revue *It's in the Air*, Dietrich made a memorably naughty impression singing a lesbian duet with Margo Lion called "My Best Girlfriend" and a song about the sexual kicks to be had from shoplifting called "Kleptomaniacs."

But by the end of the 1920s in movies, Dietrich seemed to be imitating Garbo in late silents like *I Kiss Your Hand, Madame* and *The Woman One Longs For* (both 1929), where she moves lethargically and looks like an empty vessel waiting for some kind of instruction. She seems to have no confidence in what she's doing in those films, and she got bad reviews, one critic even declaring after *The Woman One Longs For* that she "must be given up as any kind of hope."

Reviews like this must have stung the ambitious and restless Dietrich, who was seen as more of a Berlin party girl than anything else. She had been in 17 movies and had appeared in 26 theatrical productions, but she had gotten nowhere. It was Sternberg who brought her out and gave her the confidence to seem all controlling, all powerful. And that "seem" was the biggest "seem" in show business.

Sternberg's *The Blue Angel* is as important a film as when it was first released, and it is very German in that it emphasizes not sexual love but sexual hate. Sternberg was already caught in Dietrich's netting, and he uses that major pain-lover Emil Jannings as the first of many on-screen substitutes for himself, most of them wearing a droopy mustache like his own.

The Blue Angel begins with a washerwoman who splashes clean a poster of Dietrich's cabaret artiste Lola Lola as if to wash away her filth, but after finishing the job the washerwoman compares herself to the poster. This is the first of the contradictory images in their films, the need to obliterate Dietrich followed by the need to have her, even *be* her, for the famed comment by Kenneth Tynan that Dietrich had "sex but no positive gender" hits the nail on the head (she signed her pictures "Daddy Marlene" for her lesbian fans). The word "Dietrich" in German means "skeleton key" or "passkey"—an opening for all locks.

One of the deepest insights of their work is that sexual adoration, stripped of all the vestiges of romantic love, is maybe the most powerful of all emotions. Far from a shallow worship of flesh, it is the idealized hope behind Sternberg's camera that best illustrates the depth of devotion to a sexual object. The seven films he made for her are all offerings, like dozens of roses Dietrich looks at with an unreadable glint in her eyes, impressed with them, maybe, but moving on, falling in love again, always wanting to, always wanting more.

The Blue Angel reeks of sadomasochism. When Dietrich's Lola Lola first appears, she looks arrogant, coarse, impatient, and as she sings, a vendor yells, "Sauerkraut!" Lola displays herself with speculative contempt and then turns a spotlight on the audience, exposing the voyeurs and giving them a taste of their own medicine. She is a sexual careerist, shouting songs in a high, contemptuous voice quite unlike Dietrich's later low foghorn.

Dietrich is juicily full-bodied here, looking like the easiest lay in the world, though Lola says she has put prostitution behind her. "I am an artiste," she sniffs airily. Her legs are phenomenal, poised mouth-wateringly, though Dietrich explained that, "The legs aren't so beautiful, I just know what to do with them," living up to her belief in artificiality, her daydream of herself, which enslaved everyone, as it does Emil Jannings's schoolteacher in *The Blue Angel*.

Lola meanly blows powder at Jannings's Professor in her dressing room and then grows mock maternal. No matter how precisely Sternberg sets out to show Dietrich in all her rampant ugliness and hypocritical romantic attitudes, it never has the intended effect. He loves her too much, and love of such extremity adores the beloved's sadism and vanity as much as their beauty, even loves the negative more if we are dealing with sadomasochism.

The Professor shoos a persistent customer out of Lola's dressing room, and this display of chivalry elicits a memorable, wide-awake close-up of Dietrich, who looks like a shark that senses blood nearby. When she sings her famous hedonist theme song "Falling in Love Again" to Jannings's Professor, he is reduced to a grinning child by her iconic, leg-up pose on a barrel.

When the Professor proposes marriage to her after he is drummed out of school, Lola's rollicking laughter is the cruelest reaction imaginable (Lola seems more heartless in the English language version of *The Blue Angel*, mainly because Dietrich provides more ambiguous facial grace notes in the German print). Over 20 years later, Arthur Kennedy told a story about working with Dietrich in *Rancho Notorious* (1952), a western directed by Fritz Lang. There was a scene where she had to laugh, and Lang made her do it over and over again, but it never sounded like a real laugh. Kennedy felt that Dietrich had "technique to burn, but no spontaneity" at this point, and there were some things she just couldn't do. Lang was a notably unsympathetic director of actors, and she shrunk under his sadism.

So how did Sternberg get that big laugh out of her in both the German and American versions of *The Blue Angel*? It feels both lifelike and also somewhat mechanical, as if she is doing exactly what she has been told to do, throwing her arms up in exactly the same "spontaneous" way both times. Can you really tell the difference between true spontaneity and "spontaneity"? Yes and no. There is always a murky area where nearly everyone gets fooled. Which is why the Sternberg-Dietrich films are such key works when it comes to judging, or trying to judge, acting, or "acting."

In this proposal scene, Sternberg gives Dietrich a "look up, then look down," eye mannerism that carries through the rest of their work, and she used it often when she didn't feel like "acting" later on. In something like *Pittsburgh* (1942), perhaps the nadir of Dietrich's star career, she spends the entire film mechanically looking up and looking down until it becomes very creepy, the clearest case of the "puppet without her puppeteer" argument against her. Even in the Sternberg films, this up-down eye thing can be disastrous, but it does not mar Lola Lola.

At the end of *The Blue Angel*, Jannings goes even farther down than he did in F.W. Murnau's *The Last Laugh* (1924), down to the depths of humiliation, which was this actor's specialty. Married to Lola, the disgraced professor is reduced to walking out onstage in clown make-up to loudly jeering former students. We see Lola kissing an admirer, her eyes directly on her husband to catch his reaction. Her last line is a protective, "I haven't done anything!" (This is the defensive position Dietrich took at the end of her life in the 1984 documentary *Marlene*.) Finally the humiliated Professor tries to strangle Lola-Dietrich, and according to Dietrich, Jannings really *did* strangle her for stealing his picture and left bruises on her neck. Surviving, of course, Lola chants her theme song "Falling in Love Again" with masculine swagger, lapping up applause as her due.

Dietrich's performance as Lola Lola remains eternally fresh, insolent, very seemingly natural, yet packed with an excitingly self-conscious eroticism, as if she knows she's being ogled and sometimes wants to make it easier for us to look her over from stem to stern. Or, as stem-to-Sternberg himself wrote her in a cable as she sailed to America, "You have permitted my camera to worship you and in turn you have worshipped yourself."

Sex in the theater will always be sexier than sex in movies because theater is a hot medium, immediate, happening right in front of you, with real bodies moving in space, right there to be looked at and lusted after. What Dietrich intuited is that a similar excitement can be created on film if the one being watched makes it as clear as possible that they *know* they are being watched by a limitless everyone out there, whereas Louise Brooks and Marilyn Monroe are sexy precisely because they seem so totally *unaware* of being watched. Like Lillian Gish, a drastically different performer, Dietrich installed a mirror by the camera to watch herself, and by the time she left Sternberg, she knew more about lighting than any cameraman. In her 1961 book *Marlene Dietrich's ABC* under "camera" she wrote, "A friend of mine. We understood each other."

Dietrich's awareness is risky, because self-consciousness can often lead to bad, stiff acting, which is very unsexy, but she contrived to be an aware sexual presence, not an actress. She offers a state of mind. She does not need parts or plots. All she needs is light, costumes to put on and take off, and maybe a little dialogue to purr. The dialogue needed to be as non-committal as possible. She suggested that all this—movies, life—was foolish and empty. But it was just a suggestion. It was all the same to her. All is vanity, but who will not own to liking a little of it?

When the director and his actress came to America, Sternberg's view of

Dietrich became much more guarded, for he could not serve the American public the ruthless Lola and expect his protégée to become a star in Hollywood. In Germany, tales of sexual degradation were practically the most popular genre, but America would require different tactics.

In New York before she took a train to California, Dietrich wrote her husband Rudi that she had been taken to a speakeasy by Walter Wanger, Paramount's east coast head of production and the promoter and mocker of Louise Brooks, and he had groped her on the dance floor. "As you know, I wasn't so angry because a man had given me a little squeeze on the behind, that's what it's there for. What I disliked was that it seemed to be taken for granted, that this was in my contract."

In her American films, Dietrich would escape and mock such pressing male demands by blurring and confusing the rules of the game when it came to gender, but she had to follow some of the rules at first. In *Morocco* (1930), her first American collaboration with Sternberg, Dietrich looks pale and undernourished in her opening scene, the ample flesh of Lola Lola sacrificed to crash dieting, reflecting on the comment Louis B. Mayer made about Garbo before she came over to the U.S.: "Tell her that in America they don't like fat women." Sternberg views Dietrich's entertainer Amy Jolly as his equal, a buddy, as she readies herself in her dressing room in her second scene. She is wearing a man's suit, and she pops her top hat out.

Gary Cooper's legionnaire Tom Brown sits in the club outside with his long legs stretched out on a table, the camera giving him an erotic attention that seems to stem from Dietrich's all-encompassing sexual state of mind, which Sternberg picked up. She enslaved Sternberg and liberated the hedonist within himself, so that he can look at Cooper sexually as he would at a pretty girl.

Her Amy Jolly strolls on stage in top hat and tails to the jeers of the crowd outside, as if Sternberg is sensing the reaction Dietrich will get from American audiences. Cooper's Tom looks at her and is intrigued by her masculine attire, and he shushes the crowd. Dietrich observes this display of chivalry tenderly, the opposite of the surprised way she saw Jannings's similar protectiveness in the Blue Angel dressing room.

Dietrich's Amy sings "Quand l'Amour Meurt" with relaxed circumspection, as if she's rather amused that love is dead. Dietrich is at her best when she sings, completely on, and always conveying a dizzying array of subliminal messages. Amy approaches a female audience member and takes a flower from the woman's hair. She inhales it lustfully and then, after a masterful hesitation—which prepares the audience and lets her get away with it—she kisses the woman full on the mouth, a still surprising, super-charged image. She walks out to violent-looking applause and throws down the bisexual gauntlet by tossing the flower to Tom.

When Tom lights Amy's cigarette, it acts as the top hat does, as a symbol of the masculine power she has appropriated with smiling humor. Which brings us to Dietrich's smile, surely the most healing and liberating of any star. It is warm and inviting, letting us in on her secret, on her enjoyment of so much in life that people deny themselves. The hate in *Blue Angel* is flipped, and we have Sternberg the adoring lover.

"Count to six and look at that lamp as if you could no longer live without it" was a typical piece of Sternberg direction to his star, and we can actually feel Dietrich counting to six to convey mystery in *Morocco*, or counting one-two-three in between phrases. She does look "mysterious" but also starved and uncomfortable, and when Cooper's Tom eventually puts on her top hat, it's as if he's taking his manhood back.

Morocco turns into a conventional love story, the defiant frissons of the nightclub scene paid for with Hollywood sentimentality, but the ending, where Amy tosses off her high heels and follows Tom into the desert, shows the full destructiveness of obsessive love. After she saw the film, Dietrich put a note into Sternberg's pocket that read, "You—Only you—the Master—the Giver—reason for my existence—the Teacher—the Love my heart and brain must follow." But Maurice Chevalier was soon sampling her scrambled eggs.

The coup complete, they made their most underrated movie, *Dishonored* (1931), their funniest picture, the most obvious parody of the Hollywood films of that time, and one of Dietrich's most unconventional appearances. It opens with her lady of the evening fixing her stocking, and Sternberg's camera seems simultaneously adoring and contemptuous of her sumptuous body. "I'm not afraid of life, though I'm not afraid of death either," Dietrich's working girl says, simply. As an elderly woman, Dietrich herself would memorably snap in the documentary *Marlene* that you should be afraid of life but not of death, with the hindsight of ruined old age.

In *Dishonored*, she is calmly rampaging, sexually out-there, sincere and amused by life, yet also contemptuous, indifferent, fatalistic. Sternberg is allowed to be more honest about his obsession after *Morocco* had made Dietrich a star. *The Blue Angel* encapsulated the hell of loving Dietrich, *Morocco* was an offering and a sharing of her sexual freedom, and *Dishonored* is the gleeful fun of two rebels laughing at what they are getting away with.

Sternberg uses lots of lap dissolves in *Dishonored*, two images lingering over each other like lovers, and his third film with Dietrich is defiantly non-narrative and lushly dissociated and best approached as a purely experimental feature. A wholly believable pavement pounder, Dietrich quips, "I don't mind walking," before the Austrian government signs her up to become a spy. Her sense of humor has flowered, as has her ambiguity. "What appeals to me is the chance to serve my country," she says. Do we believe her? Sternberg gave Dietrich absurdly unrealistic cadenced line readings that refuse to settle definitely on anything.

Dietrich has a sure grasp of the emotional depth behind this absurdity, and this is her own quality, for it turns up in the reading of her last lines in Orson Welles's *Touch of Evil* (1958), in which she intones: "He was some kind of a man. What does it matter what you say about people?" These lines always get a huge laugh at revival houses, but Dietrich plays them both ways down the middle and up yours, so that they are funny, silly even, but also touching, a boomerang, for Sternberg taught her never to trust one idea or emotion but flutter around several. This is her bewildering post-modern talent, and no other screen performer has anything remotely like it. The impulse to send up anything and everything always blurred into Dietrich's most romantic feelings and ideas, which she believes in spite of herself, and which Sternberg loves even while he is brutalizing them with his humor, which eventually adds to his own romantic regret.

For the scenes in *Dishonored* where her character poses as a peasant girl, Dietrich looks plain and chubby without makeup, crowing, "Count ten!" like a spacey idiot. This is a hoot, but it displays Sternberg's egotism, as if he is showing her up as the little German girl he has elevated to goddesshood. He reveals the tricks of his trade only to arrogantly place Dietrich back up on a pedestal so expertly that we forget this unveiling of her un-made-up face.

When the peasant interlude is over, Dietrich strokes a cat, an iconic image, and her face is as enigmatic as the kitty. At one point late in *Dishonored*, she has a crazy close-up where she moves her eyes side to side and up and down, practically putting her eyes through hoops, and this serves as a contemptuous parody of "acting," something Dietrich can rarely be accused of.

At the end of *Dishonored*, when Dietrich's spy is awaiting execution, she requests a piano and her hooker garb: "When I was serving my countrymen, and not my country." Before going out to face the firing squad, she fixes the veil of her hat in the reflection of a sabre and gives away her black pussycat to a priest. She crosses herself and puts a hand on her hip as she faces the guns, and then she offers a deathly slight smile, just like Catherine Deneuve smiles as she offers a view of her naked body to a boy at the end of Luis Buñuel's *Tristana* (1970). This slight smile is impenetrable, all image and armor.

One soldier, an old admirer who has not been granted her favors, refuses to kill her and brings a brief halt to the execution with an anti-war speech. Rolling with the punches, Dietrich takes this opportunity to retouch her lipstick and fix her stocking. The state of mind she created with Sternberg refuses to accept all humane sentiment, even outrage at war, and the soldier's speech is seen as touching but pointless, even amusing. Later, in concerts, Dietrich would movingly sing "Where Have All The Flowers Gone?" to lament the ravages of war, but in *Dishonored* applying lipstick is of graver importance than such political matters. Dietrich's spy is shot dead without any further ado, quickly and meanly on screen, to Sternberg's evident delight.

Shanghai Lily enters next, in the best screen clothes ever seen on anyone in the classic *Shanghai Express* (1932)—a veil, pearls, black feathers, furs. This image was all Dietrich's contribution, for she slaved with costume designer Travis Banton to achieve the looks for Sternberg's films. Lily is a whore, of course, like most of Dietrich's characters. "A woman who lives by her wits along the China coast!" crows one passenger.

Dietrich's face shimmers and glows as she utters her most memorable line: "It took more than one man to change my name to Shanghai Lily." The way her voice lingers over the "shang" in Shanghai emphasizes her foreigner's ability to find new life in English words, putting the flavor back into them. In Alfred Hitchcock's *Stage Fright* (1950), for instance, Dietrich says, "He was an a-bom-in-able man," and the word "abominable" is uttered as if for the first time, sounding exactly like what it means.

When Lily puts on the hat of former lover Captain "Doc" Harvey (Clive Brook), she is man and woman, all flexible, up for anything. She glides down the train corridors seemingly thinking about unspeakable perversities, yet the fact that Dietrich is probably just counting backwards from 100 exposes how we read so much into a beautiful woman that may or may not be there. She seems sly, but that might be just a matter of moving her eyes a certain way and Sternberg's peremptory editing, which cuts on her dialogue whenever she has said something flagrantly insincere.

"Your hands are trembling," says Harvey at one point. Dietrich looks vulnerable when he says that. Sternberg would like to protect her, which would let him possess her. "That's because you touched me, Doc," she sneers, and this moment feels like Sternberg's first discovery of Dietrich's bitchery, her indifferent contempt, which only allows him adoration that spirals into loathing, self and otherwise.

Sternberg and Dietrich are alone in the wordless scenes towards the end of *Shanghai Express* as she wanders about the train, and the best close-up of her career comes as she leans against a wall smoking a cigarette and gazing upward, an untouchable. It is a moment of the purest reflection and idealization and capture, and if you have been keyed into what the films are really about, it is overwhelmingly moving.

Garbo had the sort of face that brought about a shock of recognition and then contemplation, and its severity was plain, unadorned. Dietrich is the other master of becoming *the* human face, but she is a satirist, and we can see all the work she puts into creating the perfect nose, eyes, and lips. She did not really possess an extraordinary face but created one from scratch with makeup and discipline and by moving a certain way in certain light.

The ultimate close-up of Marlene Dietrich's career in *Shanghai Express*.

Finally, the most devastating conclusion of these Sternberg movies is the fact that this ideal, enslaving woman, Marlene Dietrich, is an entirely artificial illusion, and it is this insight, at the bottom of their visual inventiveness, which wounds the most. When her husband Rudi visited America, she laughingly told him that Sternberg wanted to "do it all the time," but she could handle that and him and anything else. Why? Because she, essentially, didn't care about anything except her own glorification and gratification.

At the end of *Shanghai Express*, Harvey says, "How in the name of Confucius can I kiss you with all these people around?" a parody of English propriety. "But Doc," Dietrich's Lily says caressingly, "There's no one else around." Sternberg could not possess Dietrich in life, but he kept her in film. They are completely alone, creating dreams, and this is his triumph of art, for they are both physically dead and now indivisible. "Ms. Dietrich is me. I am Ms. Dietrich," Sternberg once said.

Blonde Venus (1932), which came next, is essentially a mother love picture in which Dietrich played scenes of sexual and maternal self-sacrifice with a subversive air of amused indifference. There had been a kidnap threat involving her daughter Maria, and Sternberg was jealous of Chevalier, so this was a hectic, strained time for Dietrich, whose feelings or "feelings" for Sternberg must have been fairly complex at this point, both respectful and removed and just teasing enough to keep him going. She is unconvincing as a mother in *Blonde Venus*, bearing out her daughter's book, where Dietrich comes off as a vicious drag queen unrelievedly sharpening her tongue on anything and anyone within her grasp.

Dietrich's daughter Maria Riva observed in her memoir that you don't have to have a beautiful soul to get the camera to love you, which is of course the central joke of the Sternberg films. There is a lot of rage and disapproval in the Riva book, and she does not seem to notice that her writing style reflects exactly her mother's default mode of sarcastic speech, where everything seems to end in an exclamation mark.

Blonde Venus features Dietrich's most bizarre musical number, "Hot Voodoo," where Afro-wigged women in chains carrying spears writhe around and Dietrich emerges from a gorilla suit, her expression a gleaming mask of warrior confidence. To sing "Hot Voodoo," she puts on a blonde Afro with lightning bolts shooting out of it, and her rendition of the song is somewhat inhibited, as if she is saying, "Jo, this time you have gone too far."

Sternberg was losing his grip on her, and his jealousy mounted. *Morocco* and *Shanghai Express*, which had sent up and then celebrated romance, had been hits, but *Dishonored* and *Blonde Venus* were financial flops. He had little time, and so he went for broke with Dietrich for *The Scarlet Empress* (1934), his movie about Catherine the Great, which he called "a relentless excursion into style."

The first half of Dietrich's performance in *The Scarlet Empress* is an extended dumb show pantomime meant to indicate innocence. Riva describes Dietrich in the early scenes as "the village idiot in a bassinet," and though she has inherited her mother's bitchery, she is correct. This "village idiot" act seems a large miscalculation on Sternberg's part and can only charitably be seen as some sort of parody of innocence that doesn't come off.

Her leading man is tall John Lodge, who sports a Sternberg mustache and dresses all in black in contrast to Dietrich's white dresses. Sternberg reveals his vanity by viewing Lodge's full-lipped surrogate here as a splendidly sexual figure. Lodge's Count Alexei looks like a wild animal, and Dietrich's overplayed innocence contrasts with his full-blooded lust (if Lola Lola was the best and easiest female lay in the world, then Lodge's Count is her male equivalent). He kisses the young Catherine and then gives her a whip. "You must punish me for my effrontery," he says, getting the S&M into full swing.

When Catherine arrives to be married in Russia, her groom is a grinning Harpo Marx loony played by Sam Jaffe. A doctor examines Catherine's vagina (on screen!) to ascertain her childbearing abilities and loses his wig in the process. Louise Dresser plays the Empress as a mean Midwest matron. "We women are too much creatures of the heart," she snaps, as Sternberg laughs.

The Scarlet Empress is a film of out-of-control set decoration: gargoyles, netting, incense, and candles surround Dietrich's face, which is shot in a series of huge, gorging close-ups. In the world of this movie, it seems that sexual pleasure is the only joy worth pursuing, and Catherine is a ripe plum, ready to find that her sexuality is the greatest of powers and makes a hash of politics and rational thought. "You spend your time in bed reading books!" cries Dresser, who wants a male heir. Finally, thoroughly disillusioned, Dietrich's Catherine picks up a guard in a forest, and another sexual careerist is born.

Dietrich comes into her own once sex asserts itself, appraising a rival (Ruthelma Stevens) with a rich mixture of contempt, hauteur and the hint of a come-on. (Hot for Stevens herself, Dietrich in her dressing room drolly asked Sternberg, "Want to share?") But Catherine's appraisal of her troops is Dietrich's best scene. Wearing a towering fur hat, she swaggers down the lines, looking downward for erections, and the expressions on the faces of the soldiers confirms Mae West's 1944 play title *Catherine Was Great*. Dietrich's Catherine looks one soldier over and says, "I'm sure you're very efficient," while playfully flicking her fur.

Empress becomes a tribute to depravity, Catherine's and Marlene's, as she takes charge of her army of lovers, a misshapen Christ on the cross staring out forlornly behind them, a wan figure overtaken by her sexual conqueror. Sternberg has given up his fight and gives Dietrich's warrior selfishness the most delirious tribute. The 1812 Overture by Tchaikovsky soars on the soundtrack, and Dietrich "grins" manically, in an entirely and creepily artificial way, completely drunk on her own power.

Off screen, Sternberg and Dietrich indulged in elaborate fights and psychological power plays, and she always won. They were made for each other, certainly, if not evenly matched in the end. Chapter nine of Sternberg's 1965 memoir *Fun in a Chinese Laundry* is a deadpan sarcastic and incisive explication of his working relationship with Dietrich, full of cryptic remarks that are only meant to be understood by her. Yet if she did read it, the subtleties of most of his pins and needles surely escaped her, which is why the French call this kind of obsession "l'amour fou"—a lonely thing, with only the smallest and bitterest and most ironic satisfactions.

Empress was another financial flop. For his final Dietrich film, Sternberg dared to give the American public a heroine even crueler than Lola Lola. In his other movies with Dietrich, there is always the furtive hope that she will eventually come to her senses and love him, only him, but Galatea was made to spurn him and move on, as he himself realized in their first film, and the wooing is over. That Dietrich survived the scathing *The Devil Is a Woman* (1935) is a testament to her determination. It also shows her fleeting awareness of Sternberg's miserable genius that this was her favorite film, for, paradoxically, his need to destroy his creation with this unflattering portrait backfires. As usual, his love makes even his impulse to kill her shed flattering lights on her manufactured face.

As Concha, a barbaric tease with winged eyebrows, Dietrich first appears in *The Devil Is a Woman* on a float awash in streamers. (Sternberg creates a fake Spain much like his fake Morocco, Shanghai, and Russia.) She smiles her mad, fake *Empress* smile and laughs a loud, very un–Dietrich-like laugh, for her Concha is playful and pleased with herself. Antonio (Cesar Romero) is bewitched by Concha, but the embittered Don Pasqual (Lionel Atwill), the deadest ringer of Sternberg's filmic surrogates, fills this younger man in on the dangers of "the gentler sex." This is a film so brimming with sexual hate as to be overpowering. "I'm romantic. So romantic!" Concha sings, and we can see what a mockery she makes of that word as she looks at her hundreds of male admirers.

"Are you afraid of death?" asks Don Pasqual, on the brink of killing her. "Why? You going to kill me?" Concha asks, bright-eyed with sexual energy at the thought of such a crime of passion, yet contemptuous, taunting him, knowing he will never give her a "little death," but playing with him, for fun. Pasqual spills his soul while she fixes her bangs. "One moment, and I'll give you a kiss," she says, all business. A bullfighter enters. "Have you seen him fight?" she asks, lewdly. "I've read the reviews," Pasqual sniffs. "Ah, critics don't value genius," Concha says, Sternberg's arrogance flooding in.

Dietrich overdoes Concha's flightiness, but she has one scene of real power when she confronts an enraged Pasqual. "How dare you come in here and create this utterly ridiculous scene!" she cries. "He threatens me! This is superb. Are you my father? No! Are you my husband? No! Are you my lover?" Thunder booms. "Well, I must say you are content with very little." Atwill's eyes flash with real Emil Jannings rage as he strangles her.

The next day, Concha is shot through shutters, her eyes appearing monstrous. "I came to see if you were dead," she announces to Pasqual. "If you loved me enough, you would have killed yourself last night!" Here we have Dietrich's own romanticism at its ugliest. She wears a necklace with a heart attached,

Dietrich at her most beautiful, artificial, and deadly in *The Devil Is a Woman*.

and coos, "Look, I'm black and blue!" Dietrich's up/down eye mannerism is at its most maddening here, no doubt on Sternberg's orders. "That woman has ice where others have a heart!" Don Pasqual cries.

It is clear why the general public in America couldn't take Dietrich at all by this point. Concha enjoys destroying men, making what was implicit in Lola Lola explicit, damagingly. Her Concha is a conquering beast, an unsparing demonstration of sexual power, and this is a harrowing movie, a fitting way to close off their relationship, and, perversely, this kiss-off movie may be the most adoring of them all.

The seven films remain. Dietrich went on, but it took her a while to regain her footing without her mentor. She is expert, very glamorous, and contemptuously sexy in *Desire* (1936), with Gary Cooper as her leading man and Ernst Lubitsch and Frank Borzage guiding both her comedic and dramatic moments, so that the showy miscalculation that afflicted her last two performances for Sternberg was subdued. But *The Garden of Allah* (1936) and *Knight Without Armour* (1937) were costly flops in which she seemed like a stranded monster, and she was eventually named box office poison by film exhibitors. Paramount paid her $250,000 *not* to make her next picture for them.

For the goddesses on this poison list, such as Garbo and Katharine Hepburn, it was essential to stage a comeback where they could be seen as more down to earth. *Ninotchka* (1939) had Garbo laughing, and *The Philadelphia Story* (1940) had snooty Hepburn getting her comeuppance. For Dietrich, there was *Destry Rides Again* (1939), her most successful performance as an "actress." Sternberg approved of yanking his goddess down to earth. "Good for the box office," he said, cuttingly, knowing his role was now over, but sure enough in his arrogance to know that his Dietrich would burn brightest.

In *Destry*, Dietrich plays Frenchy, a rowdy barroom temptress, on all systems go, pulling out all the stops. She is confident and in charge, using technique to get her through the rough spots, opening her mouth wide in laughter to simulate vitality a half-second after a joke. Audiences took delight in Sternberg's untouchable goddess getting all mussed up, most strikingly in a catfight to end all catfights with a game Una Merkel that allows Dietrich to show off her genuine savagery and her iconic legs.

Destry was made at Universal, and she stayed on there for a few years. Her Bijou in *Seven Sinners* (1940) is a drag queen performance, with femininity signaled and sent up at every turn, but Dietrich still manages to convey the libertine side of her character in this energetically junky burlesque. "May I have an American [pause] cigarette?" she asks, with a naughty gleam in her eye. She shoots her most lascivious looks at leading man John Wayne, who looks trapped by her lust, and has a relaxed time of it, singing "The Man's in the Navy" in baggy white tie and tails with smiling, androgynous pleasure.

The camp in *Seven Sinners* and elsewhere is done with spirit, but it all begins to seem tired around the time of William Dieterle's *Kismet* (1944), where she cavorts with gold-painted legs. Soon after, Dietrich went to war to entertain the troops, both on stage and in bed, which added to her knowing, shadowy reputation as Lili Marlene, a woman who might restore men's might. She gave up her country and her language to fight the Nazis, and she stoically paid the price for that. After the war, she appeared opposite her lover Jean Gabin in the little-seen French film *Martin Roumagnac* (1946), where she played a merry widow and sometime prostitute. The frank sexual chemistry between Dietrich and Gabin in that film is highly arousing.

There are two more film performances that rank with her best work for Sternberg and *Destry*. Billy Wilder's *A Foreign Affair* (1948) is really Jean Arthur's movie, but beware of Dietrich, who finally lets her riotous and sadistic real-life bitchery come to the forefront. Her character Erika is an ex-Nazi who survives by her wits and sings at a smoky dive called, appropriately, the Lorelei. Wilder, an old Berlin friend, made Dietrich feel at ease, and she sheds most of her inhibitions, or seems to, chanting Friedrich Hollander's biting song "Black Market" in a shimmering dress, expertly undulating her sinuous arms, her singing voice much stronger than previously.

Hollander's "Illusions" is the archetypal Dietrich song, and she sings it with her face squinched in mockery, her eyes half-closed: "Want to buy some illusions? Slightly used, second hand." She displays the outright treachery of Concha here, but it is more believable, for this feels like the real Dietrich we're getting, not the ravings of an obsessed Svengali lashing out. She's in full control of the character's coldness, her sexual charge, and her survival skills.

Dietrich is given all the best lines in Hitchcock's *Stage Fright*, and she has as much fun as she did in *Dishonored*. She wipes the floor with poor mousy Jane Wyman, the putative star of the film, and her selfishness here is highly amusing, never off-putting. Her entrance is a top-notch parody of "fear," exaggerating this emotion until it floats around and evaporates; yet she somehow manages to suggest the depth underneath the put-on, as in her last scene, where she has an arbitrary conversation with a policeman about dogs.

She tells of a dog she loved who hated her. "So I had him shot!" she snarls. We laugh, but are taken off balance. "When I give all my love, and receive nothing but hate, it's as if my mother had slapped me in the face," she says. There's no narrative reason for this little speech, but it is a perfect demonstration of Dietrich's grasp of a sort of absurdity that enhances deep feelings. It seems like an important piece of this jigsaw puzzle, Marlene Dietrich, and the line about the mother slapping her is suggestive. It is a hint, and then she backs into the darkness again.

She took an "acting" challenge in Billy Wilder's whodunit *Witness for the Prosecution* (1957), playing a stiff German wife who impersonates a Cockney woman, an impressive but irrelevant bit of trickery. The last part of her career was devoted to a very successful concert tour, and she found another Svengali in composer and conductor Burt Bacharach. (Sternberg had asked to be hired as her introducer for the concerts, but she turned him down, telling her friends later, "Imagine!")

Extant footage from her concert days shows how Dietrich grew as both singer and "actress," and it is essential to see her doing the songs, to be ensorcelled by the gowns she wore, which carefully gave the impression of nudity. "Dietrich must be a sensation," she told her daughter, "and that we can only do with what I wear." She underestimated what she could do with a tune, though she often indulged in an unfortunate Teutonic sentimentality. Dietrich was indeed a sensation everywhere she played but she had trouble back in Germany, where some people held signs that read, "Marlene Go Home." Leaving her hotel to go to the theater one night, she was accosted by a young girl of 18 who yanked at her coat, spat in her face, and cried, "Traitor!"

As time went on, Dietrich's face was pulled further and further back into an imperious mask, but she dared us not to believe her myth. On the song "I Get a Kick Out of You," she changed, "You obviously don't adore me," to "You might decide to adore me," and we do, of course, those who have been let in on the secret, have given ourselves over to what she represents. There was work to be done with Garbo and Dietrich. They asked something of you. Moviegoers in the 1930s needed these fantastic and nearly blank naked creatures to project upon, and we simply don't do that anymore.

She managed to put together "Marlene Dietrich" well into her seventies, which must be some sort of record for sexual sorcery. Then, inevitably, came the long decline into hermithood. Dietrich wanted to protect what she had achieved at all costs, which is why she refused to be photographed for that revealing movie that closes her career, Maximilian Schell's *Marlene* (1984). Needing cash, she agreed to be interviewed by Schell, but they did not hit it off, to put it mildly. He struck her as pretentious, and he certainly is that. The film became a battle between them, Schell helplessly falling into Sternberg's role as lover of a foul goddess who hurls abuse at him. She calls most of her movies "kitsch" or "abortions."

Marlene is a film about old age and old lady rage where Dietrich feels entitled to insist that who she wants to be is who she is, a retiring girl from a good family who let that decadent Mr. von Sternberg shoot those strange films, though she was really not much interested in them, you know. She insisted that it was all just a job, and that she was "practical."

Her daughter and others in her inner circle bore the brunt of her lies and exaggerations and her viper tongue, "always negative, critical, cruel, often ugly," wrote Riva. Dietrich knew Riva was writing a book, and she encouraged it. What kind of book did she imagine her daughter would write? Surely not the one we got. For all that it reveals, Riva's book leaves us just as puzzled as ever because the extracts from Dietrich's letters seem much more self-aware, warmer, and more intelligent than the portrait of an exuberantly sharp-tongued, consummately selfish, deluded queen that Riva remembers in page after page of harrumphing dialogue.

In *Marlene*, Schell has no idea how to talk to her so she will reveal what he wants and needs, herself, Marlene Dietrich, whoever that may be. She refuses to tell who is really behind the mask. Schell and Dietrich square off on many subjects, arguing constantly. At one point, he asks her who the real Marlene Dietrich is. "That's superfluous!" she thunders. Perhaps it is.

The film's most poignant moment comes at its end. Dietrich is obviously in her cups, and Schell reads a poem that her mother loved: "O love while still tis yours to love. O love while love you still may keep. For the hour will come, the hour will come, when you will stand by graves and weep." This woman in her eighties, who conquered the world, becomes a heartbroken little girl. "I can't read that. My mother really loved it," she says.

But what really killed her were these lines: "So quickly came the hateful word. O God, 'twas never meant to hurt." This made Dietrich sob out, "*I never meant to hurt.*" Dietrich liked to present herself in later life as a solitary Prussian officer, and in this last film, she tries hard to put this tough image across, but we hear her weep for a few moments here, and the sound is wrenching. "Maybe it is a kitschy poem. Maybe," she says, trying to regain the discipline which served her so well when she was creating her myth.

There is consistence in Dietrich's inconsistency, or inconstancy. She meant to intrigue, for, at her best, she shoots us two or three different subliminal messages at once, towards the crotch, towards the intellect, and towards a variety of emotions, which no one else navigated with such tender, basically detached amusement. Many men and women clustered to her off screen too, "Dietrich's victims" her daughter called them, moths to the flame, and she gathered them up: Maurice Chevalier, Brian Aherne, Richard Barthelmess, Ronald Colman, John Gilbert, Douglas Fairbanks, Jr., Jimmy Stewart, Erich Maria Remarque, Hemingway, Gabin, Edith Piaf, Kirk Douglas,

Frank Sinatra, Adlai Stevenson, Harold Arlen, Edward R. Murrow, Yul Brynner; she couldn't help it, but she could help it along.

As late as 1986, when she had been bedridden for years, Dietrich was having heated conversations on the phone with Mikhail Baryshnikov. A flirt and a fabulist, a shameless jeerer and gilder of lilies, she liked her lovers and ex-lovers to be friends so they could all be at one in adoring her. She loved to order, to control, to command. She died in 1992. She was buried in Berlin, next to her mother.

It all began in the head of Josef von Sternberg, who saw Dietrich in a Berlin revue and was struck with what can only be called immortal longings. He gave her things that look absurd now, but they were absurd then, and he trusted us implicitly. He trusted us enough that he gave us this monument to frivolity, this artificial creation who turned into a camp chanteuse, and deep down he knew that we would recognize what he did with her in those seven films, which was beyond her control just as she slipped out of his. As time goes on, the films Dietrich made with Sternberg will be increasingly seen for what they are, the living explication of the act of love, erotic, obsessive, romantic, and otherwise.

Bette Davis
The Hard Way

During the telecast for the American Film Institute Life Achievement Award to Bette Davis in 1977, the camera catches her in a private moment. Director William Wyler, maybe the love of her life or at least the love of her career, has come over to say a few words to her. We don't hear what he says, but when he leaves her, Davis turns around and looks very upset. That outlandishly expressive face of hers shows a mixture of things: regret, pride, acute melancholy. They are all there, these emotions, and all at her fingertips. She had deliberately not gone to Wyler's own 1976 AFI ceremony, for reasons known only to her.

Davis is maybe the best example of a performing artist who acts because they have so much excess emotion that they have to use it or channel it in some way. Even when she had all kinds of parts to play, Davis was difficult to be around in life because high drama was her permanent mode. "She proved that you can have a career and remain honest—if you are willing to pay the price of personal loneliness," says the book flap on her autobiography, *The Lonely Life* (1962). Davis willingly, even gloatingly, paid that price.

She was born Ruth Elizabeth Davis in 1908 during a thunderstorm, she claimed. "I happened between a clap of thunder and a streak of lightning," she wrote. "It almost hit the house and destroyed a tree out front. As a child I fancied that the Finger of God was directing the attention of the world to me." How's that for barely tongue-in-cheek self-dramatization? (It was actually a mild, rainy night, but print the legend.) She took the name Bette from Balzac's novel *Cousin Bette*, a tale of revenge well suited to her electric, make-things-happen style.

Helped along by her mother after her contemptuous father abandoned them, Davis started working on stage. She was Hedwig in Ibsen's *The Wild Duck* and did a few other things, and she was already gaining a reputation for being headstrong and not following direction because she felt that she knew better. She was signed by Universal and came out to Hollywood, where producer Junior Laemmle cruelly said within her earshot that she "had about as much sex appeal as Slim Summerville," a homely comedian of that time.

Davis tested for Wyler for *A House Divided* (1931) in a low-cut dress she had been given. "What do you think of these dames who show their chests and think they can get jobs?" Wyler asked everyone on the set in a loud voice, to her mortification. Still a virgin at 23, Davis was mortified again when they had her test 15 actors in a row in a love scene, with her stretched out on a couch as one man after another came in to kiss her.

Universal cast her in *The Bad Sister* (1931), where she was the good stay-at-home sister and Sidney Fox was the bad and pretty sister. In that first movie Davis looks like Charlotte Vale before her transformation in *Now, Voyager* (1942): brown hair, heavy brows, tiny mouth, very little make-up. Her emotional style is weirdly languid, blocked, slightly stilted, and the *New York Times* found her "too lugubrious" but *Variety* said she was "the very essence of repression." Davis doesn't even know how to slap people yet here, lifting her hand into a claw and doing an odd Martha Graham–like gesture to simulate hitting her bad sister Fox. ("I worshipped her," Davis said of Graham, who had briefly taught her movement in the 1920s. "She was all tension—lightning! Her burning dedication gave her spare body the power of ten men.")

Davis was far better as a daughter in group scenes in John M. Stahl's excellent *Seed* (1931) at Universal, which showcases her intensity for the first time, but she was thinking of going back to New York before getting a call from George Arliss, or Mr. George Arliss, as he is grandly billed in the credits, to be his leading lady in *The Man Who Played God* (1932) at Warner Brothers, where she was signed and where she would stay for 18 years. They dyed her hair platinum blond, which helped her looks, and though she is still a bit gauche in the Arliss movie, it showcases the rare intensity she could bring to her lines, throbbing with emotion yet clipped. She's a tense presence, watching and waiting to strike.

Davis was in support to Barbara Stanwyck in *So Big!* (1932), an Edna Ferber saga, and Ruth Chatterton in a would-be sophisticated comedy, *The Rich Are Always with Us* (1932), where she played Malbro, a "pest of Park Avenue," desperate for George Brent and staring after him when he expresses his disinterest in her. This is the first time her energy and the energy of a role click decisively, and this unleashed her roguish, self-deprecating humor, one of her most appealing modes. The chance to play unrequited love always gives her a special vibrancy, unlocking something still and quiet in the middle of her storm of flashy, slashing movements and vocal attack.

In the socially conscious *The Cabin in the Cotton* (1932), Davis played rich Southern flirt Madge, and director Michael Curtiz called her a "Goddamned-nothing-no-good sexless son-of-a-bitch" on set as she tried to be seductive. Clearly these consistent remarks against her desirability did nothing to dent Davis's furious determination to succeed. ("If I couldn't be the best in a business, I'd go into another business," she often said.) Davis's Madge strides around and poses, enjoying her moneyed status and the sexual glow she gives off. "I'd love to kiss ya, but I just washed ma hair. Bye!" she says at one point, and that "Bye!" has a comic, campy charge. *The Cabin in the Cotton* was meant to prove Davis could be a sexpot, and she proved it, but that was never her interest.

Davis played her first gun moll in *20,000 Years in Sing Sing* (1932), bringing a distinct sexual desire to her scenes with Spencer Tracy and scoring particularly in the climax, where she is immobilized in bed after a car accident. The squirming, impatient Davis was always at her best when she was somehow physically stuck like this, so that her concentration could not be dispersed. Something very neurotic emerged in her face for the first time here, a sick quality, diseased and morbid.

Davis was then given her first starring vehicle, *Ex-Lady* (1933), a slapdash consideration of free love that was much too tawdry to suit her. By this point she had learned to make her mouth larger with lipstick, which balanced her face nicely, but she wanted to be more than just a girl selling sex in her underwear. Perpetually agitated, she was smoking cigarettes constantly, and her smoking always brought keen focus to her work, for she had the most hyperactive hands in show business and a cigarette gave her something to do with them in *Ex-Lady* when she wasn't being slobbered over by the unappetizing Monroe Owsley. "I only recall that from the daily shooting to the billboards, falsely picturing me half-naked, my shame was only exceeded by my fury," Davis remembered.

In *Fashions of 1934* she was buried under heavy make-up, false eyelashes, sculpted blond hair, and furs, under which she cannot hide her mounting irritation and ill temper. "There was nothing left of Bette Davis in this film," she said. She sparred with James Cagney in *Jimmy the Gent* (1934), giving him a hard smack with her purse, and got a startling entrance ("Bang! Bang! Bang!" she cries, popping balloons until we see her face) in the fly-by-night *Fog Over Frisco* (1934). Davis liked her part in that movie, and it's easy to see why, for this is the first of her bad girls who really enjoy being bad to the hilt, blowing cigarette smoke like a steam engine, manipulating men and pouring scorn on them when necessary, which is her prime passion on screen.

"You'll take what you get and like it!" she tells a swain in *Fog Over Frisco*, like some female Gable or Cagney with excitingly neurotic underpinnings.

Best or most telling of all here is the flash of mad anger in her eyes when she slaps a man who won't do as she tells him to. She was unleashing the beast in herself, and this spectacle would set the American film audience on its ear. Davis's reckless heiress in *Fog Over Frisco* gets bumped off halfway through for her perfidy, stuffed in the back of a rumble seat, while her creator went off to grab her own particular stardom.

Davis begged and pleaded for months to get loaned out to RKO for the extremely unsympathetic part of Mildred in *Of Human Bondage* (1934), and finally studio chief Jack Warner told her to go right ahead and hang herself. *Bondage* is a solemn, slow-moving movie, an 80-minute condensation of Somerset Maugham's long, self-pitying novel that is saddled with Leslie Howard at his most phlegmatic as Philip, the club-footed hero, but such things never stopped Davis from achieving her goals. She might not have the full technical skills here that she had later (her Cockney accent is admittedly shaky), but her closed-off, sadistic waitress is one of the major breakout performances of the 1930s, fully on the scale and level of Charles Laughton's best work of this time.

Davis does not give us any glimpses of what made Mildred what she is, as a later Method actress almost certainly would have; she plays the result, not the cause. And she plays that result in such a seething, all-out way that Mildred's stupidity, greed, inertia, and lack of any sensitivity leads Davis to a kind of pessimistic endpoint that is unsparing in its own lack of any leavening or ray of hope. Her Mildred is a crummy, low-class tart who puts on airs, and that's it, but Lord, there's a lot to that. Most tellingly, Davis plays Mildred's attempts at sexual allure as miserably ugly and failed, as if she were thumbing her nose at all the men who only valued her looks and found her wanting. In many ways, this performance is a diabolically inventive response to those sexist attacks, all lowered eyes and mean mouth and hands on hips and transparent manipulations.

And when Mildred tells Philip off directly to the camera, Davis reaches a level of operatic anger that very few actors have ever touched on screen. "After you kissed me," she tells him, "I always used to wipe my mouth, *wipe my mouth*!" she emphasizes, taking a great big swipe at her mouth, which is like a body blow to the rapacious male libido. (Of course there are some men who like this kind of thing, and it is rumored that Davis could only bring millionaire lover Howard Hughes to sexual climax by verbally abusing him.) What she's doing here *is* like singing, the stabbing gruffness of her voice giving way wonderfully in the worst final insults to a high-pitched shriek on, "A cripple! A cripple! A cripple!"

Davis makes Mildred's anger seem all-encompassing, petty, out-ofproportion, and existentially deep, all at once. A vengeful anti-intellectual, Mildred slashes Philip's paintings, rips up his books, and burns his money for school, like some uncorked hateful essence let loose on the world. But look at the way Davis's Mildred nods her head when Philip tells her, in their last scene together, that he's glad her baby died, as if she finally understands something about life. It's a telling detail like that that separates a good actor from a great one. And the way her Mildred dies of tuberculosis! Davis almost looks green under the black-and-white cinematography, like she has fully thought out a last stage of ingrowing hatred and is proudly showing us the grossly rotten fruit of her depraved artistic imagination.

Hollywood was agog at her Mildred, and so was everyone else. "Probably the best performance ever recorded on the screen by a U.S. actress," wrote *Life*. But then it was back to dreck at Warners like *Housewife* (1934), *Front Page Woman* (1935), and *Special Agent* (1935), where she seems fractious, uptight, and bored by turns, too intense and special for such breezy programmers. They released the held-back *Bordertown* (1935), which had convinced Jack Warner to let her go play Mildred, and no wonder, for her cheap, dissatisfied, mentally disturbed Marie Roark is very striking, if obvious.

Married to tubby, coarse Charlie (Eugene Pallette), Davis's Marie lets him asphyxiate in their garage so she can snare the younger Johnny (Paul Muni) and then gradually loses her mind. "Sure, *me*, I killed Charlie Roark to get you!" Marie screams at Johnny, and that "me" has the full force of Davis's own world-class ego. But then when she goes fully mad in court, Davis chooses to make the jittery Marie all worn-out, flat in affect, inept, and her final cries as she is led away are pitiably small and lost, a keening, "Ohh, ohh, ohh." Davis had to fight to play it that way. "At the end of shooting *Bordertown* I was called to the front office and told that no one in the audience would know I was insane in the courtroom scene," Davis said. "I said, if this should be so at the preview, I would willingly retake the scene and play it in the usual hair-pulling way. I was never asked to do a retake."

Of the script for *Dangerous* (1935), Davis sharply wrote in her autobiography that it "had a pretension to quality that in scripts, as in home furnishings, is often worse than junk." As Joyce Heath, a jinxed, has-been, alcoholic actress, Davis plays her first scenes in frowzy clothes and hair like straw and she sports a surly disposition to match. "Rest in peace is for tombstones," she says, speaking up for drive and desire, which catches the eye of architect Don Bellows (Franchot Tone).

Davis is impishly sexy when Joyce seduces Don during a rainstorm at night, but then the script has her act hysterically defensive when he tries to let her down easy, giving her a long outburst like Mildred's blast at Philip.

Though it is played for its full histrionic force by Davis, this speech seems a little much given the circumstances, as is the extra dose of man-hating added on to the scenes where Joyce tells off her icky, masochistic husband (John Eldredge). Davis won an Oscar for *Dangerous*, and it was perceived by everyone as a consolation prize for not even being nominated for her Mildred.

After *Bordertown* and *Dangerous*, Davis was in danger of becoming just the Queen of the Jitters, every scene a matter of flashy and sometimes forced hysterics, so she wisely slowed down to play the poetic, dreamy Gabrielle Maple in *The Petrified Forest* (1936), based on Robert Sherwood's prestigious play. She finally took Warner to court to demand better roles, and though she lost her case, her films improved slightly in 1937, when she let her hair go back to its original ash blonde. She overreacts too much in *Marked Woman* (1937), giving every little moment too much force, until we have to wonder, "What is *wrong* with this woman?" Her motor was always overheating, and she needed someone to cool it down for her, but once again, as in the last scene in *Bondage*, she took almost sensual delight in appearing as ruined as possible when her character has been beaten up and put in the hospital.

It was William Wyler's *Jezebel* (1938) that finally made Davis a full-fledged star at age 30. She won a second Oscar for that movie, and she then made 25 films in 12 years that laid the cornerstone for her reputation. She was controversial in her time, but people seemed to enjoy telling others, "I can't stand her!" because the kind of hate she was knowingly stoking can be an enjoyable thing. Davis was a perverse figure, a cathartic and unsubtle force, her huge eyes sweeping around to broadcast her every burning thought, a character actress star who put together "characterizations" as if she were still saying, "Take it and like it!" Often she overworks those eyes, sending them to the sides and around the room and up and down five or six times when just one look à la Barbara Stanwyck would do just fine. She didn't do shades of gray. Davis preferred things good or bad and both of them big, though she did sometimes like making a bad girl redeemed in the end.

She needed high drama (her three comedies from this period, *The Bride Came C.O.D.* (1941), *The Man Who Came to Dinner* (1942), and *June Bride* (1948), are unimpressive changes of pace) and a strong director, which she got in her three films for Wyler and in two undervalued films she hated—John Huston's *In This Our Life* (1942) and King Vidor's *Beyond the Forest* (1949), in which there is a framework for her to reach new heights of hysteria. "A good director! Half my career was spent fighting for one," she wrote in *The Lonely Life.*

Only devoted fans will care to trudge through 140 minutes apiece of *All This, and Heaven Too* (1940) and *Mr. Skeffington* (1944), where she pitches her voice a full octave higher than usual to play an air-headed society beauty brought low into physical grotesquerie by illness. In a part like this, it was as if Davis were paying back all the empty-headed and prettier ingénues at Warners like Anita Louise who had been so prized during her long apprenticeship. But in *All This, and Heaven Too* she has virtuoso moments in close-up in which her repressed character is trying to hide emotions even from herself. Davis could accomplish so much when she chose to hold back.

The methodical and sober Wyler made Davis harness her energy for maximum impact. He wouldn't let her fidget all over the place as she does in *Dangerous* and *Bordertown*, and he also wouldn't let her force an emotion that wasn't quite there, as she does often in *Marked Woman*. In *Jezebel* there is an exquisite tension between Wyler's control and Davis's own frenzied and semi-sick emotional charge, and this matches up with the constraints of antebellum society on her rebellious belle Julie. This was her first costume movie that took its time, and the first one where Max Steiner composed his score to her moods.

Davis's Julie insists on destructiveness, and Davis's movements are contained like fireflies in a jar by Wyler in the way she restlessly twirls a parasol as she waits in a carriage for her fiancé Pres (Henry Fonda), or the crazy forward movement of her shoulders (right, left, right, left), which seem to have a life of their own, as her carriage drives away from his bank. Those shoulders let us know how close Julie's spirit is to outright disturbance without ever spilling over into the physical spasms of Joyce Heath or Marie Roark.

Julie wears a red dress to a ball where unmarried women are supposed to wear white, and this ruins her life. A *Jezebel* could be made where Julie is purely a victim of outmoded conventions, but that is not the Julie that Davis plays. Her Julie victimizes herself first and those around her second, and it might also be said that Davis instinctively plays Julie as an essentially diseased symbol of the Southern tradition she represents. This is the first real Bette Davis movie dominated by her frank and hypnotic stares in

Bette Davis's Julie Marsden at the ball in *Jezebel*.

lovingly lit close-up, and what followed in her film career was one treat after another, some sticky sweet, some tart, some so overblown you could barely swallow them.

Her affair with Wyler drew to a close in melodramatic fashion. He left her a letter saying if he didn't hear from her in 24 hours he was going to marry someone else, and Davis didn't open that letter until after she heard on the radio that he had married actress Margaret Tallichet. But her career was in high gear now, and that was always her focus.

Davis had four films in release in 1939, and all of them added to her growing legend. The first was *Dark Victory*, where she narrowed those staring eyes of hers as a brittle playgirl stopped in her tracks by disease and then ennobled by a walk up the stairs to face death, Max Steiner's music leading the way. She has moments of little-girl vulnerability in that movie that she had never showed before and would never show again, counterbalanced only by her constantly squeezing, restless hands.

The death itself in *Dark Victory* is awfully pretty compared to Gish in *La Bohème* and Garbo in *Camille*, but Davis was not after realism in this movie. Her guard was down, and she fell for movie fantasy, and the fantasy here, which suggests a soap opera stations of the cross, has its own kind of structure, order, even integrity. Gore Vidal, not exactly an old softie, once said in an interview that he was most touched by "Bette Davis planting her plants" at the end of *Dark Victory*.

Davis had a corker of a mad scene as the increasingly unhinged Empress Carlotta in *Juarez*, impressively screaming at Claude Rains's Napoleon III, "You *char*latan!" at the scary height of her vocal range, seeming both absurdly over the top and genuinely disturbed, chewing into the scenery with campy brio. Is this good work? Well, no, strictly speaking, but it's hard to be strict given how much fun it is.

Davis faced off against Miriam Hopkins in *The Old Maid*, going from lovely young girl to tight-lipped, dried-up spinster, making her audience take and like her Acting Challenge, predicated as it was, as so often, on lost and unrequited love. Maybe Davis could only love on screen and in life when she was sure it would be unrequited, or not work out, and then she could sit back and feel sorry for herself in a luxuriously expansive way, with Max Steiner music in her head.

As Queen Elizabeth I in *The Private Lives of Elizabeth and Essex* her Queen of the Fidgets mode had an exuberantly undisciplined fling, presumably because a queen can get away with anything. Her hands here don't squeeze each other but the very air around them, grabbing it up by royal decree. Her "t" sounds were out of control, even jumping in on "d" sounds so that "You slimy toad" becomes "You slimy toat," and "kind" becomes "kint," and so forth. What had seemed overdone in a clip joint hostess in *Marked Woman* was more than suitable for a queen, or at least just more for its own sake. And she delighted in trying for the classic Elizabeth I look in Technicolor: shaved hairline, egg-white make-up, flame red wig, penciled red eyebrows, no eye shadow, orange lipstick.

Davis makes her entrance into her second film for Wyler, ironically titled *The Letter* (1940), pressing the trigger on a gun and unloading bullet after bullet into her faithless lover. Another white colonialist bitch, her Leslie Crosbie seems to be in a trance of malignant, veiled anger until she looks up at the moon with her huge, staring eyes. By all standards, this is a powerhouse opening gambit, and Davis's performance only gets tenser and tighter as it goes along. Playing such a repressed woman brings out the best in her creative character, so that she puts her more artificial mannerisms on top of Leslie's own deeply hidden feelings, as if Leslie even hides most of her genuine feelings from herself.

Davis always had a declamatory way of delivering lines. She never sounds natural or conversational, never stumbles or does little stops and starts or throws words away, as Barbara Stanwyck and Katharine Hepburn sometimes did. She just barrels ahead with her own super-charged way of talking, always, and it's a perilous style because it risks seeming put-on, but it works for her perfectly in *The Letter* because everything Leslie says is a put-on, and part of her knows it. Davis's Leslie sometimes seems to be thinking, "I wonder how much I can get away with," or even at certain points considering how little she has to do for believability, for the sexually frustrated Leslie has to take her kicks where she can get them! She compartmentalizes everything, but her compartments keep getting out of whack, sometimes ludicrously (she has a habit of playing hostess at incongruous times) and sometimes creepily.

Davis's eyes in *The Letter* are hypnotic, commanding, but also clouded by all kinds of odd issues and tangents, and if *The Letter* is among her very best work it is because it gives her such a richly duplicitous character to play. The fault of Davis's work, even in her golden period, was that it was often so obvious, so blatant, and so hectically undisciplined, but in *The Letter* she gets to filter her instincts through a glass darkly so that her performance is super-controlled and conscious yet unsettled underneath, and the result is very exciting. There are times of stress here where it seems like Davis's eyes are going to bulge right out of her head and fall on the floor, and she seems to be pulling them with all her considerable might back into their sockets.

Wyler wanted Davis to be charming and sexual as Regina Giddens in his film of the Lillian Hellman play *The Little Foxes* (1941) while she saw Regina as a pure heavy, and so they clashed throughout the shoot and never worked together again, alas. From this vantage point, it looks like Davis was right to do the part her own tough, uncompromising way, and it must have been difficult for her at times to stick to her own colder interpretation. She contrived a distinctive physical look for Regina with rice-white make-up, no eye shadow, and a tiny mouth to look older, and she has an animal-like quality here, like a lizard that sits in the sun and waits for the flies. Her Regina does have humor, but it's heavy-spirited and used mainly for deflection and intimidation. As with her Mildred, Davis never plays one moment for sympathy or understanding of this woman but plays the result of what made her what she is. And it's unpleasant, bullying, and thuggish.

"You were such a soft, meek fool," Regina tells her ill husband Horace (Herbert Marshall), who is blocking her exploitative capitalistic scheme to make money on a sweatshop. "You were so kind and understanding when I didn't want you near me. The lies and excuses I used to make to you, and you *believed* them! That's when I began to despise you." Once again, as in *Bondage* and *Dangerous,* Davis is telling off a weak man who couldn't give her what she wanted, and this stirred certain women and certain men in her audience vicariously, even when Regina lets Horace die of his heart trouble without blinking an eye or moving a muscle until she's sure he has dropped dead on the stairs behind her.

When Regina's brother Ben (Charles Dingle) tells her she'd get further with him if she smiled, Davis's mirthless showing of her teeth is a kicky feminist rejoinder to such a request, but how far Davis is a feminist icon is a tricky issue. Perhaps it is best to say that she worked out women's frustrations in colorfully sick ways, and such a purging was needed at the time.

Davis made her little mouth into a bee-stung pout for *In This Our Life,* where she plays Stanley Timberlake, a vile, sorry racist, in her twitchiest, most manic style ("I'd rather do anything than keep still," she says at one point). It is made surprisingly obvious that Stanley has been sexually abused all her life by her even worse Uncle William (Charles Coburn), and Davis instinctively plays this up by acting all dissociated in his presence, absent and empty, a frozen-in-time little girl. No doubt Davis puts her foot down on the accelerator of her hysteria too many times here, but that's what she thought her audience wanted.

It also wanted her in *Now, Voyager,* a heartfelt fantasy where her heroine Charlotte Vale goes from beetle-browed, put-upon daughter to stylish and confident woman in careful stages. "I'm my mother's servant! My mother says! My mother, my mother, my *muh-ther-er!*" she screams in her first scene, upsettingly. "Go on torture me!" she cries later, breaking down when the teasing of family members gets to be too much. "Go on torture me, you like making fun of me, don't you, you think it's *fun* making fun of me, don't you—" at which point her words get choked off and Davis offers one of those genuine flashes of madness in her eyes, cannily edited so that it breaks off just at the right time, like captured lightning. As always, Davis holds her hands in front of her and relentlessly squeezes them, something she does in practically every movie, no matter what character she is playing.

Now, Voyager is a slow film, lush and measured and campy, but Davis brings it just enough touches of psychological realism to make it play, especially in the later scenes she shares with her tyrannical mother (Gladys Cooper), where she brings subtle shadings of irony and keen misgivings to their confrontations. "I didn't want to be born and you didn't want me to be born either, it's been a calamity on both sides!" Charlotte finally cries, with a sense of relief, and it's that explosive telling of the truth that kills Charlotte's mother, and her mother's hold on her. It was clever of Davis to play an inhibited, repressed woman coming to life after all the bitches she'd been chewing on (she had to fight to get the *Now, Voyager* script), and the success of this film gave her a few more years as a top star at Warner Brothers.

Weak directors like Irving Rapper, Vincent Sherman, and Bretaigne Windust did Davis no favors, but she carried on alone. "I have never talked to a man for more than five minutes in my life without wanting to box his ears," Davis says, in amused, clipped tones, as teacher Miss Moffat in *The Corn is Green* (1945), where she is at her most controlled, bringing a fine bluestocking spirit to her role and a rare kind of intellectual excitement. She let Claude Rains shoot the works in *Deception* (1946) but contributed a cherishably campy final close-up, as if even she had stopped taking her material seriously. And then Davis left the Warners lot in a blaze of theatrics in *Beyond the Forest* (1949) as Rosa Moline, a woman who will do anything to get out of her small town and get to Chicago.

Rosa is too big for her hometown but too provincial and small (and too old) for the life she wants in Chicago, and Davis plays the humiliations Rosa suffers and her lashings out with a freakish stubbornness that she must have intimately understood herself. Audiences laughed at Davis's outsized acting here, but characters in the movie laugh at the messy, unkempt Rosa as well, and Davis digs pretty deep into this misfit, this figure of fun, who dreams of being exceptional and dreads being normal, being just like everybody else in town. Her Rosa achieves a kind of feverish grandeur in her contempt for her nice husband (Joseph Cotten) as she lies dying of peritonitis: "You really *hate* me, don't you?" she asks him. "Well, congratulations, it'll make a *new* man of you!" Director King Vidor brings out the elemental in Davis, the hunger, the absurdity, the conceit and the terror.

The camp underpinnings of Davis's performances came to an apotheosis in *All About Eve* (1950), where a lowered voice due to laryngitis gave an extra oomph to her delivery of Joseph Mankiewicz's baroque and pointed lines. As Margo Channing, a theater star starting to fade at age 40, Davis for the first time seems to be doing a kind of drag version of herself (the lowered voice is part of that), her artificiality and drama queen posing explained, as it is in a different way in *The Letter*, because she's playing an actress.

Margo's best friend Karen (Celeste Holm) says that Margo makes up for underplaying on stage by overplaying reality, but it's very hard to imagine this hyper-literate virago underplaying anything, on stage or off, as we watch her hilariously exult in her own questionable taste in words and manners. Davis's long drunk scene at a party here is admirably detailed and precise, and her readings of the most far-out of Mankiewicz's lines are consistently inventive. *All About Eve* is widely considered Davis's best film, the film of hers you have to make the least allowances for, and it defined and clarified her image for all time as a "look at me" star actress, even if what we were looking at, as the years went by, became less and less palatable.

Every consideration of Bette Davis always breaks off here and says that nothing she did after *All About Eve* was worth considering seriously or even considering at all, but that isn't fair. She did have a tough 10 or so years after *Eve*. She gained weight, her voice coarsened, and she was off the screen for three years because of health problems. Ventures in the theater didn't work, and she did episodes of TV shows without enthusiasm. Her vocal delivery fell into a curious singsong pattern that sometimes became cut off from the meanings of the words she was saying. It was as if she fed every line through some complex filtering system that was out of order, so that she took pauses and robotically cut up phrases for no clear reason.

Reviews began to accuse Davis of imitating her own nightclub imitators, and those eyes of hers worked overtime as usual and often looked bleary, even defeated. *The Star* (1952), in which she played a has-been movie actress, feels like a crucial mistake, self-exploitation that she plays with a new kind of slam-bang campiness. In the scene where she tells off her money-grubbing in-laws, grabs her Academy Award and cries, "C'mon, Oscar, let's you and me get drunk!" we could be watching a Bette Davis impersonator doing a comic takeoff of her in some bar somewhere.

But she improved on her first Elizabeth I in *The Virgin Queen* (1955), and her Aggie Hurley, a worn-down Bronx housewife in *The Catered Affair* (1956), is a surprisingly empathetic and closely observed performance. Watch the scene where Aggie falls apart and cries behind a closed door, letting all of her pent-up agony out, and then watch the way Davis plays Aggie's slow, relieved recovery from those tears. She told the director Richard Brooks that she could only do this scene once for him, and that's because she was digging far deeper into herself than she usually did. Davis was known for being able to go into a scene and come right out of it, which might suggest that she stayed on the surface of her emotions much of the time, but in *The Catered Affair* she proves she was capable of going down further. Maybe she was secretly intrigued by the Method actors of the 1950s and their search for a deeper truth. Whatever the cause, her Aggie is fine and serious work, a case made for a woman very different from herself.

Storm Center (1956), which had a politically liberal theme, helped to keep her out of features for another three years. Most of her scenes as a dope-fiend countess in *The Scapegoat* (1959) were cut, and she looks unhappy as Apple Annie in Frank Capra's *Pocketful of Miracles* (1961), where she first introduced a witch's cackle to her repertoire of mannerisms. And then she did *What Ever Happened to Baby Jane?* (1962) for Robert Aldrich, where she gleefully tormented Joan Crawford, a long-time rival, and cooked up one of her most uncanny looks: clown white make-up and heavy black eyeliner and lipstick and even a "beauty" mark (shaped like a heart!). She felt that Jane, an ex-vaudeville headliner and alcoholic, wouldn't wash her face but just add another layer of make-up a day. Many actors, even character actors, can be vain or protective about their appearance, but never Davis. She was quite the opposite, in fact. She had a perverted zeal for appearing as gross as possible from the beginning.

Davis received her tenth Oscar nomination for her controversial performance in *Baby Jane*, and it certainly is attention grabbing. Considering that old Davis movies (*Parachute Jumper* and *Ex-Lady*) were used to represent the failed Hollywood career of Jane, it might be said that this movie took the self-exploitation of *The Star* to new and even meaner levels, but there is a core of emotional truth to Davis's work here, if you look for it.

When I first saw this movie, I was a 10-year-old kid, and I found its story of a wasted life very impressive and disturbing. As a college student, when I attended a screening of *Baby Jane* in New York at the Film Forum revival theater, I was taken aback when the gay men in the audience started hooting with laughter at the early scenes between Jane and Crawford's Blanche, which played now as a drag act of their own personal hatred of each other.

Yet Davis's performance is really not too far from her childlike Stanley Timberlake in *In This Our Life*, and in many ways it's more restrained and on target (and she does suggest that Jane was too close to her father, maybe even in the same incestuous way that Stanley was to her Uncle). Davis's choices here feel more modern, more connected to the material, than in her early work, particularly in her sharply detailed scenes with Victor Buono, who plays a musician eager to get money from Jane as she plans a comeback.

Baby Jane is a camp film, on one level, in that it invites us to laugh, if we care to, at Davis and Crawford. And surely part of its commercial success came from their old fans coming to see them looking and behaving like hags, not a very nice or respectable impulse, but a human one. We're all curious about decay and failure, particularly if it comes to those who were once beautiful or successful or both. But it's difficult to laugh or remain distanced from the scene where Davis's Jane, alone and drinking by herself, goes into an old routine from childhood, screams when she sees her ruined face in a mirror, and then slowly stands up and draws herself out of this distress physically when Jane decides to make her sister Blanche a target for her anger. Davis is clearly using her own dislike of Crawford in this scene, and that's what the Method actors were doing, so in a way she was going with the times.

"They just didn't love you enough," Jane says drunkenly, as she goes over her old clippings. "They just didn't love you enough," she repeats, weighting each word. Yes, we've probably been laughing or jumping out of our seats in other scenes, but Davis still gets across the misery of an over-loved performer totally deserted in her twilight years. And in her final scene of mad relief as Jane dances on a beach for curious onlookers, Davis reaches a point of almost classical catharsis.

Davis had her own warped kind of integrity. I've seen women who look like her Baby Jane on the street, and I'm sure you have, too. Not often, of course, but once in a great while. They are the unmentionables of life, the freaks who have lost all perspective, the ones people laugh at and steer clear of. In her way, Davis shined a light on far-gone people like Baby Jane and Rosa Moline and made you understand what made them like that. And that's what a creative person is supposed to do.

Davis did another Aldrich thriller, *Hush … Hush, Sweet Charlotte* (1964), playing a

Bette Davis's Baby Jane realizes that her public just didn't love her enough.

demented Southern belle who may or may not have committed a hatchet murder, and once again she played a woman who was maybe too close to her father. It was a far cruder film than *Jane*, with a forced, screechingly overdone central performance from its star (a double bill of *Jezebel* and *Hush ... Hush, Sweet Charlotte* would make a grim contrast). Davis went to England to be *The Nanny* (1965), where she was used and lit like Boris Karloff and seems about to say "Boo!" in every other scene. And then her features drifted towards obscurity. It takes a real Davis cultist to place *Connecting Rooms* (1970), where she played a repressed cellist (and which was barely released), or *The Scientific Cardplayer* (1972), where she was entirely dubbed in Italian as a rich meanie in a white wig. To say nothing of *Bunny O'Hare* (1971), unquestionably her worst feature, where she dressed as a hippie and robbed banks.

But Davis found valuable opportunities on television in her later years. She was at her singsong, choppy worst in *The Disappearance of Aimee* (1976) and especially in the four hours of *Family Reunion* (1981), where she was a schoolteacher interminably going around visiting relatives, but there were three TV movies of this time that marked a brief renaissance for her, and they deserve to be thought of with her best work.

Davis played Lucy Mason, an embittered old woman, crusty and barnacled and defensive against daughter Gena Rowlands in *Strangers: The Story of a Mother and Daughter* (1979), for which she deservedly won an Emmy. Her Lucy is more heightened than her Aggie Hurley in *The Catered Affair*, but this is a fascinating example of acting work that is larger-than-life, underlined, shaped, made much of, yet also based in quiet, day-to-day reality (her playing here is aided by a plaintive, elegiac musical score by Fred Karlin, her best since the Max Steiner days).

Davis was never so affected by a fellow actor as she is by Rowlands in *Strangers*, not even Claude Rains, and there's such relief in the way her performance is strengthened by exposure to Rowlands's simpler and more lyrical expressiveness, as if she doesn't always have to go it alone. Davis had done bad work for years and had made a fool of herself in many films, but *Strangers* was a reward for her patience, and her ability to let herself, or her image, go.

This is never said of Davis, and it should be: she found new ways of working as she got older, without ever quite giving up the supercharged emotions that had made her so distinctive as a young woman. Yes, sometimes her Lucy is declamatory, but some old ladies are like that in their kitchens, just as Elizabeth I was on her throne. "It's a hell of a part for me, this dame," Davis told her friend Whitney Stine. "And I'm a little afraid of it. A lot of me is going into it—much more than I had planned." When the producers ran out of money, she offered to work with Rowlands until midnight to finish the scenes they had to do. She had done the same thing 40 years earlier when Jack Warner threatened to take Wyler off *Jezebel* for being too slow. Her work meant that much to her, even as an older woman who was not always well.

She was an upright widow who winds up on the street in the grim *White Mama* (1980), where an elderly weariness seemed to be sapping her usual electric energy (and this was not a bad thing, for she always had too much of it). "Oh, this life," she says in exhaustion at one point, giving the words real weight. In *A Piano for Mrs. Cimino* (1982), a far cruder TV issue movie, Davis plays an elderly woman trying to pull her mind back together, and though her work is correspondingly broader here, she still has fine little bird-like moments.

Davis suffered a stroke, and after some time for recovery she made a few more films and some talk show appearances, her mouth twisted, but her voice still emphatic. In *The Whales of August* (1987), her penultimate feature, Davis's stubborn crankiness tested even Lillian Gish's patience. She stayed seated through much of that film, those ever-moving hands of hers finally lying limp in her lap now, all worn out. Just as Davis began with *The Bad Sister*, almost 60 years later she ended with *Wicked Stepmother* (1989), a Larry Cohen cult film that she dropped out of after she saw her skeletal appearance in the rushes. The sight of her in that movie was too much even for her.

Davis was not one like Garbo or Dietrich or Crawford to retreat to protect some legend of earlier beauty. In true Davis style, she seemed to flaunt her physical afflictions and decay in old age as she did on the screen when she was younger with the aid of make-up, as if to say, "Have a look at what life can do to you." There are always going to be some people who want to turn away from that. Sometimes her narrowed eyes would take on a pleading look towards the end, but there is no need to offer her your sympathy. Davis was a body artist, a hunger artist, like the man in the Kafka story, and rugged old age gave her one more mortifying role to play.

Her four marriages were all unhappy, and her daughter B.D betrayed her with a petty memoir, *My Mother's Keeper* (1985), written after Davis had suffered her stroke. In every scene in that book, Davis cries, "Brother!" and "Jesus!" and "Shit!" and is impossible about everything. She was a warrior, or winner, who had clawed her way to the top of the heap, and her core audience were the unlovable, or at least the unloved, among women and gay men, for whom she brought solace. She herself pushed away most of the people who tried to love her, though her son Michael remained admirably loyal to her. It was Michael who tried to talk B.D. out of publishing her book, but she told him that she'd already accepted and spent most of the advance money, so it had to go forward.

That expression on Davis's face as Wyler leaves her at her AFI event shows keen regret, among other things, because she was herself as self-destructive—and destructive—as her three Wyler anti-heroines. She did it alone too much, rejecting most of her latter-day directors who tried to offer advice with a snort of "That's nonsense!" And the results she got were erratic. But there was a shy, almost embarrassed sense of decency to her best work. You have to look for it, but it turns up in fleeting moments, every now and then, when she lets her guard down just a bit.

The world did not please Davis, and she was not shy about expressing that. But she was a little scared about showing us the things that really mattered to her, the things about life that gave her moments of pleasure. She came out to Hollywood and they told her she was unattractive, as if that were the worst thing a woman could be, and she showed them plenty of other things women might be, and she made them like it. She also tried and persevered and grew as a screen actor over time. Her instincts could play her wrong, but her long record is filled with intriguing things: unvarnished, graphic hatred; naked neediness; ironic humor; and appetite. She could light a cigarette in a room and that whole room would vibrate with her colorful discontent, her presence. That presence is still there on screen in 100 or so films, still demanding attention.

Katharine Hepburn
Sadly Happy

Towards the end of her long life, Katharine Hepburn spent the better part of 20 years giving "rare" interviews, from her rip-snorting appearance on Dick Cavett's TV talk show in 1973 (surely one of her most invigorating and riskiest performances of starry self) to the TNT documentary *All About Me* in 1993. Her cheekbones tilted high, Hepburn would hold her chin to steady the trembling of her head and hold court and make firm and rapid-fire pronouncements; she was self-intoxicated and on a roll with her nasal talk talk talk. Hepburn became less an actress and even a star and more of a lifestyle choice in favor of good sense, wit, and cheerful attitude. There were few people who were as widely loved as Hepburn was in this period.

But when Hepburn was a young woman, she was an acquired taste at best. In fact, even more so than Bette Davis, there were many who said, "I can't stand her," but there was less perverse enjoyment in that stance when it came to Hepburn. She was seen as snooty and affected—perhaps because she was snooty and affected. But all her precious mannerisms were actually a protection for what she was concealing: the soft heart of a freak and a loner who actually did care very much what people thought of her. The broad "a" and the "rally" for "really" and the "yah" for "yes" were signals for a larger-than-life persona carefully constructed, sheer artifice, sheer art.

She had rough edges, and they showed particularly in her earliest film work, but Hepburn learned to sand those away in public. Butch and boyish by nature, no one could be as meltingly "feminine" and vulnerable on screen as Hepburn when she chose to be, and she chose to be that more and more during her uncertain middle period as a star, from about 1940 to 1956, when she played a lot of women who needed to compromise their own standards and specialness in some way. Hepburn doesn't change herself for a part the way Bette Davis often does but makes every part into Katharine Hepburn, bringing out or tamping down certain Hepburn mannerisms for each occasion. And so she's "always the same," as some people say, in voice and manner, either strident and sure of herself or very sensitive or overly sensitive.

Though that quacking voice of hers seemed to suggest the entitled eccentricity that might be the result of inherited wealth, Hepburn's family was actually not as well-to-do as was once thought. Her father was a doctor who specialized in treating venereal disease and her mother was a feminist who fought for women's suffrage. It was a large family, and the children were encouraged to debate and talk amongst themselves. They were all hams clamoring for attention.

Dr. Hepburn once said that his children didn't like going to a party unless they were assured of being either the bride or the corpse, and that's partly why Hepburn never went to the Oscars any time she was nominated or any of the four times she won, for she never wanted to be seen losing at anything. As a kid she cut her hair short and told everyone to call her Jimmy. Like Garbo, it seems clear that Hepburn thought of herself as a boy, with a boy's freedom and a boy's prerogatives.

She was very close to her older brother Tom, who committed suicide when they were both teenagers under somewhat mysterious circumstances. Hepburn was the one who found his body. "I burst into tears," she wrote in her 1991 memoir *Me*, describing the aftermath of Tom's death. "This is what I thought I should do. People die—you cry—but inside I was frozen." For years after that, she took Tom's birth date as her own. She said later that she felt she was living for two people, and that makes sense given her overachieving and her brave, nearly foolhardy ambition.

Hepburn told friends as an older woman that she thought Tom might have been gay. Her own sexuality is still a vexed question of debate for some people, but whatever it was, it was complicated, and it cannot be understood with modern labels. There's what Hepburn was, and there's what she wanted to be. There's what she was drawn to, and there's what she could live without. Because what she wanted to be most of all was famous, and she'd do anything to get fame and keep it.

She went to Bryn Mawr college, where some of the girls must have sounded a bit peculiar, but really nobody sounded or sounds like Katharine Hepburn any more than anyone sounds like Cary Grant. "Whenever I see a Hepburn film I start by wondering why on earth she speaks like that," said Tallulah Bankhead, "and by the end of the film I wonder why everybody doesn't."

Hepburn invented her voice, and she loved to be looked at. She even posed for nude photos for her beau of this time, Ludlow Ogden Smith (who briefly became her first and only husband), just as Bette Davis posed for a nude statue for money when she was a teenager, just as Louise Brooks and Barbara Stanwyck posed topless for photos when they were Ziegfeld Follies girls, and just as Joan Crawford—well, Joan Crawford supposedly went much further than any of them. There are no nudes of James Cagney or Cary Grant floating around, and that's at least partly because women were encouraged to see themselves in a sexual way. Part of acting is being looked at, and you are naked emotionally if not physically. And so women understood the nature of that right away, whereas most men of this time shied from it.

Hepburn tried to go on the stage, and she would get jobs only to be fired from them, again and again. She was brash and she was odd and there was something amateur about her. In fact, there was always something amateur about Hepburn, something that she carefully hid through the years by acquiring a fortress-like technique, but it turns up in something as late as *Stage Door* (1937) where she plays a brash and odd young girl trying to go on the stage.

There's a moment in *Stage Door* when Constance Collier's seedy dame Miss Luther is defending Hepburn's Terry to the rest of the girls in their theatrical boarding house that shows Hepburn's potential for disaster. Collier is the focus of the shot but Hepburn is visible in the foreground screen left. As Collier talks, Hepburn is caught "reacting" to Collier's lines, far too much and far too fast. It's the kind of mistake you would see in an amateur theatrical, pure disconnected and laughably unconvincing mugging. To my knowledge, no one else has ever pointed out this Hepburn gaffe before, maybe because she's tucked away in the frame and not the center of the shot. It's hard to imagine Stanwyck or Davis making a mistake like this, though Crawford might have early on. Maybe that's part of why Hepburn kept getting fired. Plus, who talked like she talked? What did she think she was *doing*, anyway?

Hepburn was an understudy for Hope Williams in Philip Barry's play *Holiday* for a while, and she finally got noticed in *The Warrior's Husband* on Broadway in 1932, which was basically a leg show where she strode about in a short tunic and bossed men around. This caught the interest of producer David Selznick, who signed Hepburn to a contract to play the lead in *A Bill of Divorcement* (1932) opposite John Barrymore. She came out to Hollywood with Laura Harding, who did actually come from money and who lived with Hepburn for most of the 1930s. When her friend James Prideaux asked her in the 1980s if she and Laura had gone to bed together, Hepburn replied, "Of course!" And they spoke no more of it. (This is a key exchange from William Mann's biography *Kate: The Woman Who Was Hepburn*, which was published in 2006.)

Many of Hepburn's fans still won't believe she was basically lesbian. Surely her sexuality was a source of confusion and fear for her. Her agent Leland Hayward linked himself with Hepburn as a cover for some of the 1930s, and then she linked herself to Howard Hughes because she knew that it would make good publicity. But in the 1930s, Laura Harding was the person Hepburn was closest to, and maybe she admitted that to herself, but her way in everything was to charge blindly ahead. There were things in her life that she would never discuss with anyone. She would never even discuss them with herself.

Hepburn is given a starry entrance in *A Bill of Divorcement* by her mentor director George Cukor, who went on to direct her 10 times; she floats down a staircase in a white and birdlike dress, running a bit and then skidding into the arms of her fiancé (David Manners). This entrance suggests that she is fun-loving, romantic, impetuous. But in her second scene, at breakfast with her mother (Billie Burke) and aunt (Elizabeth Patterson), Hepburn brashly shows herself in her own blunt, virile, and youthfully intolerant, nearly arrogant splendor.

Speaking of her father, who is in an asylum, she says, "The war wasn't our fault, you can't blame anyone for shell shock!" while she helps herself to food. "We can't go around with a handkerchief to our eyes all the time, we've got to *live!*" she barks, in a very strong-minded way somewhat different from her gentler "Live!" persona of 1993, when she quaveringly told us the Hepburn family motto, "Listen to the song of life."

The young Hepburn is bold, slashing, and harsh. Her decided presence cuts through everything else in *A Bill of Divorcement*, and it came (and still comes) as a relief to some, while others were merely irritated by her. It was safe to say, however, and it is still safe to say, that she was an original. Her Sydney is given to slight eye rolls sometimes, as if Hepburn moved at a quicker speed than anyone else and other people made her impatient (one of the few qualities she shares with Bette Davis). Her too-muchness in *Bill* is explained by the fact that there's insanity in her family, a fact that she must touchingly adjust to. So the first Hepburn heroine is forced, through hereditary predisposition, to plan for a life without husband and without children, a life like that of Hepburn herself and Lillian Gish before her.

She was curiously inexpressive in her follow-up, Dorothy Arzner's *Christopher Strong* (1933), as an aviatrix (a dated but pretty word) who comes to grief when she falls in love with a married man (Colin Clive). Hepburn seems closed-off here, hard and impenetrable, in both senses of that word. She's clearly the boss and she lives her own life, so it's tough to believe she lets herself get all upset over such a small thing as adultery with Clive. Hepburn is ready to be something new in *Christopher Strong*, something that would even seem new today, but her evergreen, androgynous newness was up against conventions from before the First World War, and so she is always being pulled back down to earth.

Hepburn wears pants in *Christopher Strong*, just as she did in life, just as Dietrich did on screen and off, but she also dons a shimmery white "moth" dress with skullcap for sheer freakishness here, and she seems to have a secret, an essential for movie stardom. Reviewers compared her to Garbo as the most distinctive new personality on the screen, but the words "grating," "strident" and "strange" kept coming up in her notices. These descriptive words were apprehensive, but not unkindly meant as of yet. The *Los Angeles Times* mentioned her "pleasantly unpleasant voice." How can a voice be pleasantly unpleasant? Maybe that's what "distinctive" means.

"I'm not attractive that way," her Lady Cynthia insists, when Clive tells her she's beautiful. It's something Hepburn herself might have said to discourage an interested man. She didn't want what women were supposed to want, and she had to play elaborate games to live her own life her way. RKO, her studio all through the 1930s, was a queer place where nobody seemed to be minding the store and where people might get away with odd things, and so it's no wonder that Katharine Hepburn was their reigning star turn. Lady Cynthia speaks of being lonely, but unlike many later Hepburn characters, she doesn't seem too bothered by that solitary status.

Hepburn used her early inexpressiveness and immunity to emotion and made it into a style for *Morning Glory* (1933), where she plays Eva Lovelace, a stage-struck girl not too far from being an out-there loser. Hepburn spoke here in what she called a "mistress of monotone" fashion that was an outright imitation, she said later, of the way Ruth Gordon played a role on stage in a play she had seen called *A Church Mouse*. Hepburn's Eva says she doesn't believe in marriage for the artist and that cold weather makes her feel strong. She doesn't mind if people think she's affected for "trying to speak properly." These are perfect positions for the young Hepburn.

She delivers Eva's lines with just the right amount of intensity. Another actress might have made Eva's first scenes more comic, might have made her more easy to laugh at, but Hepburn makes her so deadly serious that it's hard to laugh at her. Instead, she emanates a vague unease, especially when she says she wants to die at her zenith by "my own hand one night, on the stage." There's something morbid about Eva, and Hepburn was always secretly encouraged by any suggestion of morbidity, which turns something on in her performing style, or her imagination. She won her first Oscar for this part.

And then she had a big hit in *Little Women* (1933) as tomboy Jo March, another ideal role for her. While Bette Davis was scrounging for anything she could get, Hepburn right from the start was having vehicles tailored to bring out her unicorn gifts. Her films were never programmers, never anything she was just thrown into, and they always centered on her exclusively. Like her Eva, Hepburn's Jo is high on life and egoistic, but she is also loyal and self-correcting, as wholesome, clean, and energetic as a snowball fight.

It was an easy part for Hepburn. Her Jo doesn't like wearing dresses and being girly because she's a boy at heart, like Tom Sawyer, rough and ready and straightforward, full of basso yelps to release her high spirits. When she dances alone by herself at a ball, she is too self-intoxicated to want any romantic attachments of any kind. Hepburn maybe pushes certain effects a bit too hard sometimes here, but Jo herself might do that, so it works out fine. Of the major actresses in this early talkie period and beyond, only Barbara Stanwyck never pushes or forces emotion, as Davis and Hepburn sometimes do, because she doesn't need to. Any deep feeling that Stanwyck wants is right there for her at only the slightest touch.

Hepburn's Jo gets her hair cut short to sell the shorn hair for money. "It's boyish, becoming, and easy to keep in order!" she says of this new hairstyle. Hepburn's Jo today plays very much as a gay girl finding any excuse to avoid getting trapped into traditional femininity, even if the script does make her cry over her lost hair later. Then again, who's to say born rebels don't long for what they aren't? That's always been a potent subject for outsider artists.

For someone who in later life was constantly railing against moaners and self-pitiers, Hepburn always cries on screen with luxurious abandon, as she does in *Little Women* when her sister Beth (Jean Parker) is sick and dying. Her tears dried, Jo rejects the ardent Laurie (Douglass Montgomery) in favor of an older professor (Paul Lukas) who is not likely to make many, or any, sexual demands on her. It seems clear this is the kind of arrangement that Hepburn herself always favored.

Everything had been charmed for Hepburn so far, but now she experienced her first string of failures (success and failure seemed to come for her in steady cycles). She disastrously went back to the Broadway stage in *The Lake*, about which Dorothy Parker allegedly said, "Miss Hepburn ran the gamut of emotions from A to B." This supposed new Garbo, this new star, they were saying now, was limited, monotonous, an amateur. People began to wonder if her earlier work had been a fluke as Hepburn made flop after flop.

In *Spitfire* (1934), where she was crazily cast as a barefoot hillbilly faith healer, Hepburn was very reckless with her accent and her goofy choices (that's part of what her "amateur" star quality is maybe). She coyly affected a Scottish brogue for some scenes in the J. M. Barrie adaptation *The Little Minister* (1934), a failed attempt to recapture the charm of *Little Woman*, and she struck over-intense poses with Charles Boyer and flared her rocking horse nostrils in *Break of Hearts* (1935), a drippy romance.

Hepburn's bad movies of the 1930s are filled with long extreme close-ups of her face where her eyes are glistening with shed and unshed tears and she speaks in a rapt, trance-like way. Once thought too hard and tough, she was now in danger of putting everybody to sleep with this new "feminine" mode, and her over-sensitivity was beginning to seem more than a little absurd. She has a moment in *Break of Hearts* (that title!) where she is playing some music that reminds her of Boyer, and she suddenly stops playing and jerkily puts a hand up to her face. It's one of those mistakes that lets us see that Hepburn, when she didn't have enough control or direction as a girl, was entirely capable of acting as badly and artificially as Norma Shearer at her worst.

And so *Alice Adams* (1935), one of her very best performances, was the first of many comebacks for Hepburn. As an affected young girl who puts on airs and wants to rise above her station, Hepburn exposed all of her own vulnerability as a misfit and outsider, and the result was nerve-wracking, in the best sense. After being totally rejected and humiliated at a party (she makes it even worse several times by trying to pretend how much she's enjoying herself), her Alice has a brief moment where she says she wants to go on the stage, but her simple father (Fred Stone) gently shoots that down in a way that Dr. Hepburn did not.

Trying too hard, in snobby and even racist ways, is Alice's problem, and Hepburn judges her effects so carefully here that they never feel alienating because we can always discern the pure and romantic spirit underneath that is misguidedly animating Alice. As she sits on a date with her suitor Arthur (Fred MacMurray), she talks about being "sadly happy," that melancholy, mixed, isolated exaltation that Hepburn does so touchingly, so distinctively.

Towards the middle of the film, Hepburn's Alice comes to a kind of self-awareness, even referring to herself as a "tricky mess" in comparison to Arthur. At the end, she is all ready to go to secretarial school and earn her own living, but the film

Katharine Hepburn as Alice Adams.

gives her a hard-to-believe reprieve when Arthur comes back for her. This is a film that *explains* Hepburn's acting style, just as *The Letter* does for Bette Davis, and the result is very moving.

But then Hepburn made another career mistake, a more personal kind of mistake. "I'll be a boy, and rough and hard, I won't care what I do!" she cries at the beginning of George Cukor's *Sylvia Scarlett* (1936), where she cuts off her hair and poses as a boy, or re-discovers her true self, the boy named Jimmy she had not forgotten. *Sylvia Scarlett* was a very damaging flop in its day, and it's easy to see why: it's precious and nearly plotless, gayly moving from one episode to another, and the sexual ambiguity of the characters was seen as unsettling and unfunny. Hepburn admitted that she'd lost confidence in the film halfway through, and she often said that confidence, especially in this early period, was all she had.

Most of her leading men of the 1930s—David Manners, Colin Clive, Douglass Montgomery, and John Beal—actually were or read as gay. She was so hard that they often put her with softer men, and this added to her androgynous, disturbing impact, which came to a head in *Sylvia Scarlett*. Three more flops followed, each more harmful than the last. She was *Mary of Scotland* (1936) for John Ford, a stiff and shadowy pageant that Ford lost interest in. "Outside the narrow range in which she is superb, Katharine Hepburn often acts like a Bryn Mawr senior in a May Day pageant," sniffed *Time*. She was a Victorian feminist in *A Woman Rebels* (1936), a picture that has no right to be as lifeless as it is. And she was Miss Phoebe Throssel in *Quality Street* (1937), another film from a J.M. Barrie source, in which she was very coy. It seemed again that Hepburn was limited, out of her depth, getting along because of her unusual looks and manner and voice.

And so she went back to the source of her success in *Stage Door* (1937), playing a young rich girl named Terry Randall who wants to go on the stage. "If I can act, I want the world to know it, if I can't, I want to know it," she says. This was more of an ensemble movie, so the pressure was off of Hepburn to carry it, and the film also offered a formula for her. This is the first time where one of her movies acknowledges Hepburn's highfalutin manners and upper-crust way of talking and throws barbs at her until the time comes for her to prove herself as a goodhearted type when the chips are down.

Terry has no romantic interest and her sole concentration is her career, and she stays on at an all-female theatrical boarding house even after she has a success on stage. To put it bluntly, Terry does not seem all that heterosexual, and the film does not saddle her with a choice between man and career, as some later Hepburn films do and as *Christopher Strong* did. Aside from the amateur mishap noted earlier, Hepburn does clean, smart work here, and it feels subtly personal, particularly at the end when Terry tries to talk roommate Jean (Ginger Rogers) into not going out on a date with an available man. In her covert way, Hepburn was offering options to women and others that the movies generally didn't endorse, and she would continue to do that, where she could, for the rest of her career.

A long time was spent shooting Howard Hawks's *Bringing Up Baby* (1938), which is why, though it made money, it was not a financial success. Some of the problem they had on set at first was that Hepburn was playing her farcical part in too silly a way, as if she were enjoying her own jokes, and Hawks had to teach her that comedy like this is best when it is played in all seriousness. It took her a while to get it, but she eventually learned and learned quickly, prodigiously. This was her first out-and-out comedy, and the first and also the last time where she played a really scatterbrained lady, a dizzy heiress named Susan Vance who charges right ahead and drags repressed David (Cary Grant), the man she has a thing for, with her. Her performance is based in the sometimes-lunatic confidence that had made her a star in the first place. She imposes herself here like a younger sibling who is always willfully tagging along.

Susan keeps saying "Everything is going to be all right," and she exists in a state of continual improvisation and chaos that the movie posits as fun and as the best way to live life. Hepburn makes this position convincing because she herself is having such a good time with the part underneath Susan's hell-bent seriousness (so much so that she didn't want the shooting to end), and we share in her fun, especially in the scene where she pretends to be a tough gangster's moll to get out of jail. *Bringing Up Baby* feels like a liberation, an advance for Hepburn, even if there could be no further to go with this particular type of anarchic heroine. Some people at the time felt *Bringing Up Baby* was too much, tiring and obnoxious, but today the film plays perfectly, always, through endless viewings. It has lasted.

Hepburn then got to be the unhappy rich girl Linda in *Holiday* (1938) on the screen. "Looks like me," she says, as she turns a childhood toy giraffe named Leopold to profile. "Don't you say a word about Leopold, he's very sensitive," she cautions her sister's fiancé Johnny (Grant again), and of course she's really talking about herself. A child of privilege, Hepburn's Linda is left wing and dissatisfied and would like to retreat into a created world of her own, even a movie, maybe, like the one we're watching. She's a failed painter and, of course, a failed actress, and she has integrity.

Hepburn can make you believe in things like integrity and character, and hope for something better, whereas Barbara Stanwyck is too detached and too far-gone for that and Bette Davis too neurotic and destructive. When

Hepburn gets upset on screen, it's for a constructive reason, because she hopes to change something, whereas Davis wants to scorch the earth and Stanwyck is protesting on a much purer and abstract plane, the battle already lost or maybe never even fought. One of the few things Linda has in common with Susan Vance is her belief in the ameliorating playfulness of a romantic or at least sisterly attachment, this time in the midst of a group of like-minded friends. Hepburn never did anything on screen more touching and suggestive than *Holiday*, or more revealing of herself and what she wanted.

And so Hepburn had now made three major films in a row, imperishable classics all of them, but they did her no good, maybe because she played rich girls in all three and in the last two her rarified point of view was indulged and vindicated. Reviewers who used to be kind and tactful about her flops had turned against her. She wrote in her memoir *Me*, "It seemed to me that I was in a very odd situation. Certainly I had done some very boring pictures. But then, I had done four really good pictures, and they had just not done well."

After being labeled box office poison by a group of film exhibitors, Hepburn went home to Connecticut and tried to think what to do before Philip Barry came to her rescue with a cleverly made vehicle, *The Philadelphia Story*, in which she played a snooty rich girl brought down to earth by drink and by men who tell her that she needs to get off her high horse. Howard Hughes bought her the movie rights to the play, which was filmed in 1940 and made another smash comeback for her.

The basic problem with *The Philadelphia Story* is that all the male characters keep telling Hepburn's Tracy Lord that she is inhuman and intolerant but we never actually see enough of what they are saying in her behavior. She physically gets knocked down in the wordless opening, pushed in the face by her ex-husband Dexter (Grant again), and that's all the film does to her verbally for the next two hours.

The scene where Dexter blames her for his drinking is one thing, but then the subsequent scene where her father (John Halliday) blames her for his affair with a younger woman is something else again. How does the father get away with this? Why, he says, if Tracy had been a loving and tolerant daughter, he wouldn't have felt the need to stray from his marriage. Which is a profoundly icky sentiment if you even think about it for a moment. But audiences didn't. They liked seeing Hepburn knocked over and over again, and they enjoyed her long and inspired and starry and discreetly sexy drunk scene with Jimmy Stewart.

At 33, Hepburn was finally offering just a bit of sex appeal to sweeten the deal, and she enacted Tracy's coming down to earth with wide-eyed credulity. She was willing to play all kinds of comic games with her dignity for a laugh, and in this she is set apart from Gish, Davis, Stanwyck, and Crawford, for she made her deepest impact in this period in romantic comedy material (only Stanwyck conquered screwball comedy, briefly but triumphantly, in *The Lady Eve* (1941), through sheer force of talent and will).

The Philadelphia Story established Hepburn again at a new studio, MGM, a very different place from live-and-let-live, screwy RKO. She sold another package to MGM for *Woman of the Year* (1942), which paired her for the first of nine times with Spencer Tracy. Hepburn's Tess Harding is a high-powered political columnist with a tacitly gay male secretary and links to the old feminist movement. Tracy's Sam is a sports writer on the same newspaper who starts a column war with Tess before he actually meets her. When they first lay eyes on each other here, Tracy comes into an office and the camera privileges his point of view by focusing on Hepburn's shapely legs until it sweeps up to her face. Pow! Chemistry.

No question about it, this chemistry between Hepburn and Tracy in these first scenes of *Woman of the Year* is momentous, and very sexual in a way she had never been before on screen. She does this "I can be made submissive" thing with him physically where she drops down to his shoulder level, and her eyes are softer than ever before, her voice hushed and tender. The scene where they drink and talk to each other in a bar and he tells her he sees the freckles on her face feels so private that you almost feel like you shouldn't be watching it. This is the only time that Hepburn played a woman who uses sex to get what she wants, and she's surprisingly convincing at that, no doubt because her real feelings for Tracy at that point were all there for her.

Time magazine approved of her this time, saying, "For once, strident Katharine Hepburn is properly subdued." Those recurring words, "strident" and "metallic" and "mannish" began to get dropped from her reviews. She seems almost entirely new in *Woman of the Year*: streamlined, less high-strung and anxious. In the scene where Tess listens to a wedding ceremony after Sam has left her, Hepburn achieves a remarkably focused intensity, a far cry from some of her more scattershot and overreaching RKO close-ups.

Hepburn hated the ending they tacked on to *Woman of the Year*, where Tess tries and fails to cook Sam breakfast, but she allowed it because she knew it was essential for a commercial success, and she cared very much indeed now what people thought of her. She was very moved by Tracy, and he by her. Hepburn had been an oddball and outcast heroine, but now she was briefly a "citadel that can and must be taken," as Dexter says in *The Philadelphia Story*.

For the rest of the 1940s at MGM, Hepburn was in a string of poor films, and her outspoken condemnation of the House Un-American Activities Committee got her into trouble as this new string of flops petered out. Her bad MGM movies are easier to take than her RKO flops, smoother, less egregious. She was getting more mannered, more likely to offer a Hepburn "turn" with teeth flashing and spirits high no matter what the part. Her youthful grimace where she rolled her eyes slightly turned into a persistent tic where she made her face a blank and looked around jerkily and helplessly for a few moments. She increasingly found herself playing helpmates to men, which is how she saw herself in her unconventional off-screen life with Tracy.

This was a sedate period for her on screen where she fell back on things she had done before. In Vincente Minnelli's dreamy *Undercurrent* (1946) she was put through an ordeal at the hands of husband Robert Taylor, and the film winds up with a scene where she is almost crushed by a rock, her eyes widening ridiculously at the prospect. When she gets up, Hepburn absurdly shakes her stiff hands in front of her to indicate her upset. Again, this scene proved that directors still needed to keep a close watch on Hepburn.

She brings a surprising amount of razzle-dazzle charm and intensity to her loyal wife to Tracy in *State of the Union* (1948), so that the movie is lucky to have her but she's not too lucky to have the movie. Her slump was broken by a bright comedy with Tracy, *Adam's Rib* (1949), in which he teased her just enough to make her palatable as she quacked those nasal "a" sounds of hers like Donald Duck in anger. Hepburn and Tracy are very cozy and playful in most of that movie, in a way that couples on screen rarely are, comfortable and mellow and secure.

The 1950s and 1960s were in some ways a golden period for Hepburn's career. She decided to challenge herself on stage, playing Rosalind in *As You Like It* on Broadway and Shaw's *The Millionairess* in London and New York (she wanted to make a movie of that Shaw play directed by Preston Sturges, but they couldn't find financing, unfortunately). She played Portia in *The Merchant of Venice*, Katharina in *The Taming of the Shrew*, Viola in *Twelfth Night*, and she was Cleopatra with Robert Ryan as her Antony. Her basic talent expanded to meet these roles, and her reviews were mixed but respectful of her hard work. Starting in 1951 with *The African Queen*, she worked in film sparingly, but every movie Hepburn made seemed to bring her an Oscar nomination (she racked up seven of them in this period).

Hepburn's screen persona now was the Spinster Who Finds Love, and this started off with her psalm-singing, skinny old maid Rosie Sayer in *The African Queen*, a double act with Humphrey Bogart's drinking man Charlie Allnut. The film is similar to her collaborations with Tracy in that Bogart's

Charlie makes fun of her high-toned righteousness until he falls for her, which allows us to laugh a bit at her and then fall for her too.

Bogart is a far more stylized performer than Tracy, a guy's guy who lingers over lines for the fun of it, and he stimulates that same sense of fun in Hepburn, daring her to outdo him in bold line readings. "I never dreamed that any mere physical experience could be so stimulating!" she cries ecstatically after they've gone down the river rapids for the first time. She pulls at her hair and even does a little mini-orgasm.

Hepburn risks being overdone in her swooning reaction to Bogart's drinking of gin, and in the way Rosie doesn't understand Charlie's jokes, but her effects are sure here, professional and controlled yet nicely abandoned, too, like when she snorts with laughter at his hippo impersonation, or in all the romantic changes she rings on saying his name: "Charlie, *Char*lie." It could be said that Hepburn and Bogart stay on the surface only, as Method actors of this period might have judged them, but what fun the surface can be.

They are both basically detached from their "turns" in *The African Queen*, but they bring them to a head of steam like the craftsmen they were, so that the sweatier and dirtier their characters get, the starrier Hepburn and Bogart seem. "Realism" is a moot term when it comes to acting like this. Their work here is a resourceful, created thing: up, not down, profoundly enriching and reassuring, in the best way. Star acting like this means structure and possibility, borne from and ignoring chaos and defeat.

On a roll again, Hepburn made her finest movie with Tracy, *Pat and Mike* (1952), in which she played an athlete who can never do her best when her fiancé (William Ching) is watching her. She is very mannered and highly strung in that film, doing all kinds of strenuous, but surface level, emotions, while Tracy eyes her understandingly. And then she went to Venice to be Jane Hudson, a "fancy secretary" from Ohio looking for what she's been missing all her life in David Lean's full-bloodedly sentimental but pragmatic *Summertime* (1955).

In *The Time of the Cuckoo*, the original Arthur Laurents play on which *Summertime* is based, Jane Hudson is a drunk and apt to throw barbs at people. Hepburn's Jane still drinks too much, and she is nervous and puritanical, but she is different from the woman in Laurents's play, more melancholy and wistful, and more conformist than any of Hepburn's 1930s heroines. "Well, I guess I'll settle with the majority," she says defensively in her first scene, insistent that she's *got* to like Venice because she has saved up for her trip for so long. In a scene with Isa Miranda's hotelkeeper, Hepburn says that she's looking for "a wonderful, mystical, magical, *miracle*," and the full measure of her talent is displayed in the searching, musical way she reads that line.

A pratfall into a canal for *Summertime* gave Hepburn an eye infection for the rest of her life (always prone to tears, her eyes were ever-glistening and overflowing from this point on). When Rossano Brazzi's married man comes to court her, Hepburn's Jane wonders if he sees her like a sister, a revealing moment for Hepburn, who in her on-screen persona was usually seeking a brother-sister bond with men.

Her Jane wants romance, but sex scares her. She wants it, but she doesn't want it, and in this she is close to what we know of Hepburn herself. Jane has her affair and then she leaves to go home, waving to her lover from a train with lyrical abandon so that he can keep seeing her arm moving as long as possible, a lovely, dancelike movement. In the end, Hepburn's Jane seems content to be alone again.

Hepburn finished her spinster cycle ignominiously with the poorly filmed *The Rainmaker* (1956), where she played a long-in-the-tooth cow country maiden desperate for a man. Desperate, for Wendell Corey! There's no way for anyone to play this self-pitying role without embarrassing themselves (Geraldine Page was stuck with it on stage), and Hepburn sells it hard without flinching, talking in a soft, wondering way about how she isn't a woman without a man to take care of, bemoaning her supposed plainness. In the other scenes where she gets upset, indicating distress with cartoonishly widened eyes and stiff arms held akimbo, Hepburn pushes her own fluttery, all-aquiver mannerisms so forcefully that the effect finally feels contemptuous, a coarse parody of her best early work.

They gave her another Oscar nomination for *The Rainmaker*, but it was a low point for her, as was *Desk Set* (1957), a feeble comedy with Tracy, where the name "Bunny Watson" could not disguise just how macho she was as a managing reference librarian who floats the idea to co-worker Joan Blondell that they can forget about men and just move in together and keep cats. (Blondell even makes fun of Hepburn's put-on "femme" and excitable mode here to her face for a moment, and Hepburn swats her on the rear in response.) Hepburn goes through all her old routines in *Desk Set*, including a detailed but obnoxious drunk scene that she had done far more cleanly and sharply in *State of the Union*. It was as if she had placed her old mannerisms in a deep fat fryer or something, with all kinds of girlish-rancid bubbles and gurgles percolating underneath them.

But then Hepburn challenged herself and grabbed another Oscar nomination for her prolix mother monster Mrs. Violet Venable in *Suddenly, Last Summer* (1959), where she digs deeply and entertainingly into her Tennessee Williams lines like she was trying to figure them out. When she first appears here, Hepburn sometimes seems like she has no idea what she's doing but is plunging gamely ahead anyway, and she even seems to be sending up her role, ever-so-slightly, but then the material activates the part of her that is encouraged by morbidity and she comes colorfully alive.

"Most people's lives, what are they but trails of debris," she says, pronouncing the last word with an emphasis on the first syllable. "Each day, more *de*-bris, more *de*-bris—long, long trails of *de*bris, with nothing to clean it all up but finally death!" She brings surprising conviction to this sentiment (the risky rhythm of the writing helps her), and then when she goes into Williams's long monologue about sea turtles being ripped apart by "savage, devouring birds," Hepburn tears into her florid lines with extraordinary brio and attack and appetite, building and building the speech and taking it fully seriously.

Hepburn is always a serious presence, a kind of bluestocking, ever-curious, and she is incapable of being campy. Mrs. Violet Venable could be played on a camp note throughout, but she plays it as searchingly and grimly as possible, and the result is resplendent. The bird monologue is such a difficult speech in so many ways, with its repetitions of words and its flowery turns of phrase, but Hepburn makes a meal of it, never losing her grip on it. It showed just how much technique she had acquired in her stage work with the help of her coach and friend Constance Collier, who had played with her in *Stage Door*. George Cukor was surprised by her Violet Venable and told Hepburn that he never knew she could be so evil. There were more surprises to come.

It would take more than technique to play Mary Tyrone in a film of Eugene O'Neill's *Long Day's Journey Into Night* (1962). It would take courage and daring, and asking for help. Hepburn admitted that she needed as much guidance as she could get from Sidney Lumet, her director, but the result speaks for itself. Who would have thought that the unskilled, monotonous girl who had flopped on stage in *The Lake* would one day do the definitive Mary Tyrone, the most difficult, demanding, and rewarding role for a woman in the American theater? "Not a great actress, by any manner of means," Robert Benchley had written about her in *The Lake*, "but one with a certain distinction which, with training, might possibly take the place of great acting in an emergency." Here at last was the great emergency, after much training.

Hepburn uses some mannerisms from her comedy roles in the early scenes of *Long Day's Journey,* but then she jettisons and subsumes them under the weight of Mary's anger and sorrow and passive aggression, which she never underlines, never making it feel conscious on Mary's part; she is just blindly striking out at her family, and surely Hepburn understood that kind of blind energy. It's like both Hepburn and Mary are exploring room after room of a darkened house for us, tentatively at first, and then with increasing, hell-bent stamina.

After Mary has caved in and taken her morphine, Hepburn's face becomes starker, and her voice is stonier and more accusing, but distant, too. As in *Suddenly, Last Summer*, Hepburn's formerly flat, thin hair seems to be augmented here, or thicker and curlier, which visually gives her more weight and substance. The bones in Hepburn's face stand tall like columns found in some Greek ruin, her freckles showing, her hair helplessly tumbling down in a picturesque mess, her eyes sometimes hard and mocking, sometimes as helpless as a trapped animal. She makes intimidatingly seamless transitions between girlish, high-voiced gentility and basso rage, laying a deadly guilt trip and then putting her hand in front of her face as she apologizes, waving it as if she'd like to efface herself entirely (and this is look-at-me Katharine Hepburn making this gesture full-out!).

Katharine Hepburn's ruined Mary Tyrone in *Long Day's Journey Into Night*.

Hepburn burrows deeper and deeper into the play, using up all of her skill and talent and imaginative capabilities until finally, *finally*, she has reached a point of naked, helpless responsiveness. "See!" her Mary cries to the family servant Cathleen (Jeanne Barr), holding out her crippled hands like a little kid to show what life has done to her, retreating further and further into the past as if it were a maze and she's never sure what she might come upon.

When Mary's son Edmund (Dean Stockwell) tells her he has to go to a sanitarium for his health, Hepburn's Mary lets out a short yell and then smacks him across the face and then pulls him into her arms, bam, bam, bam, staccato and fast yet also somehow fluid. Pure instinct. Hepburn is not too scared to go all the way with that savage and mixed reaction (she understandably hesitated over it when they were rehearsing), and she's not too scared to do anything at all here, ringing so many changes on self-pity that they become symphonic, a cry for help and clemency to the almighty God that Mary feels has deserted her.

When Edmund says, "It's hard to take at times, having a dope fiend for a mother," Hepburn stays very still, as if Mary has been permanently annihilated by this remark, and when she moves again it's like looking at smoke still rising on a battlefield covered in dead bodies. She murmurs to herself when Edmund leaves that she hopes she will accidentally take an overdose of morphine sometime. "I could never do it deliberately," she says, quietly and flatly. "The Blessed Virgin would never forgive me then."

Hepburn reaches a liquid point here, all disintegrated, all dissolved. It's quite a sight, quite a feat, quite a revelation of understanding, an end point that brought her, finally, to where her brother Tom had been when he choked himself to death. In Mary's last scene, where she drags her wedding dress and then remembers her convent days, Hepburn is simplicity itself, all affectations gone, pure water, with a few drops of poison in it.

You can hardly advance on a performance like this. There is nothing left to prove after having stretched so far and given it. Hepburn retired for a few years to look after Tracy, who was in ill health, returning only to support him in his swan song, *Guess Who's Coming to Dinner* (1967), for which she was given a second Oscar. She got a record third leading Oscar the following year for her Eleanor of Aquitaine in *The Lion in Winter* (1968), small potatoes or even potato chips after *Long Day's Journey*, thin, bitchy material that she plays in all seriousness and which some people took in all seriousness. In his DVD commentary, director Anthony Harvey said that he had to talk Hepburn into really doing up Eleanor's self-pity and vulnerability, both of which are laid on very thick here with pink cheeks, quivering head, and eyes overflowing with copious tears.

Hepburn had a personal success in a Broadway musical about Coco Chanel called *Coco* in 1969, proof that the public was willing to love her now in absolutely anything, even when she tried to quack and warble out some talky songs, pushing her voice harshly and rolling her "r" sounds. "Life is such a very solitary holiday," she talk-sings at one point on the cast album, pushing her loner point of view.

Hepburn's highbrow theater taste let her pick plum after plum on film in this golden autumnal period. While Davis was doing *Bunny O'Hare* and Crawford was doing *Trog* (1970) and Stanwyck had basically retired, Hepburn was playing Hecuba in a film of Euripides' *The Trojan Women* (1971) and Agnes in a movie of Edward Albee's *A Delicate Balance* (1973), demanding roles in the richest possible material.

The surprise of Hepburn's Hecuba is that she chooses to play it with her lowest possible voice, howling and growling away and finding all kinds of low-toned vocal variation, which is no small feat. Perhaps there shouldn't, then, be much surprise that she tackled the wordy Agnes in perhaps Albee's best play with skill, verbal accuracy, and appetite. Hepburn said that she didn't understand *A Delicate Balance*, but that did not impede her intelligence from feasting on every word and intellectual shift in it. Agnes is a talker, coming out with great articulate streams of thoughtful dodges and evasions, and Hepburn emphasizes the fact that this woman mainly talks to entertain and hold her husband Tobias (Paul Scofield). If not as definitive as her Mary Tyrone, this Agnes still could not be bettered.

Davis, Crawford, and Stanwyck would never have thought or pushed to take parts like Agnes in *A Delicate Balance*, whether they could have played them or not, but Hepburn gravitated towards the best and tried her best. She even wedged an Amanda Wingfield in *The Glass Menagerie* (1973) in there on TV, knowing full well she was miscast but gamely pressing on anyway with her old *Spitfire* accent. As her friend Ruth Gordon would say, we can draw the veil over things like that.

Hepburn won a well-deserved Emmy for *Love Among the Ruins* (1975), a charming and very sensitively written soft-focus period romantic comedy for TV about love lost and found in old age where she played opposite Laurence Olivier and was directed by George Cukor. That same year she made a western with John Wayne called *Rooster Cogburn*, extolling the value of his steady masculinity, if not his politics, to any interviewer on hand. She had truly covered the waterfront of male co-stars.

In the late 1970s, producer Hal Wallis wanted to team Hepburn with Bette Davis in a script called *Whitewater*, but he couldn't find the financing. When a photographer from *Life* sought to photograph them together, Davis was all for it but Hepburn said it was "a shitty idea" and begged off. It's impossible to imagine Hepburn in any of Davis's major parts, though Davis played a Hepburn-type role in *The Petrified Forest*, and fairly well, and she might have handled Mrs. Violet Venable, too, though she probably wouldn't have had the patience or need to attempt Mary Tyrone.

They gave Hepburn a fourth Oscar for supporting another swan song for a male actor in *On Golden Pond* (1981), where she helps Henry Fonda to his own first Oscar. "There's something to be said for a deviant lifestyle," Fonda tells her at one point in that movie, in reference to an "old lesbian" who lived to be in her nineties, a remark that Hepburn just smiles at absently. It was at this point that she became a kind of elderly Katharine Hepburn impersonator, absurdly high on life or at least high on herself, indulging any sentiment that might make her popular and adorably old-lady-ish.

Hepburn headlined one more feature, the barely released dark comedy *Grace Quigley* (1984), and then she appeared in a string of TV movies, each worse than the last. There were five of these in all, and so that's a lot of veils to draw, but luckily TV films from this period don't circulate much. "I hear she shakes all the time now—but still lets herself be seen, even does television!" said a shocked Marlene Dietrich, safely hidden away from view in her Paris apartment, to her daughter Maria. "She must be rich—so why does she show herself like that?"

The people directing and writing these ramshackle vehicles shamelessly used Hepburn's own image as their guide, and there is no way to judge her performances in these things because her head was now shaking so badly that she could barely bark out her lines between tremors. Hepburn's mind was beginning to go, alas, and so those around her just kept wheeling her in and cashing in on her star persona long after it was feasible to do so.

Warren Beatty would not take no for an answer and Hepburn was not all there mentally anymore, and so her last feature, unfortunately, was a forgettable and forgotten remake of *Love Affair* (1994), where Beatty insisted she utter the phrase "Fuck a duck." Hepburn did mutter that for him, finally, but at least she was sharp enough momentarily to get off a good line about him. Speaking of his wife and co-star Annette Bening, Hepburn told her friend Scott Berg: "They're both in love with the same man."

Hepburn lived nearly 10 more years after that, her mind elsewhere, and died at last in 2003. "I want to be put next to Tom," she told her brother Bob, and so she was. She had stayed too long at the party, as Jane Hudson says she always does in *Summertime*. What Hepburn was basically saying was: I am alone, you are alone, we are all alone, but, as Susan Vance keeps insisting, everything is going to be all right, just stick to it! The world isn't quite as much fun without Hepburn in it. Have you noticed?

Joan Crawford
A Woman's Face

At a Halloween party in Manhattan a few years ago, I was watching the parade down Sixth Avenue when I heard a girl next to me say, "Look! There's Mommie Dearest!" When I mentioned the name Joan Crawford, she didn't know who that was, but she did know the image of "Mommie Dearest." That's fame, of a sort.

Her adopted daughter Christina Crawford wanted to destroy Crawford's name and image with the 1978 memoir *Mommie Dearest*, and she did, in a way. This girl at the Halloween party didn't know the name Joan Crawford. But online, just the mention of that name is enough to inspire whoopingly energetic enjoyment and debate. No other Hollywood star of her time gets discussed more often or more vigorously than Crawford.

And Crawford still has fans like she did in her heyday. There are elaborate sites devoted to her where you can read some of her obsessive correspondence, enough to make you think that maybe correspondence was Crawford's real art. She answered every bit of fan mail and sent thank you notes for thank you notes, currying favor and using intimidation tactics if she needed to. The central joke about Crawford is about how transparent she was, how nakedly aggressive and permanently aggrieved under her arch manners.

The touchy Crawford had more grudges than she could keep track of, and her anger animates most of her screen performances, but that anger came to dominate towards the end of her career. She went from shopgirl's delight to something wholly other in 20 years, her face hardening into a mask that she held up and out to us, daring us to find her thickening eyebrows pathological, her wide red mouth clownish, her staring eyes unforgiving and barbarous.

She was born Lucille LeSueur in San Antonio, Texas, but there is no reliable year of birth. It could be as early as 1904 or as late as 1908, which is the year she liked to claim. Her mother moved Lucille and her older brother Hal around, shacking up with men here and there. Little Lucille gained a stepfather, Henry Cassin, and a new name, Billie Cassin, for a time, and in his book *Joan Crawford: The Essential Biography* (2002), Lawrence J. Quirk, who knew Crawford, says that Cassin sexually abused her around the age of 11.

Quirk was a gossip and at times unreliable, and his stories must always be taken with a grain of salt, but if this is true it might explain some of her subsequent behavior. She described herself as a "highly sexed woman," and she was notorious for many years for using sex to get what she wanted for her career and also, undoubtedly, for her own personal pleasure. She liked sex, it seemed, but her relation to it might have been tainted by this first experience with Cassin.

Cassin left after a time, which broke Billie's heart. She couldn't finish school because she was on a work scholarship that left her little time for class. She was beaten, snubbed by snooty girls, and generally ill-treated, all of which would later be perpetually regurgitated as stories for fan magazines. "If there was a laughingstock, a class joke, it was little Lucille," she remembered. "I guess maybe I didn't want to conform, and I paid the price for that."

Her mother ran a laundry, and Lucille was expected to help iron shirts and put the clothes on hangers. She entered dancing contests and got herself chorus work, and there are stories of her stealing dresses and doing anything she could to get ahead. She got to New York and danced in a show called *Innocent Eyes* (though her eyes were never innocent), kicking her heels behind the ageless French star Mistinguett and then doing a dance afterward at Harry Richman's club. Rumors of a stag film she allegedly made at this point would dog her all her life.

In 1925, she got herself signed to MGM and took all kinds of bits and extra work, including doubling for Norma Shearer in *Lady of the Night*. Under her real name, she got a part in *Pretty Ladies*, where she plays a chorus girl who is a warm friend to star ZaSu Pitts. There was another little showcase part in Frank Borzage's *The Circle*, enough to suggest that someone at MGM, probably producer Harry Rapf, was looking out for her. "The casting couch? It was better than the cold hard floor!" she once supposedly said. To get a role she desperately wanted in *Old Clothes*, she admitted to sleeping with child star Jackie Coogan's father, whom she later called "a dirty pig." She was willing to do what it took to pull herself out of where she came from.

After her name was changed to Joan Crawford, the result of a fan magazine contest, the newly named starlet got a good role in Edmund Goulding's *Sally, Irene and Mary* (1925). Though Goulding predicted a starry future for her, Louise Brooks was unimpressed (and also jealous). "She played her part like a chocolate-covered cherry—hard outside, and breaking up all gooey with a sticky center," Brooks said. "I didn't care for her.... She isn't truly like a chocolate-covered cherry; she is like biting into a delectable piece of wedding cake and hitting the brass ring."

Crawford played leading lady to comedian Harry Langdon in *Tramp, Tramp, Tramp* (1926) and to her friend William Haines in *Spring Fever* and *West Point* (both 1927); those Haines vehicles have touching moments where he seems to be trying to kid her out of her anxiety and self-seriousness. Many of her silent films are lost or at least inaccessible, which is a shame, for in something like *Winners of the Wilderness* (1927), a costume drama where she plays a French noblewoman, Crawford shows that she has some largely undirected talent at this early stage aside from her ravenous need to be noticed.

Her first really challenging part came in *The Unknown* (1927) with Lon Chaney, where she played a girl who cannot stand to be touched. In the first scene, Chaney throws knives at her with his feet so that her clothes are somehow stabbed off, and she looks saucy and aggressive, full-bodied and nearly butch. In *The Unknown* she has a close-up where she closes her eyes and seems to commune with her own love of being looked at, as if the camera were one more lover to use and conquer, the most important of all.

Crawford was learning her craft, and in her off-hours she relentlessly chased after publicity, entering Charleston and Black Bottom contests, trying to be noticed. Her skirts were shorter, her heels were higher, and her manner was brighter than anyone else, and her mouth was 1920s small then, her eyebrows dark but thin—only her large flashing eyes signal the later Crawford of the sound era. There was no publicity photo she wouldn't pose for, nothing she wouldn't do to get a mention in a column, and already she was writing to the people who wrote to her, begging their loyalty.

MGM paired her with John Gilbert, and in *Four Walls* (1928), which seems to be lost, they worked up some chemistry. "For getting down to earth with the practical sort of lovemaking that folks like, our hat is off to John Gilbert and Joan Crawford," wrote *Photoplay*. "John certainly takes that girl in hand, and boy, how she loves to be taken!"

Our Dancing Daughters (1928) established Crawford as a star playing a girl who does the Charleston and pulls off her skirt so that she can move faster. She gets a whip-cracking entrance here, her jittering feet seeming to appear by magic in her shoes until we see her whole body vibrating to music as she gets ready in front of a mirror. In her first close-up, Crawford looks at herself in the mirror and her eyes cloud over with pleasure and self-love until her face hardens and she lifts her chin up in a proud but protective way.

Running downstairs, Crawford's Diana takes a sip from all the boys' drinks and then she drinks a toast: "To myself!" Egotism plus hedonism, all on Art Deco sets, and still irresistible. When Diana dances on a table at a boisterous shindig, Crawford makes herself distinctive from other flappers of this time by being just a little crazy-eyed, so that her calculation and desperation plainly shows, and that image sums up a certain part of the 1920s ethos. Crawford had an unerring ability to be what she needed to be for her times, and to change, sometimes drastically, when one era ended and another began.

Of all the stars of this period, Crawford believed the most in the Hollywood system and all that went with it, always going further with it than anyone else, so that if you look just a little closer you can see and feel with her that something is more than a little cracked, disturbed. In many of her films, from as early as *Our Dancing Daughters* to the bitter end, Crawford would shrug as if to indicate that she was a good sport, and what is most remarkable about this consistent and lifelong mannerism is how unconvincing it always is. Crawford would become an object lesson in the fact that you cannot fool the camera.

She married Douglas Fairbanks, Jr., the "crown prince of Hollywood," all in a flurry of publicity. Though MGM kept casting her as heiresses, it was made clear in the press that she was a working girl from nowhere who had trouble fitting in at Pickfair with her new husband's father Douglas Fairbanks and his stepmother Mary Pickford.

"I never selected a fork until I'd checked to see which one Miss Pickford used," Crawford wrote in her memoir *A Portrait of Joan* (1962). To impress Fairbanks, Jr., she "tried to devour Shaw, Ibsen, Proust, and Nietzsche all at once. I read my way to mental indigestion." Improving herself would become one of her obsessions, but she could never seem to read enough or learn enough to get past her own engrained vulgar taste in everything.

Crawford somehow survived her first talkie, *Untamed* (1929), where she plays a wild-girl heiress named Bingo. In both that movie and *The Hollywood Revue of 1929* she dances in a hilariously galumphing, spasmodic fashion and sings haltingly. *Untamed* is the first of her enjoyably bad movies where Crawford tries so hard that she makes all the trying funny and touching.

Our Blushing Brides (1930) was the first time she played a shopgirl, and it was the real shopgirls who became her most devoted fans, taking solace in the fact that she was one of them and she had made it. But Crawford pleaded with her bosses for a bigger chance: "I was fighting for emotional, dramatic parts because I am dramatic and emotional. I wanted self-expression," she said. And so she got an emotional part in *Paid* (1930), where she played a burned-out working class woman falsely convicted of a crime.

This was an ideal opportunity that stoked her sense of grievance, and in her first scene in *Paid* where she is sentenced in court, Crawford uses her huge eyes to express frozen anger and disbelief, as if she's staring off into her own grim future in jail. She tries very, very hard to push out as much feeling as possible, but you have only to imagine Barbara Stanwyck playing this scene to realize that Crawford is working with a limited amount of emotional expressiveness and desperately shoving as hard as she can with it. That desperation carries its own kind of power, in a way, and it was this peculiar kind of sympathy for what she was *trying* to do that always won her fans over.

Crawford has a certain store of raw talent in these early movies, and surely this would have been noted if she had taken an acting class in a later period. What she needed was someone to help her shape and control her talent, but she was all alone, really, and had to try to do everything herself. And eventually she came up with her own queer way of doing things. Ninety percent of the time on screen Crawford is working in the dark, without any firm foundation for what she is trying to do, and yet she often does somehow find her own singular path, especially in close-ups where her eyes can do a lot of the acting for her.

In most of her Pre-Code movies, even her flapper parts, Crawford plays girls who are steadfastly holding on to their virtue, a part of the special hypocrisy that makes her so fascinating. She was still learning. In *Dance, Fools, Dance* (1931), she has a scene after her father dies where she is asked to burst into hysterical laughter not once but twice, and she seems to have no idea what she's doing, so that it's like watching a little goldfish flopping around on the floor after someone has dumped it out of its water.

But in her best early talkie, *Possessed* (1931), Crawford is far closer to her real life character as a girl who works in a factory who wants more out of life. She stares at a train filled with swells like a movie fan drinking it all in, and when she decides to go to the city, she makes no bones about going after rich men and swiftly becomes the mistress of a business tycoon (Clark Gable).

Like Crawford herself, the woman she plays in *Possessed* tries to improve herself, to dress well and to speak with distinction so she can order the right wine for dinner, but her fallen state makes her socially vulnerable, and it is only through proving her love for Gable that she finally attains some security. "I left school when I was only 12," she tells Gable. "I never learned how to spell regret." This is the first time that Crawford takes a loaded line and socks it over with a ringing kind of camp frisson. It was her burning belief in her own material that made her so funny in her unaware way.

The surprise of her stenographer Flaemmchen in the all-star *Grand Hotel* (1932) is how assured and natural she seems interacting, under enormous pressure, with the heavyweights around her. With John Barrymore, she flirts in a free-spirited, captivating way, and he responds as much as he can, giving her an affectionate but quietly lustful pat on the behind. With Wallace Beery's magnate, she keeps her sexual options open: "Oh, I'd love to be in the movies!" she tells him, very sweetly. With Lionel Barrymore's vulnerable and dying clerk, she opens up in an entirely new sort of compassionate way. All with Garbo overacting upstairs, far from Crawford's youthful vitality and big-eyed authority, which stops the movie cold in several star close-ups under director Edmund Goulding's watchful eye. When Crawford has to get upset towards the end of *Grand Hotel*, Goulding carefully protects her by keeping her face in shadows and then letting her collapse behind a bed to cry.

Like her character in *Possessed*, Crawford's Flaemmchen is appealingly straightforward about the possibility of trading her body for some good clothes and food, and she's so bright-eyed and full of life that she still has a kind of untouched glory, a childlike cherishability. Of course, Crawford's version of naturalism is a highly self-conscious one, as if she is watching herself in a mirror as she poses her slim body at tilted angles for our inspection. She turns up her personal charisma as far as it will possibly go, and she glows in the black and white, so that this is star acting of a very high order, a performance of a persona or self, fully conscious and heavy, yet also somehow suggesting lightness and fluidity.

Crawford had a big personal success as *Letty Lynton* (1932), all decked out in Adrian gowns for suffering and steamy emotions. This was the first film that really unlocked her appetite for unbridled melodrama, for hiding in the shadows and wishing a man dead, her hypnotic eyes staring with ugly neediness and fear, her large mouth made defiantly larger with lipstick.

But then she flopped with critics and public as Sadie Thompson in *Rain* (1932), a film Crawford hated for the rest of her life. It has become traditional now in studies of her career to say that she was underrated in this movie, and she has her moments, particularly when she's telling off the Reverend Davidson (Walter Huston). She tries very hard, as usual, but she is laboring under the very heavy-handed direction of Lewis Milestone, who leaves her unprotected in long takes where she cannot build the emotion of a scene the way a more trained or skilled actress could.

Joan Crawford in *Grand Hotel*.

Called upon to write a screenplay for Crawford in the 1930s, F. Scott Fitzgerald watched some of her films and came away with these insightful remarks: "She can't change her emotions in the middle of a scene without going through a sort of Jekyll and Hyde contortion of the face, so that when one wants to indicate that she is going from joy to sorrow, one must cut away and then cut back. Also, you can never give her such a stage direction as 'telling a lie,' because if you did, she would practically give a representation of Benedict Arnold selling West Point to the British."

In her best films, Crawford is allowed to totally immerse herself in one emotion and then the camera cuts to allow her to do another emotion. A total creature of the cinema, she was never tempted to work in live theater. Crawford can't do two or three things at once as some performers can, but it could be said that no one else plunges into single emotions as extravagantly or fully as she always did. She can't do transitions, but she can sustain one extreme mode of feeling for as long as necessary or possible. As an older woman, Crawford made a specialty of being in one emotion, getting tempted briefly by another one, and then returning decisively to the original emotion, which is maybe part of the obsessive-compulsive side of her persona.

After *Dancing Lady* (1933), a star vehicle with all the trimmings where Gable was again her leading man and she got to dance, theoretically, with Fred Astaire, Crawford finished out the 1930s with a series of formula films where her exaggerated Adrian clothes and ever-changing hair styles seemed to be more important than her scripts, directors, and co-stars. This is her least interesting period as a star, a kind of cinematic desert of light cocktail comedy-drama.

As if to compensate, she took the business of being a movie star off-screen more seriously than ever. "Even in her bath, Joan Crawford looked as if she were about to make a public appearance, just in case a crowd happened to drop by," said columnist Radie Harris. She married Franchot Tone and tried to attain some culture to suit him, reading Shakespeare plays aloud at home and then going to the studio to do fluff like *No More Ladies* (1935) and *The Bride Wore Red* (1937).

On radio, Crawford actually attempted to do Nora in Ibsen's *A Doll's House*, which she plays fairly well until the last scene, where she flat-out doesn't seem to understand why Nora has to leave her husband. On screen, her eyelashes got longer and her voice got more strained and syrupy, until finally she was named, with Hepburn and Dietrich and a few others, box office poison.

There was a steady stream of men in her life, including a 17-year-old Jackie Cooper. "She was a very erudite professor of love," Cooper wrote in his memoirs. "She was a wild woman. She would bathe me, powder me, cologne me. Then she would do it again. She would put on high heels, a garter belt, and a large hat and pose in front of the mirror, turning this way and that. 'Look,' she would say. I was already looking. But that sort of thing didn't particularly excite me. I kept thinking: The Lady is crazy."

Crawford nervily grabbed the unsympathetic role of Crystal, the hard-boiled, phony, bitchy shopgirl who wrecks Norma Shearer's home in George Cukor's *The Women* (1939), and though she has only four major scenes, she makes them pay. This movie was the first time her face started to look very hard, stiff, mask-like (she plunged it into a bowl of ice every morning before coming to the studio).

Desperate to branch out further, Crawford then took Serious Acting roles for Cukor in *Susan and God* (1940) and *A Woman's Face* (1941). As a flibbertigibbet society woman who claims to have found spiritual solace in *Susan and God*, she tries very hard to give a tricky sort of high-style comedy performance and almost succeeds, but the effort shows far too much. In *A Woman's Face*, Crawford's sense of grievance was suggestively explained by a scar on her face, and she has fine moments in that movie of deluded romantic hopes, bitterness, and violent lashing out, at least in the first half, before her face gets changed back to that star mask she was cultivating. After nearly 10 years of light fare, *A Woman's Face* proved that Crawford was at her best whenever her material was dark and cynical. It also proved that she very much needed a strong director, for her work in *A Woman's Face* is as much Cukor's achievement as it is her own.

Crawford left MGM after 18 years, and she might not be remembered too well today if, like Garbo and Norma Shearer, she had left it at that. But Crawford wanted to last, and she was willing to do anything to do so. She waited two years before getting the script she knew she needed, *Mildred Pierce* (1945), even making a screen test for it, and she won an Academy Award for that movie, which heralded a full comeback.

Crawford was signed to Warner Brothers now, where at last she found the kind of red-blooded melodramatic material she fed so greedily on. Crawford was out of place in those MGM drawing rooms, but she was a dominating if increasingly grim and set screen presence at Warners when asked to plot and scheme in film noir shadows, her large eyes staring out of the dark in fear or anger or both.

Her work as the mother and entrepreneur in *Mildred Pierce* is somewhat cautious except in the pay-off confrontations with her selfish, snobby daughter Veda (Ann Blyth) where Crawford unleashed something elemental in her own character, a brute rage and mistrust. She was far more assured in

Humoresque (1946), where she played a glamorous, myopic, alcoholic collector of talented men, self-loathing and self-loving by turns. Crawford was stimulated to go to an auto-erotic extreme in close-ups where she listens to her lover (John Garfield) play the violin, and her self-pity in that movie has real grandeur as she tosses off her fruity Clifford Odets one-liners. This film captures her suffocating, self-dramatizing, jealous concept of romantic love better than any of her earlier or later work.

In the 1981 film of *Mommie Dearest*, the infamous "No wire hangers ever!" scene seems to occur during the making of *Humoresque*, judging from the hair style Faye Dunaway is wearing and the lapse of time after the Oscar win. This suggests the disturbances waiting to crack the hard, and then harder, surfaces Crawford was offering the camera.

She was exceptional again in a heavy melodrama, again called *Possessed* (1947), where she played Louise, a pitiful woman who loses her mind over unrequited love for a sexy cad (Van Heflin). Crawford took all this very seriously, going to an asylum to study the mentally ill, and her work has specificity, particularly the sidelong look in Louise's eyes when her mind becomes unmoored from reason.

Crawford could be said to be an early exponent of Lee Strasberg's version of the Method, for she always used memories from her own life to give her the emotion she needed, which is why her work has a limited, enclosed quality. It took her a while to get into an emotional scene, which were her favorite scenes to play, and it also took her a while to get herself out of the emotion once her director called cut.

This was a woman who was already drinking heavily who always felt like she was being slighted and insulted, and her extreme touchiness could lead her to retaliate in monstrous ways, especially when the two children she adopted, Christina and Christopher, proved more rebellious than she had hoped for. Christina was like a mirror for Crawford in which she saw herself all too clearly, and what she saw became intolerable to her until she felt the need to somehow wipe that mirror out. It was the battle of a lifetime, and it spilled over into her on-screen life later, so that in *Strait-Jacket* (1964) and *Berserk* (1968) her daughter is revealed as the killer at the end of both films, and Crawford stares at them in hammy sorrow just as Mildred Pierce looks on her Veda with all the bitterness she feels towards life itself.

Crawford was far more restrained in Otto Preminger's *Daisy Kenyon* (1947), where his austere style deeply probes her self-pity and her hurt feelings all alive behind the static architecture of her face. That film offers a new way of looking at her, but this way was not taken. *Humoresque* and *Possessed* have their campy underpinnings, though they can be taken fairly seriously. It was in *Flamingo Road* (1949), however, that Crawford crossed the line into becoming a camp version of herself. If I were to pinpoint the exact moment, it would be when we first see her dancing a tense hootchy-coo in a carnival, her face stiff with affronted dignity behind her veil, as if she knows she's too old for her role.

In *Harriet Craig* (1950), where she was ideally cast as a domestic tyrant, her lighting starts to get overelaborate and her eyebrows have comically and frighteningly darkened. Crawford lets her image play that part, all on one tense note, as if it had been tailored to her measure. She doesn't play it like an actress would, thinking it through and making specific choices, but like an increasingly rigid star monotonously imposing herself.

Her contract at Warner Brothers ended, and she made another comeback with the independently produced *Sudden Fear* (1952), a juicy thriller where she was menaced by Jack Palance and Gloria Grahame. The centerpiece of that movie is a nearly 10-minute scene, very carefully edited, where Crawford silently reacts to a recording of Palance plotting with Grahame to kill her, a real overblown diva tour-de-force that ends with her bugging her eyes and putting her hands over her ears. Her acting here is like extremely tasty junk food that you know you should stop eating but before you know it you've finished the whole bag of it and want more. Crawford's face had become forbidding and unaccountable by this point, burned-up, as if something essentially human had been painfully stripped off of it.

She returned to MGM for *Torch Song* (1953), a small color musical showcase and a key transitional work into pure camp. As tyrannical musical comedy star Jenny Stewart, Crawford's emphatic way of talking makes even the most ordinary lines of dialogue sound like camp epiphanies, and she excelled again in another long wordless sequence where Jenny tries to fill an empty Sunday, pacing around her bedroom, restless as a resentful child. Crawford didn't need words in *The Unknown* or *Our Dancing Daughters*, and she certainly didn't need them to communicate 25 years down the line. She was absurd now but she was embracing that absurdity, evoking queer meanings that were beyond her and beyond her control.

The gulf between what Crawford wanted to be and what she obviously was had grown so wide that nothing but laughter could bridge the gap. That's what camp can be. Marlene Dietrich masterfully closed that gap and seemed to be in control of everything, even the camp elements of her image, and in the movies "seeming" can be enough, as if Dietrich were clothed in her immaculate foundation garment for us and not turning at all. Crawford was totally naked and exposed and spinning out of control on screen but *acting* as if she had Dietrich's control, and this was a laughable and a pitiable thing.

Crawford dances stiffly in *Torch Song* and lip-synchs some songs, including the notorious "Two-Faced Woman" number, which she performs, for some unknown reason, in blackface. It isn't Al Jolson blackface; Crawford retains her bright red lipstick mouth and even wears rhinestones in her eyebrows (in *That's Entertainment III* (1994), Debbie Reynolds tactfully calls this "tropical make-up"). Surrounded by listless chorus girls—who are also in half-done blackface—and a bunch of adoring chorus boys, Crawford goes through with this very ill-advised number as she did everything else, with completely oblivious chutzpah.

Her manliness was openly acknowledged and prodded in Nicholas Ray's gender-bending, psychosexual western *Johnny Guitar* (1954), a film she hated. Does she "act" in that movie, now highly valued by most film critics? She had become elemental by this point, with her livid blue eyes and imperious falseness and the schizophrenia of her voice, syrupy sweet sometimes and slashingly ugly at others, like someone who always has a headache and needs to lash out about it.

Crawford is hardest to take when she tries to indicate amusement and good humor, neither of which she had one iota of, and again we can compare this to Stanwyck's heroic good sport mode for contrast. Stanwyck, in fact, was her friend, but in a widely listened-to recording of a late-1960s phone conversation between publicist Shirley Eder and Stanwyck that was uploaded to YouTube in 2012, it was made clear that even her friends found her trying. (Only Myrna Loy stuck up for Crawford convincingly in her 1987 memoir, but surely Loy's good humor and patience were out of the ordinary.)

In the central scene in *Johnny Guitar* where she re-connects with her former lover Johnny (Sterling Hayden), Crawford transcends her limitations, partly because the scene begins with Johnny asking her to lie to him and tell him that she waited for him and still loves him. Crawford's Vienna repeats each of these lies back to Johnny in her stoniest, most artificial voice, and suddenly the reason for her way of talking like that becomes clear through the power of Ray's imaginative and very sensitive direction.

Johnny Guitar is a film with a lot of cutting within scenes so that Crawford doesn't have to make transitions. When Crawford drops Vienna's resentment and lying, so close to her own, and levels with Hayden's Johnny about the sacrifices she had to make to keep going, she hits a level of feeling that feels overwhelmingly true in the context of all of her usual fakery. This is probably the most touching scene she ever played because it reveals what is behind her weirdly ossified late style. Crawford has a kind of gallantry in this movie—even a sort of moral discrimination—that does not show in any of her other later work. Vienna is like the remains of her Flaemmchen after years of bad luck.

Her vehicles became even more hard-edged and knowing. In *Female on the Beach* (1955) and *Queen Bee* (1955), Crawford offered a narcissistic camp drag version of herself, sending up soft femininity with her every sneer and put-down. Whereas *Johnny Guitar* is a film about Crawford's metamorphosis into Medusa, these two movies were gleeful exploitations of it. Her mannered acting in these pictures is very bad by any standard, totally disconnected from normal human behavior, from the script, and from her fellow players (such as they were). But Crawford was so stiffly formalized now and so intensely stylized that she seemed to be seeking to create her own new acting rules— her own new kingdom of blatant melodrama where she could be both king and queen, making love to herself and beating herself up. Just try to look away!

Crawford was then cast surprisingly and rewardingly against type as Millicent Wetherby, a lonely typist from New England in Robert Aldrich's *Autumn Leaves* (1956). Millicent is a prim, modest lady who slowly falls in love with a younger man (Cliff Robertson), marries him, and then discovers that he has severe mental problems. Everything about this rich and unsettling film seems to stimulate Crawford in all the right ways, from getting to play a woman very far from herself to having to deal with and help someone else. Many of her best moments here catch Crawford's character in moments of silent reflection and melancholy reverie, which she reveals to us in an extra-legible way with very rigid and definite shifts of her huge eyes. She is very touching in this movie mainly because it seems as if she is imagining the emotions of Millicent Wetherby rather than feeling her own feelings.

When I interviewed Robertson about *Autumn Leaves*, he told me that his image of Crawford came from watching her 1930s movies. "In my mind she was this older, sexy, slightly wicked woman," he said, smiling. Crawford was on her fourth marriage by then, to Pepsi magnate Alfred Steele, and she was beginning to travel with him for the company. Steele was there when Robertson rehearsed with her, at Robertson's request, out by her pool.

Maybe because of Robertson's youthful desire for her, there is a romantic chemistry on display in *Autumn Leaves* that Crawford hadn't had with anyone else since her early films with Gable. Reacting to Robertson, Crawford really makes decisions like an actress for the first time since *Grand Hotel*. There are moments in the scenes where Robertson is courting her where she actually seems a bit girlish, and when she is queenly or condescending it is strictly set within the perimeters of the character she's playing. This is probably the best, most varied, most controlled work Crawford ever did, and still much underrated.

After Steele's death, Crawford was left with financial debts, and so she accepted the smallish role of waspish book editor Amanda Farrow in *The Best of Everything* (1959), a curdled career woman who tries marriage briefly but then comes back to the job when she realizes she doesn't have any love to give. In the scene where Crawford tells off her married lover on the phone, her rhythms seem off, or abrupt, a sign perhaps that the 100 proof vodka she was favoring was creeping into her performing style.

Crawford was vividly masochistic for Aldrich in *What Ever Happened to Baby Jane?*, a film in which there are moments when she sits quietly in her wheelchair and seems genuinely annoyed that Bette Davis is chewing so much scenery that there is really very little left for her to munch on. She then made four more crude and embarrassing features where she overacted all over the place and was more than willing to be as inappropriately emotional and sexual as possible. And her drinking really started to show.

In *I Saw What You Did* (1965), her second picture for William Castle, Crawford is feeling no pain, and in her 1968 appearance on an episode of a sitcom with Lucille Ball, she is clearly drunk, slurring her words. On her last movie, *Trog* (1970), Crawford didn't even get a dressing room on location but was expected to dress in her car. Little Lucille LeSueur had been an exhibitionist at school and everyone had laughed at her, and she was still up to her old tricks, still doing anything for attention, even acting with a troglodyte.

The fearful laughs intensified with the publication of *My Way of Life* (1971), a sort of memoir and self-help book that offered Crawford's own cockeyed, totally out-of-touch advice on living graciously. Every word of that book is a lie or an illusion, so that it's a veritable Bible of self-deception. "All the beauty products in the world can't disguise a disagreeable expression," she wrote (or dictated). "Have you ever noticed that when you say 'no' you begin to resemble a prune-faced schoolmarm? Not that any woman can go through life saying yes to everything, but it's a nice example of how important an expression is in giving an impression of youth." Crawford finally retired from the public eye after

Joan Crawford as Millicent Wetherby in *Autumn Leaves*.

unflattering photos were taken of her at an event in 1973. "If that's the way I look, they won't see me again," she said.

Crawford stayed in her apartment in New York for the few years she had left before her death in 1977. My friend Bruce Benderson knew her a bit then, and he found her helpful and charitable, maybe even a little mellowed. When a mutual friend of theirs told her a bartender was fired from the gay bar Julius for staying home to watch some of her movies on TV, she commanded him, "Bring me my phone." She called Julius and asked to speak to the manager. "This is Joan Crawford," she announced, in her smoothest tones. "I have been told that a young man in your employ lost his job because he stayed home to watch some of my pictures on television. I *do wish* you would give him his job back." And of course the awed manager bowed and scraped happily and said, "Of course, Miss Crawford!"

Her adopted daughter Christina's memoir *Mommie Dearest* was published a year after her death in 1978, and the film with Faye Dunaway compounded the damage in 1981. There have been arguments and debates about both book and film ever since. For what it's worth, I interviewed Christina over the phone in 2013 when she did an embarrassingly ramshackle show in New York called *Surviving Mommie Dearest* (anything for attention). Though she was an elderly woman in her seventies at this point, Christina sounded like a nervous, eager-to-please little girl on the phone.

When I tried to ask her what might have been wrong with Crawford to cause all her bad behavior, Christina wouldn't stand for excuses or any attempts at understanding. She still had her own livid sense of undying grievance, and like her adopted mother she was motivated chiefly by hatred and revenge. Her stories had gotten more unlikely with the years, and she was claiming now that Crawford might have murdered Alfred Steele, among other things.

Camp aficionado and cult director John Waters has called the *Mommie Dearest* film "the first comedy about child abuse," and his sharp remark gets at the uneasiness of that movie's camp reputation. Dunaway plays on a large scale that exposed her to the ridicule Crawford had heaped on herself in her last films, and sometimes she certainly does go too far, but she finds a decisive identification with her role. Dunaway burrows deeply into understanding the psychological reasons behind Crawford's violent, erratic behavior in a very thoughtful, point-by-point Method way that would have confounded Crawford herself.

If you want to see the difference between Hollywood screen acting of the studio era and the post-studio era of the 1970s, look no further than late Crawford playing herself versus Dunaway playing late Crawford. Dunaway gives

Crawford's American dream misguidedness a kind of unhinged grandeur, and that includes a hearty slice of the grotesque and the baleful still horribly insisting on its own freshness and good cheer.

The saga of Joan and Christina has become a potent and undying camp routine played out in gay bars, riding on the spectacle of an overbearing, competitive mother and a spoiled, revengeful daughter who hates but would like to be that mother. Christina's lifelong attempt to destroy her mother's reputation has only added years and texture to Crawford's fame, an instant hook, and this cannot be what Christina wanted. Crawford has become an endlessly amusing character to dish about, an ambitious climber who put on airs and who would stop at nothing to maintain her image and satisfy her appetites. This public character was deepened considerably when Jessica Lange offered her own far more sensitive and complex interpretation of Crawford in the TV series *Feud: Bette and Joan* in 2017.

Most of us would like to be something we are not, at least when we are young, and Crawford took that urge to revealing extremes all her life. In spite of extensive personal and professional limitations, she holds her place with Stanwyck, Davis, and Hepburn as one of the key movie women of her time. All the stories surrounding her that are probably apocryphal only add more color to her legend, which shows no sign of fading.

Ingrid Bergman
You Must Change Your Life

"My father was a genius," says Isabella Rossellini, in her searching Guy Maddin-directed short tribute to her father Roberto, *My Dad Is 100 Years Old* (2005), which marked his centenary. After this statement, she pauses briefly and then says, "I think." Her confusion is sweet and quite understandable. Rossellini has had evangelical fans, especially the directors of the French New Wave like François Truffaut, Jean-Luc Godard, Jacques Rivette, and Eric Rohmer, all of who wrote tributes to his difficult, ambiguous films. Martin Scorsese devotes long passages to Rossellini's key early works in his documentary on Italian cinema, *My Voyage to Italy* (1999), and there's an air of special pleading in his endorsement, particularly when he talks up *Europa '51* (1952), as if he knows that many people won't give it a chance because of its out-of-synch soundtrack.

When she saw Rossellini's *Rome, Open City* (1945) and then *Paisan* (1946), Ingrid Bergman was so impressed that she sent him a rather shameless fan letter. "If you need a Swedish actress who speaks English very well, who has not forgotten her German, who is not very understandable in French, and who in Italian knows only 'ti amo,' I am ready to come and make a film with you," she wrote him. At that time, Bergman was the biggest star in Hollywood, and everything she touched then turned to gold.

Bergman's father took lots of photos of her when she was a little girl, and she was a real camera nut all her life, always posing for and shooting photos herself. She made 10 movies in her native Sweden in the 1930s, and they let her learn her craft. Aside from her natural charisma, Bergman acquired an estimable technique in the 1930s, though there are sometimes chinks in her armor in these Swedish films: narrowing her eyes to express anger, say, or putting her hands to her forehead in distress too quickly. She feels things a little too abruptly, but intensely, and that was part of her youthful appeal.

Intermezzo (1936) was the movie that got her noticed, a small love story where her face was radiant with love and self-love, especially in a luminous scene, photographed in celestial light and dark shade, where she falls in love with a married violinist (Gosta Ekman) and flings herself over to him and to the camera, quivering with joy and nerve and hope for herself but also for her music, her burgeoning career as a pianist, which she might share with this established and much older performer.

Her abandon here is so sexy because she doesn't seem to know how brave it is to be offering yourself up like this, to be so completely exposed, and it speaks to Bergman's special brand of confidence, which had no concern for bourgeois morality. Many children play pretend by themselves in their rooms, and on that level Bergman is the best play-pretender-in-my-room of all time, rapt and completely immersed in play, yet also somehow untouched by anything, pure.

In the 1939 American remake of *Intermezzo*, she put across that same self-intoxication, but slightly scaled down, mixed with appealing doubts and tugs towards modesty. Bergman loved being photographed, and the camera seemingly loved photographing her—but was that all? Was there much more there beyond the glowing love for posing and smiling for us, and weeping and suffering in a way that felt oddly sturdy and healthy? When she is acting out an ordeal in a movie, Bergman is clearly *enjoying* doing so, because for her acting is a sensual pleasure, and this is not a modern attitude. The modern actor is supposed to suffer as the character suffers, to be wrung out emotionally by a heavy role, whereas it feels like Bergman goes the distance and then emerges fresher than ever.

Surely Bergman's musical, emotionally throbbing voice helped her win our love, for it was such a pleasure to listen to, giving out the same uncomplicated pleasure that could be drawn from looking at her. (Listen to Hedy Lamarr's awkward, borderline unpleasant speaking voice in English for contrast.) Of all the actors from Europe who made a career in another language in America, Bergman is the one who never seems to stumble or hit an off note in English. Every word and phrase she says is fluent and unerringly on target.

She displayed a frank yet also shy interest in sex as Ivy in *Dr. Jekyll and Mr. Hyde*

Ingrid Bergman in the first version of *Intermezzo*.

(1941), which helped her along in Hollywood. Then she made the classic *Casablanca* (1942), exhibiting grace—and real glamour—under pressure. She's so sensitive in that movie that even her nostrils feel the sway of romantic emotion, and she is happy to let glycerin stand in for her very convincing tears, like Louise Brooks dabbing water from a fishbowl on her face in *Love 'Em and Leave 'Em* to get her man. "In *Casablanca* there was often nothing in my face, nothing at all," Bergman wrote in her autobiography, "But the audience put into my face what they thought I was giving. They were inventing my thoughts the way they wanted them: they were doing the acting for me."

This is very much what Garbo, Dietrich and Brooks sometimes did, but there was a difference. There was no darkness in Bergman, no real mystery or irony, and even her rich and slightly naughty sexuality seemed somehow scrubbed-clean. If anything, Bergman is a bridge from Garbo and Dietrich to someone like Audrey Hepburn, who offered simple pleasure to those who responded to her (practically everyone).

People liked Bergman. They were happy when she smiled and slightly sad when she cried, or pretended to cry, whereas this simple concept of "liking" is not something that can be applied to Gish, Garbo, Dietrich, Brooks, Davis or Katharine Hepburn. (With Crawford, there was identification, a very different and less secure transaction.) Of the romantic comediennes, Carole Lombard comes closest to innate likability, whereas Irene Dunne, Myrna Loy, Ginger Rogers, Jean Arthur, and Claudette Colbert are more complex propositions. And the memorably perverse Miriam Hopkins is so essentially unlikable that her brief stardom really does seem anomalous in this context.

Audiences were happy to fill in thoughts for that face Bergman had. She moves stiffly, like a much older matron, so her movies of the 1940s almost always keep her in close-up so we can feast on her smooth, pearly skin, her elegant long nose, her generous mouth. In two of the films from her high 1940s Hollywood star period, *For Whom the Bell Tolls* (1943) and *Saratoga Trunk* (1945), both directed by Sam Wood, the literary sources (Hemingway and Edna Ferber) fall away and what we are left with are curiously inert, trance-like movies obsessively devoted to filming Bergman's face in close-up. Bergman's career was controlled by producer David Selznick, who surely had something to do with these close-up overdoses, which also occur regularly in the movies starring Selznick's wife Jennifer Jones.

At this point, Bergman was very lucky in her directors. George Cukor assisted her to an Oscar for *Gaslight* (1944), a virtuoso piece of work in which she descended to fearful depths of somehow lovably neurotic despair and very fetching hysteria. Cukor got that performance by verbally filling Bergman in with thoughts until her mind and face were brimming for the camera. "Cukor explains everything in such detail that sometimes you feel like saying, 'Please don't say any more because my mind is so full of explanations,'" Bergman said to interviewer John Kobal. "I used to tease him by saying if it were a little line like 'Have a cup of tea,' he would say what kind of cup it was and what kind of tea it was until you got so worried you couldn't say the line."

She made a huge hit as the nun in Leo McCarey's *The Bells of St. Mary's* (1945), teaching a little boy how to box to defend himself from bullies with shameless but irresistible comic timing, the nun's wimple effectively putting her into automatic close-up. McCarey allowed her to grow and build this routine naturally. "The boxing sequence ... was completely unrehearsed," said Bergman to Kobal. "We didn't know what would happen. So McCarey gave me the words and showed me what to do and then we shot it several times and new things would keep coming in. Just little touches—doing things with your feet, looking worried about your clothes, a way of pushing your hair back, that sort of thing."

And just try resisting her tousled and motherly psychoanalyst in Alfred Hitchcock's *Spellbound* (1945), or her boozy party girl Alicia Huberman, daughter of a convicted Nazi, in thrall to Cary Grant in Hitchcock's *Notorious* (1946), where she made self-loathing, illness, and ordeal seem erotic. "Now I go to jail," her Alicia says mordantly in *Notorious*, when she is pulled over for reckless driving. "Whole family in jail!" she cries, "Who cares?" Not many stars have ever hit such a note of rebellious nihilism as she does on those two lines, especially in the way she throws away that "Who cares?" And not many stirred up more enraptured sexual abandon than in the love scene where she lightly kisses Grant over and over again on a terrace. And not many were as touching as she was in her attitudes of queasy fear and suffering and wasting away as the thriller plot of *Notorious* played out over a background of vicious recrimination between herself and Grant.

But then Bergman's luck changed for a bit. (When a little man calls her beautiful in *Saratoga Trunk*, she smiles gloatingly and says, "Yes, isn't it lucky?") She foundered in *Arch of Triumph* (1948) and *Joan of Arc* (1948), both heavy, solemn, unconvincing movies in which she seemed to be running out of conviction. The intensity she was capable of for Cukor and Hitchcock was wavering, yet she returned to masochistic form in Hitch's *Under Capricorn* (1949), excelling especially in a nearly nine-minute confession scene done all in one long take. There is not a long take in cinema that is more emotionally complex than this, and its quality has as much to do with

Bergman as a performer as it does with Hitchcock's direction. He's working very closely with her here, and together they create a sequence that is frequently transporting in its intense evocation of past events.

When her eyes retreat into the past during this long take confession, it is clear that Bergman is seeing and creating specific things, and she makes us see them vividly: her lover's face, his hands, the horses they rode, the large home of her youth, and, most potently, the early promise of sex with the man she loved. "We used to ride for miles and miles," she says, closing her eyes, savoring the memory. Bergman touches herself a lot during this speech, putting her hands on her neck and elsewhere for comfort and reassurance, so that we can see what a sensual woman she is. Her imagination is at its height in this confession scene, and all of her skill, and it is still modern, what Bergman is doing here, even when she puts a fist to her forehead in distress at the very end of her speech as a climax—she re-activates this old-fashioned theatrical gesture by making it as intensely as possible and stuffing it full of raw emotion, as Lillian Gish might have.

Though Bergman was unhappy with the long take methods of *Under Capricorn* during the shoot, in a letter quoted in her autobiography she admitted that "some of those damned long scenes work out very well." About the eight minute-plus confession scene Bergman wrote, "I must admit, much better than being cut up and edited." The point where Hitchcock and Bergman match up most deeply as artists is on the necessary issue of guilt, its causes, its spasms of pleasure, and the way it can be burned away if you just stay with it long enough. Such Catholicism would be maximized in her subsequent collaboration with Rossellini.

Bergman thought she was fed up with the artificiality of studio filmmaking, and if you look at her 1940s movies all in a row, you can understand why. She seemed to long to be shot down in the streets as Anna Magnani was in *Rome, Open City*, the tops of her stockings erotically exposed in death. Rossellini didn't know who Bergman was when he got her letter, but when he was told of her top-of-the-heap stardom in Hollywood he moved in on her with all the considerable charm at his disposal.

For their first film, *Stromboli* (1950), Rossellini keyed into Bergman's guilt-ridden and torrential 1940s sexuality and touched off an international scandal when he won her away from her husband and child and then got her pregnant out of wedlock. This caused an uproar in America, with Senator Edwin C. Johnson denouncing them from the Senate floor, calling Rossellini a "love pirate" and "degenerate."

Remarkably, *Stromboli* doesn't advocate the rejection of caution for passion but is partly a film about how sexuality simply isn't enough to get by on.

Bergman plays Karin, a displaced woman in a refugee camp who marries a simple fisherman (Mario Vitale) who takes her to live on Stromboli, a nearly deserted island dominated by an active volcano. When Isabella Rossellini plays her mother in *My Dad is 100 Years Old*, she gives Bergman a kind of spacey ruthlessness that matches up with what we see of Karin on *Stromboli*. Isabella's Ingrid briefly ponders how she hurt Anna Magnani by stealing Rossellini away, and then she blithely and practically says, "Too bad." Bergman was a woman who famously said that happiness was "good health and a bad memory." But when she was with Rossellini, he made sure that she never fell back on such winner-like evasiveness.

Rossellini calls Bergman on her opportunistic-actress sexuality, but he also celebrates her beauty, for the first and last time, lingering on her sensual mouth, her sexy long hair, and her behind in tight slacks. It's as if he's considering this woman, his quarry, and he's not sure he likes what he sees (it took Sternberg six films with Dietrich before he could be as tough with himself as Rossellini is from the very beginning).

In a moment of true religious salvation, Bergman's Karin accepts blessed responsibility for the child inside her, just as Bergman and Rossellini decided not to abort their child, which would have saved them so much trouble. The (actual) child in her stomach is a miracle, but Karin doesn't know if she's up to the challenge. She ends the film shouting to God for the strength and courage to carry on as Rossellini cuts to white birds flying free in the sky.

Stromboli, also called *Stromboli terra di dio (Land of God)*, embodies the invocation of the Rilke poem "Archaic Torso of Apollo," which ends with, "there is no place that does not see you. You must change your life." Like so many of Rossellini's other movies, it is a stirring call to spiritual revolution. And it seems clear now that Bergman instinctively felt what he was saying but didn't quite understand it.

In her next film with Rossellini, *Europa '51*, Bergman has shorter hair and seems much more matronly. The sexual interest we feel in *Stromboli* has ebbed away, but in its place is a loving celebration of Bergman's stubborn will and her longing for a higher purpose, which is what led her to Rossellini in the first place. It's a generous gift of a film from a director to an actress and it has a stark, altruistic purity, for it seems clear that Rossellini did not mesh well with Bergman on a personal level past their initial coming-together, though they did marry and have more children under the pressure of the world's outraged gaze.

Bergman plays Irene, a flippant, rushed society woman who fatally ignores her young son, who throws himself off a steep staircase during a dinner party and dies. As the film goes on, Rossellini focuses increasingly on Bergman's face, her eyes filled with sharp, conflicting ideas, as if she has absorbed her director-husband's own torrential intellect. Her Irene is a prim woman, unlike Karin, but she learns to love and understand everyone, moving towards people who need her: the poor, prostitutes, even criminals. Her upper-class husband (Alexander Knox) doesn't understand this spiritual conversion, and he eventually places Irene in an insane asylum. Such martyrdom always suits Bergman.

In *Voyage in Italy* (1954), her third movie with Rossellini, she played with George Sanders as one half of an unhappy married couple on holiday who are assaulted at every turn by the rude vitality of Naples. Rossellini got what he wanted from Bergman and Sanders by keeping them off balance, never giving them a set script or telling them what *Voyage in Italy* was about. He knew what the film was about: Bergman and Sanders not knowing what the film was about, their performer's anxiety standing in for the dread of the people they are playing. Bergman and Sanders are framed so that their faces are stuck uncomfortably off-center, as if they were butterflies pinned to a wall. She's a tight-ass and he's a smart-ass, and they step on each other's nerves until they impulsively agree to a divorce.

One day, Rossellini set up his camera as an excavation was being done and a dead couple was revealed under the dust, and when this happened, he knew he had the ending of his movie. Bergman's Katherine cries out when she sees the bodies, and she wanders away with her husband. "Life is so short," Katherine says, the deepest thought this limited woman can come up with to meet the ultimate revelation of her own mortality. "That's why one should make the best of it," replies Sanders's Alex, in an English public school get-on-with-it tone that is pierced by an awareness of the wholly inadequate quality of such a response.

When Alex hears his own tone of voice, the message he gets couldn't be clearer—you must change your life, not by divorcing your wife but by trying to love her honestly. Rossellini uses a crane shot, unusual for him, to express the miracle of their coming back together during a parade. The ending suggests that marital compromise is a kind of salvation. The couple in *Voyage in Italy* pledge to stay with each other. Rossellini and Bergman moved closer to separation.

Their next collaboration was a movie of the Paul Claudel/Arthur Honegger oratorio *Joan of Arc at the Stake* (1954), which they had toured extensively throughout Europe. It's an almost purely joyous film and stands as Rossellini's final gift to his wife, who had earned the right to play Joan the saint with her steady commitment to her husband's vision. Many of her scenes are played in long shot against a backdrop of stars, as if Rossellini was finally allowing that Bergman is a star as well, and a special one.

The whole film describes how Joan conquers her fears and stays true to herself, and the stirring climax comes when she flings up her arms and shouts, "I'll burn up like a candle!" She accepts her martyrdom blissfully, though in the end, at the actual stake, some of her doubts return, just as Bergman both believed in and doubted her husband's artistic methods. The Honegger music is drug-like in its ability to produce euphoria, the mise-en-scène is simple and affecting, and Bergman reaches her Rossellini-era apotheosis as she cries, "Hope is triumphant! Faith is triumphant! God is triumphant!" This fourth major Rossellini-Bergman film is barely ever screened, and it should be shown more often, preferably with the Italian soundtrack that uses Bergman's own voice.

The last Bergman-Rossellini film, *Fear* (1954), is a dark-hued, plot-driven tale of blackmail and forced emotional torment that doesn't seem to interest Rossellini all that much. He observes the rote agony of his wife with a rather contemptuous eye now, especially her climactic profession of love to a husband who has spent the whole film torturing her. After this, they divorced and she went back to Hollywood while he moved away from narrative into documentary and scrupulously uninflected historical re-creations for television. Their films had been trashed by most reviewers, barring the critics of the French New Wave, but they have steadily been reevaluated and honored over the years.

Bergman herself was aware of this reevaluation of her Rossellini films, and belatedly, cautiously happy about it after all the fuss and trouble of those years when she made them. "They come on television all the time in Italy, and they write the most marvelous things about them—which they certainly didn't do in the beginning," she said in 1972. The Bergman-Rossellini films seem to me crucial examples of a performer being stripped down to bare essentials where Bergman is totally naked and revealed and then revealed even further until what is being brought out can only be called soul, or humanity.

When she would feel uncertain about a scene with Hitchcock, he would say to her, "Ingrid, fake it." And so she learned technique for him, artifice even, but with her own self and creativity bubbling underneath it, the two of them at one or feeding each other, just as Hitchcock's camera feeds her. The confession scene in *Under Capricorn* required a great deal of technique to put over the way Bergman does it, formality, control, structure. And Rossellini took all of that away from her.

Look at *Under Capricorn* and then look at *Stromboli*, or *Notorious* and then *Europa '51*, and you will see drastically different work from Bergman, classic Hollywood studio acting and then the kind of naturalism that Brando was pioneering. (Luchino Visconti wanted to cast Bergman with Brando in

Senso [1954], and surely that movie would be better as a duel between those formidable actors. Would Bergman have matched Brando's naturalism with her own, or would she have fought him with the artifice of her *Under Capricorn* technique?)

Sheer artifice took over again for her after she left Rossellini. Bergman reemerged in America to make a comeback in *Anastasia* (1956), winning an Oscar for an expert but somewhat mechanical star turn. Her features after that were disappointing, but she excelled as the sexually repressed governess in a TV version of *The Turn of the Screw* (1959) and cheekily took on Jean Cocteau's *The Human Voice* for TV in 1966, a part that Anna Magnani had done for Rossellini in *L'Amore* (1948), playing it less imperiously than Magnani and more for sympathy.

Bergman worked sparingly and commandingly in the 1970s, picking up a supporting actress Oscar for her dopey Swedish missionary in *Murder on the Orient Express* (1974), in which she hilariously dominates a five-minute take with weird furtive glances and "just how dumb is she?" broken English. And then she brought all her old emotional intensity to the role of the Contessa in Vincente Minnelli's last film *A Matter of Time* (1976). There's gravity to everything Bergman says in that movie, and she has a grandeur that seems to come naturally, a statuesque hauteur, so that she papers over every crack in the scenario with her authority.

When the Contessa's former husband (Charles Boyer) asks her why she is speaking about sex at her age, Bergman stares out a window longingly and cries, "Because I'm alive. I'm alive!" In a moment like this, which could so easily be corny, Bergman locates the genuine emotion in an old woman's clinging to what she knows and loves, and some of the depth must come from Minnelli's handling, too, the way he frames her and lavishes attention on her posturing, and the way he identifies with her (he also was becoming a bit addled with age).

She had her swan song with her namesake Ingmar Bergman in *Autumn Sonata* (1978), a film where she plays Charlotte, a concert pianist and neglectful mother to the embittered Eva (Liv Ullmann). Bergman engages in something of a tug-of-war with her director in *Autumn Sonata*. Many times in that movie, Ingmar tries to find some sort of discord in Ingrid's healthy, aged face, but he fails, and he seems to know he is failing. You can feel his frustration, but perhaps this failure gave him a bit of unaccustomed joy, too? Ingmar can't fully follow his own pessimist party line as he stares at this simple, oblivious, wondrous creature. Ingmar wants her naked and naturalistic, but she refuses that to stay clothed in her technique, her armor.

The collision of Bergman and Bergman carries an exciting tension between his intentions and her star valor. They fought constantly during the shoot, and Ingrid quite rightly questioned much of Ingmar's script (according to Ingmar, they even briefly came to physical blows at one point). Ingmar doesn't love Ingrid as Hitchcock, McCarey, and Rossellini did. But his righteous, carnal hatred cannot vanquish her. Ingrid's Charlotte is always acting, always "on," and Eva refers derisively to her "performance" of gracious affection when Charlotte is faced with her other daughter Helena (Lena Nyman), who suffers some unspecified, degenerative disease.

Late Ingmar Bergman films are all about searching for truth in acting, and here he sees Ingrid Bergman as an example of old-fashioned, phony movie star playing. He wants to show her up as a relic, but Ingrid's acting is only *slightly* old-fashioned, an overly ornate frame around a beautiful canvas. Her performing style still carries its glamorous, old Hollywood charge, and Ingmar cannot work through the small, largely irrelevant chink of fussy outdatedness in her armor, even when she's at her most presentational and abrupt.

Ingmar Bergman tries to present both sides of the conflict in *Autumn Sonata* equally because he too is torn between the outrage of an abused child versus the protective pride of a bad parent, and it all comes down to, "I should never have been born," Bergman's modernist credo, shared with Samuel Beckett and many other important artists. But isn't it worth being born just to look at Ingrid Bergman and her self-absorbed, crisply erotic play-acting?

Ingmar wants Ingrid, hates her for getting older, identifies with her abandonment of a child for Rossellini, feels that the basis of her performing style is false, and wants to strip her naked of all artifice, but he winds up giving her a last hurrah that led to a final Best Actress Oscar nomination. *Autumn Sonata* is not a major movie, for either Ingmar or Ingrid, but their encounter with each other is poignant. She was dying of cancer as she acted, and he was at the end of his creative invention on film, yet they eke out one last stand here for each other. Ingmar says, "No." Ingrid says, "Yes." They're both right and both wrong, but it is Ingrid, in her last feature film performance, whose "Yes" carries more conviction and authority.

Bergman wrote a very charming if unreliable memoir that was published in 1980 and made one last film for TV, sympathetically playing Golda Meir in *A Woman Called Golda* (1982), an old-fashioned great lady biopic performance, just transformative enough in voice and look, filled with her own warmth and shyness, before her death in 1982. Her place in movie history is secure, and the films Rossellini made with Bergman are essential viewing and open to many new interpretations. No other star of her time worked in such radically different performing modes, and that's because Bergman was as stubborn and adventurous as she was beautiful. Isn't it lucky?

James Cagney
Hard to Handle

As Tom Powers rises to the top of the criminal underworld in *The Public Enemy* (1931), his ascent involves access to certain available women, and one of them is Kitty (Mae Clarke), a pretty but forlorn girl with a whiny voice. Over the breakfast table one morning, Kitty starts in whining, and this whining is mainly about "wishing" certain things could be different. Powers looks at her hard for a moment and then says, "I wish you was a wishing well, so that I could tie a bucket to you and sink you." It's a medium-cool laugh line, and most actors of this time could have gotten a mild chuckle with it.

But Tom Powers is played by James Cagney. It's the part that made him a star. So just imagine his voice, if you haven't seen the film, leaping on that line. It comes out: "I wish you was a wishing well," which he does in a light singsong tone, followed by a lethal little pause. Then: "So that I could tie a *bucket* to ya and *sink* ya!" he snarls, putting all of his punching force behind this line so that it's hilariously tight and aggressive, a sock in the jaw, "silly" but also deeply disgusted. Watch out! Tom eventually smashes a grapefruit in poor Kitty's face, of course, but he's already done that verbally with those lines about the wishing well and sinking her. That's because Cagney is the first major male *talking* picture star.

He moved beautifully, and he could have pranced and crawled and excelled in silent movies as well (he made an empathetic success playing Lon Chaney in *Man of a Thousand Faces* [1957]). But talking is what he does best, rat-a-tat-tat like gunfire, faster sometimes than bullets. He played gangsters and tabloid reporters and con men who looked down on "book learning" as just another racket. He stood for the low-down side of life, and the world was his personal playground, a stage where he could trip down the stairs or dance out a door. Proudly born in the gutter and hyper-alert, his characters seemed to feel more sensations per minute than some people feel their whole lives, and Cagney offered that alertness to us as a goad. Like many first-rate actors, he was observant. Of one of his persistent mannerisms, the hitching of his trousers, he said, "I got that from a fellow who hung out on the corner of 78th Street and First Avenue ... that's all he did all day!"

Cagney leapt on slang words like "beezark" or colorful locutions like, "Am I gonna stink pretty!" as he bathed in *Picture Snatcher* (1933), and he didn't just play with words; he was also a delighted maker of nonsense sounds (there's a series on YouTube called "James Cagney Makes Weird Noises," and it's fairly lengthy). A one-man melting pot, Cagney gave the impression that he was super-human, or more than human, the most exciting and volatile of actors, capable of morphing into anything, like some man-made cartoon.

He was built for the speed of Warner Brothers movies, where his playfulness could find full expression, and though his scripts at Warners were sometimes very routine, especially in the mid-1930s after the Production Code took effect, Cagney is always worth watching as closely as possible because he's so receptive to stimuli. Look at how he listens to every other actor in a scene, like a man searching for a life jacket on a stormy sea.

He actually came from the mean streets of New York and he was fully capable of street fighting if street fighting were necessary. Cagney played in a drag chorus line on stage, he played in vaudeville, and he danced like no one else (he even ran a dancing school when times were tough). He paid his dues throughout the 1920s.

Al Jolson bought the rights to the play *Penny Arcade* and sold them to Warners with the stipulation that Cagney and Joan Blondell were to repeat their stage roles on film. Thus Cagney made his debut in *Sinners' Holiday* (1930) as a highly vulnerable and hysterical mama's boy. His voice was pinched and nasal, very New York, but his face was wondrously open and responsive.

His apprenticeship in films was brief. Before *Public Enemy*, he stops William Wellman's *Other Men's Women* (1931) cold with one of his eccentric dances, and he paid his respects to a very different kind of star actor, George Arliss, in a single, urgent scene in *The Millionaire* (1931), bursting in to sell him (and his fusty acting style) some life insurance. He made Edward G. Robinson seem a little stiff in *Smart Money* (1931), where he steals scenes just by listening closely (his pantomime to describe the full amatory impact of a sexy girl he knows is particularly audacious and suggestive). It was clear that he was bursting with talent and invention, and his next few movies let him run delightfully amok.

He made a comic and then very romantic match with Blondell in *Blonde Crazy* (1931), one of his most creative and most vulnerable early performances. From the moment he sees Blondell in that movie, he's both lust and lovestruck: "What a woman," he says when she fake-haughtily slaps him a second time, in an unclassifiable goofy, foggy-toned voice.

"I've wanted you since the first day I saw you," he tells Blondell earnestly. "But if I can't have you, I'll have somebody else," he says, very quickly and distractedly, in a way that lets us know that "somebody else" actually won't do for him, even if he has to settle for that. It's a shivery little moment, a sharp insight into the would-be pragmatic emotions of a tough guy, a model of suggesting several things all at once, which was what Cagney's female equivalent, Barbara Stanwyck, was even more adept at.

When Blondell tries to kiss him towards the end of *Blonde Crazy* and Cagney just closes his eyes and tries to avoid all the emotion this gesture brings up in him, we are seeing a man who has mastered his expression of feelings in order to express the uncontrollable feelings in the character he is playing. Look at the way he tenderly grabs on to the fur trim on Blondell's coat in the last scene and see the far more empathetic precursor to Brando's supposedly groundbreaking interactions with women in the early 1950s.

How many times in Cagney's Pre-Code movies did he look a woman over from stem to stern, noticing her every little bodily quirk and idiosyncrasy? Is there any other male star who looks so deeply excited by the prospect of sex with a woman? Women of that time knew that there was nothing sexier than Cagney's total, specific attention, just as women now can see Cagney's romantic and purely sexual appeal beyond the famous grapefruit-smashing, hair-pulling, and smacking that was really just rough foreplay.

Cagney himself was married to one woman all his life, and he faithfully turned down all the women who threw themselves at him, with one exception: Merle Oberon. In John McCabe's 1997 book *Cagney*, a friend of Cagney who wished to remain anonymous told a story about a time when Cagney succumbed to Oberon's advances during a train trip. Halfway into their coupling, she suddenly cried, "I'm being fucked by Jimmy Cagney!" This so alarmed the real man behind the movie icon that he ended the sex right then and there and scurried back to his own compartment. The on-screen aggressor hid a somewhat retiring person intimidated by his own iconography.

All of his early 1930s performances are jam-packed with grace notes and jolts of pleasure. He moved faster and thought faster than anybody else, and he wasn't afraid of following his most daring instincts for fun. Look at the way he picks up Blondell's underwear in *Blonde Crazy*, holding it against himself and becoming a hot girl for a couple of seconds, his unabashed femininity completing and sealing his greatness as a performer. Look at the semi-alarmed but intrigued way he reacts to a gay tailor measuring him for clothes in *The Public Enemy*.

Even at his toughest, he was always playful, extraordinarily loose but never messy, knockabout and sometimes agitated but also curiously serene within himself. He had a Shakespearian extravagance, so that he could be the best Bottom in *A Midsummer Night's Dream* (1935) just as Mickey Rooney was the definitive Puck. In that movie, he sometimes seems to be doing a loving send-up of John Barrymore's purplest physical and vocal mannerisms, one kind of ham paying tribute to a very different kind of ham. When he was really super-charged, there really was something non-human and uncanny about him, something elemental.

They called him "the Professional Againster" at Warner Brothers because he was always complaining about low salary, exploitative working conditions, and poor scripts. But when he had some control over his work, as he did on the low-budget and amateurish *Something to Sing About* (1937) and *Boy Meets Girl* (1938), the hair-raisingly virtuous *Johnny Come Lately* (1943), or the sentimental *The Time of Your Life* (1948), they were enough to show that he sometimes didn't know what was best for him on film.

There aren't many major stars who survived as many nondescript programmers as Cagney did, particularly after 1934 when he was paired far too many times with Pat O'Brien in films that had little distinction. But he had quite a spree from at least *Blonde Crazy* to the musical *Footlight Parade* (1933), eight films in two years that made his reputation like a bunch of firecrackers going off. *Hard to Handle* (1933) is probably the funniest and *Picture Snatcher* the most disturbing, but even these films tend to run together in the mind. "Come out and take it, ya dirty yellow-bellied rat or I'll give it to ya through the door!" he sneers in *Taxi!* (1932), a line that would be misquoted as "You dirty rat" by a thousand nightclub impressionists of Cagney who would often add, "You killed my brother!"

Cagney was for the working man, and his early films often reflected that. In *The St. Louis Kid* (1934), he makes a very leftist anti-capitalist speech in favor of the workers, and Cagney himself was involved in union organizing in Hollywood, which was another reason for his bosses to be unhappy with him. The formulaic nature of his vehicles really came out by the late '30s; when in doubt, his films end with a big physical brawl, so that he was always serving up punches left, right, and center. He was expected to teach a moral lesson to the Dead End Kids by faking fear as he is led to the electric chair in *Angels with Dirty Faces* (1938), and he did his best with such pious tasks as his films got cleaner and cornier. He grabbed any opening he could for humor, mainly triple-take, cross-eyed slapstick when his wisecracks as written grew tamer.

In his later films for Warner Brothers, like *The Fighting 69th* (1940), Cagney is always being put in his place, his rebelliousness squashed, as if he were a street-fighting, male Katharine Hepburn. Most of his films of this time are cut-rate, like the boxing movie *City for Conquest* (1940), though he did seem tickled to be opposite a lusty Ann Sheridan in the satirical *Torrid Zone* (1940).

Cagney took the Oscar for his all-out performance as George M. Cohan in *Yankee Doodle Dandy* (1942), calling on all the training of his vaudeville days and adding a touch of superhuman madness to the squareness of that movie. It's an old-time biopic where everything is squeaky clean and just too good to be true, but who can forget the way he dances up on his toes and then slides along the stage seemingly on the sides of his legs, or the way he tap dances down the steps of the White House, so scrumptiously pleased with himself and his own audacity?

His best director of this time was Raoul Walsh, who brought out a rare delicacy and shy decency in Cagney in *The Strawberry Blonde* (1941), where his outer energy, humor, and toughness is balanced by a sense of restrained grievance and loss. Walsh also gave Cagney ample room to be the psychotic Cody Jarrett in *White Heat* (1949), a tough guy who is so in love with his mother that he sounds like an animal caught in a trap when he is told of her death.

Cagney had given his all to the death scene of father Walter Huston in *Yankee Doodle Dandy*, but that was just a sketch, a warm-up, for what he does in *White Heat*. This was Cagney at his most daring, dredging up the kind of raw, ugly, mature despair that would never have been countenanced in his Pre-Code days. It's the most outsized performance he ever gave, the meanest and toughest and also the most pitifully vulnerable, jacked up to the most primal and literally explosive level.

In *White Heat*, the gangster is "explained" to us by his debilitating headaches, his mother fixation, and the fact that his father died in the nuthouse. If Cagney still makes Cody Jarrett charismatic and attractive while casually shooting people right and left,

A portrait of James Cagney, who was always at his best in motion.

that's our problem, and one of the key problems of the movies, one of the major reasons why some people were offended by them and scared of their influence, and eager to censor them.

Even deep into the 1940s, Cagney was still capable of taking an ordinary-to-good line of dialogue and making it sound like a wisecracking epiphany. In *Blood on the Sun* (1945), a violent thriller, Sylvia Sidney assures Cagney that Japanese women aren't allowed to think. Cagney thinks this over for a split-second and then raps out, "Well, they probably bootleg a thought every now and then." He gets a huge laugh with this line because his timing is the fastest in the business, but also because he manages to make it such an all-encompassing raspberry to hypocrisy or mistaken attitudes. No fuss, a clean, brutal thrust and BAM!, Sidney's pious, silly remark is k-o-ed and out cold on the mat.

Cagney got a bit thicker physically as he aged and a bit more querulous emotionally. His films did not improve much in the 1950s and they also tend to run together in the mind just as his mid-to-late '30s movies do. Even when he had a fine director like Nicholas Ray, the film they made together, *Run for Cover* (1955), proved unexceptional.

His performance as the touchy captain in *Mister Roberts* (1955) might have been given by a Cagney impersonator, but he did manage to measure out just the right doses of bullying intimidation and tormented torch-carrying in *Love Me or Leave Me* (1955) with Doris Day, a film he thought highly of. When he watches Day sing in that movie, he does so with a mixture of pain, pleasure, and embarrassment, as if he doesn't want anyone around him to know about his unrequited passion for her, because men aren't supposed to show their feelings, or feelings like that. Which is why men, particularly in the classic Hollywood period, are usually not as interesting to watch or expressive as women are. But in the early 1930s, the thrill of Cagney's work was that he showed all of his feelings and impulses, without censoring himself. He showed us more than we could have dreamed of, and he made us enjoy it.

Cagney played his last lead role in Billy Wilder's Cold War farce *One, Two, Three* (1961), where he sped through the crude jokes at a breakneck pace that broke his own belief in himself. When he had trouble remembering all the lines, Wilder suggested that it was time to hang it up and pack it in, and so he did. He retired to a farm with his wife and did not emerge for 20 years before taking one final role as a police commissioner with an elaborate mustache in *Ragtime* (1981), a film in which his movements were restricted by age and illness but his vocal power was undiminished. He was sadly diminished, however, by the time of his last TV film, *Terrible Joe Moran* (1984), playing an ex-boxer in a wheelchair. Cagney's stroke-impaired voice was dubbed by impressionist Rich Little.

As far as male movie stars of the classic Hollywood period go, Cagney's only real rival is Cary Grant, who did almost as much on-screen whinnying and nonsense noise-making as Cagney did, but in a much darker, resentful key. Grant is Post-Code to the max, screwball comedy incarnate, whereas Cagney is Pre-Code always, leaping on Joan Blondell or an opportunity for larceny with equal relish. He's a totally cinematic tonic who insists crime does pay, money is great and sex is better, and wisecracks rise out of a baseline decency that needs to be discovered again in America.

Cary Grant
Just a Butterfly

Cary Grant is the embodiment of what most movies, or at least most Hollywood movies of the late 1930s and early 1940s, were all about: fantasy, fun, and escape, but with a disquieting edge. A flawless comic technician, he registers as a phantom blur of black, thickly glossy hair, springy, athletic movement, and booming yet strangled vocal attack. Grant is close to being a filmic abstraction, the Platonic idea of a leading man, so constantly and dazzlingly in motion that he can never be pinned down for close scrutiny. Is he even really good-looking, or are we attracted and dizzied mainly by his impeccable clothes, his unmistakably classy but classless voice, his restless physical authority?

If we look as closely as we can at Grant, it is possible to discern what drives him: unappeasable rage. This rage is underneath everything he does on screen, and it keeps him dynamically tight, contained yet always leaping around; he's never able to relax for an instant. His rage gives his fabled charm a murderous quality that was developed most disturbingly by Alfred Hitchcock, who proved Grant could just as well kill you as kiss you. Leo McCarey and George Cukor brought out the teasing playfulness that made him the idol of millions of women, turning him into a screwball, off-kilter first boyfriend who was only flirting with effeminacy.

He seemed like he'd show a woman a great time at nightclubs, put a lampshade on his head to make her laugh, and then kiss her at the door and go home. As he grew older, Grant added "befuddled" to his arsenal of comic mannerisms, usually overdoing this quality, while his whinnying frustration, which seemed to signal his unreleased sexuality, narrowed into gray-suited crankiness and boredom, with saving glimpses of his hardened ironies. Perhaps his best part was the amoral newspaperman Walter Burns in Howard Hawks's *His Girl Friday* (1940), where he gave his anti-social tendencies full rein without losing a bit of his magician's appeal.

He was born Archibald Leach in 1904 and came from a working class British background. His mother was committed to an asylum when he was a small boy without his being told anything about it. Was she even his real mother? He related differing stories about that as an older man. His father was a drunk who treated him very badly, and his Grandmother Leach treated him even worse, calling him a "nancy boy" and shunting him aside contemptuously.

Leach understandably left home early to tour with music hall performers, and while in New York he lived in Greenwich Village with the future costume designer Orry-Kelly. He sold ties on the street when times were tough. Stage star Noël Coward, who was briefly his lover and always his friend, taught him how to talk in a more cultivated manner as he worked on stage and then went out to Hollywood and signed with Paramount in 1932.

He made his debut as an Olympic athlete carrying a javelin and an attitude of free-floating aggression in *This Is the Night* (1932), an antic and fairly dirty sophisticated comedy. Right away, it was clear that he moved and spoke like no one else, yet it wasn't obvious just what kind of parts he should play. Asked to throw a punch in his first scene in Josef von Sternberg's *Blonde Venus* (1932), he looks like he'd much rather not.

His screen character at this point is clearly urban, well-dressed, and uneasy. But with just *what* he was uneasy, it was difficult to say. His eyes flash with brute anger and impatience sometimes, but why? That is never quite clear in these early films. A former stilt walker, he moves in a tense, definite way, as if "walking" were a performance that amused him slightly. He is suntanned, slender (he always told himself to "think thin"), and tilted, as if he can't even stand or stride across a room without doing so from a rakish, cockeyed angle. His hair was so sculpted and Brilliantined that it looked like imaginary hair, like movie fantasy hair.

I once knew a boy in high school who came from Jamaica. He didn't talk like anyone else I've ever heard, before or since. He had gotten rid of most of his Jamaican accent, or smoothed it out, but when he talked the words would come out in a wholly original way and rhythm all his own. Of course everyone in school was in love with him, and Grant inspired such feelings world wide with his smoothed-out working class British accent, which he turned into a triumphantly original way of expressing himself: jaunty, sexily and sometimes scarily emphatic, neither here nor there. He had the perfect movie voice—not quite real, but with an echo somewhere of unforgotten reality. It was a voice that gives you permission to fantasize, a voice that gives you permission to want to live in the movies.

Grant seemed embarrassed by the sexy cleft in his chin and his well turned out, glistening good looks, but this embarrassment and uneasiness is intriguing, whereas, say, the same quality in a young Paul Newman is not.

Why is that? Because even in his early films, Grant was stylizing and heightening all of his behavior for the camera while the young Newman was disastrously influenced by the psychological realism of the Actors Studio, which made him feel inadequate on all fronts.

Different eras bring different holding contexts. Could James Cagney and Barbara Stanwyck have thrived in the 1970s on screen? Yes, most probably. Could Grant and his best screen partner Katharine Hepburn have done so? No, I think not. They needed the distancing of 1930s cinema, the stylization. Nor is it possible to imagine Grant's other best partners, like Irene Dunne, Ingrid Bergman, Grace Kelly, and Audrey Hepburn, operating in the Method atmosphere of the 1970s.

When he presses his attentions on Marlene Dietrich in *Blonde Venus*, Grant seems shy and not at all happy about having to push himself and his desire on a woman. Some writers have chalked this up to youthful callowness on his part, but it actually seems like he is simply not meshing with his role and not convinced by Dietrich (her kind of obviously sexy haughtiness doesn't interest him).

He was cast with Randolph Scott in *Hot Saturday* (1932), and he convinced Scott to move in with him. They lived together for almost 10 years, and there has been much speculation about Grant's sexuality ever since photos appeared in fan magazines of the two of them being domestic with each other. Grant had racked up five marriages before he was done, and one major relationship with a photographer, Maureen Donaldson, in the 1970s. He talked about being very much in love with Sophia Loren, with whom he co-starred in *The Pride and the Passion* (1957) and *Houseboat* (1958), but Loren, aware of the gay rumors about Grant, chose to marry producer Carlo Ponti instead. His third marriage to actress Betsy Drake, a kind of imitation Margaret Sullavan-Katharine Hepburn type, lasted the longest, from 1949 to 1962. Addressing the sexuality rumors in a 2004 TV documentary on Grant's life, Drake said that she didn't know what he had done in his youth, but that they were "too busy fucking" to pay attention to what people said.

There is no reason to disbelieve her. And there is also no reason to disbelieve Bill Royce, who befriended Grant in the 1970s and wrote a frank and detailed memoir of their friendship called *The Wizard of Beverly Grove* (2006). In that book, Royce recounts a long conversation where Grant opened up about his love for Randolph Scott. "The only problem was that Randy never fell in love with me," Grant said. "Anyone who knows him knows he loves two things—golf and money … the most Randy felt for me then was the affection one would have for a brother. He knew how I felt, and whenever I'd try to take things to the next step, he'd shrug and say, 'Ah, Cary.'"

Grant's first marriage to actress Virginia Cherrill was taken on purely as a cover, and he treated her very poorly while he continued to focus on Scott. Grant told Royce:

> I told Randy that if we were going to be accused over and over again of being lovers, then at least I wanted to experience what we were being accused of. Our first get-together was a disaster. Randy made a half-hearted, stumbling attempt at making love—and that only made me feel worse.... We were able to resume our friendship on its previous terms because I later realized that there was no way Randy would have experimented with me—and that's really what it amounted to for him, an experiment—if he didn't truly love me on some profound level.

By the early 1950s, when Grant was married to Drake, he was undergoing extensive psychoanalysis and taking LSD partly, it seems, to wash away his gay desires. From all the available evidence, it would seem that Grant was bisexual with gay leanings in his youth and that he tried to direct his feelings more towards women as he aged. This personal conflict of his must account, at least in part, for the richness and ambiguity of all his relationships with women on screen, because on screen, at least, only women and partnership with women really interested him. And this was simultaneously part of his gayness and also very much part of his straightness as a performer. He didn't relate to women as a man's man of that time would have but as an equal partner, a foil, and a catalyst. His feelings were fluid, and they brought an immense and tantalizing romantic freedom to the screen. The complexity of his achievement as a screen actor and a movie star was predicated on the very real sexual complexity of the man himself.

"You're considered much too dangerous for local consumption," Nancy Carroll tells his rakish rich guy in *Hot Saturday*. He is already an honest screen presence in his early days, never quite hiding what he is actually feeling, but managing to keep just a bit of it to himself. He took chances with clothes then and dared you to think that his sartorial taste was just a tad loud or vulgar, yet Pre-Code sexual frankness seems to upset him. It was only when the sex urge went underground Post-Code that he was allowed to really assemble all the pieces of his shifting, imaginative, peek-a-boo dream man personality.

He was just able to keep a straight face when asked to stand still for inspection by the lurid Mae West in *She Done Him Wrong* (1933). The indefatigable Mae asks him to "come up sometime, see me" as she looks him up and down. "I'm home every evening," she groans, to which he responds, "I'm busy every evening." He's hard to get, but Mae tells him, "You can be had." Can he? When he does come up to see her, she tells him, "Loosen up, unbend, you'll feel better," but Grant never loses his coiled vitality, his watchful, catlike responsiveness. Telling him to unbend is like telling a big cat to relax: impossible.

In their follow-up, *I'm No Angel* (1933), he is made to tell her, "I could be your slave," but this is comically unlikely. What's really funny in their tête-à-têtes is how smirky and blatantly insincere he is with West. She really zings one of her men (Kent Taylor) here: "I like a sophisticated man to take me out," she says. "I'm not really sophisticated," Taylor says in response, to which she replies, "You're not really out yet, either"—a comment that would make no sense at all to a general audience but would make perfect sense to her gay audience.

In *The Woman Accused* (1933), Grant was asked to administer a surprise whipping to the villainous Jack La Rue, and Paramount was sometimes trying to make him into a touchy tough guy, as in the grim *The Eagle and the Hawk* (1933), where it is clear that he has some dramatic talent but doesn't possess the technique quite yet to control it. That movie showed that he was open to playing an unsympathetic character without any varnishing, but he was always more interested in romantic comedy, where he could get it.

Thirty Day Princess (1934) has a witty Preston Sturges script, but Sylvia Sidney is too serious-eyed for her comic role, and she has no chemistry with Grant. This problem with chemistry will come up again and again in his early years on screen. Grant needed a woman to play against, someone who would challenge him, preferably a high-class lady like Katharine Hepburn or Irene Dunne. He was cast twice with Joan Bennett in two films, *Big Brown Eyes* and *Wedding Present* (both 1936), and she's much too coarse and simple to interest him. But *Wedding Present*, does have an archetypal Cary Grant moment. When a cuckoo clock goes off unexpectedly in a quiet room, Grant shoots Bennett a quick, knowing look. This sharing of delight in absurdity with a romantic partner was his key mode of intimacy on screen, and it made for a daunting, seductive model for living.

He finally met his ambisexual other half, Katharine Hepburn, in Cukor's *Sylvia Scarlett* (1936), where she was dressed as a male for most of the running time and Grant's Cockney adventurer was eager to go to bed with he-she, thinking Hepburn's Sylvester would make a "proper little hot water bottle." This dainty and off-color film frees Grant to be as bold as he wants to be physically, like a boy who ran away from home to join the circus and loved it.

Though it is not a star part, Cukor lights and presents Grant like a star here, and though the movie was a flop for Hepburn and Cukor (too gay, too daring), it showed Grant in a new and favorable light. He's much fleshier in *Sylvia Scarlett*, and his movements are correspondingly looser. Being a Cockney on screen allows him to be more good-humored, less worried and angular.

This movie releases some of the spirit that would come out fully in the great comedies he made from 1937 on, and it allows him to really swagger. In what is probably his gayest picture, Grant was never more masculine.

He sang to Jean Harlow at MGM in *Suzy* (1936), and then he settled in to his unparalleled run as a romantic comedian with *Topper* (1937), where he is first seen driving a car with his feet and sparring with his wife Marion (Constance Bennett), acting as serious about being silly as it is possible to be. This is the movie that finally established the classic Grant character, an acrobat in a drawing room, restlessly playful, floating high, wide, and extremely handsome through every nightclub in town, attached to the woman who challenges him the most and brings him the most fun, something a fully heterosexual man of this time might have scorned or had trouble with. The version of pleasure-seeking practiced by Grant and Bennett here is a little too relentless to be appealing, but that was soon fixed in *The Awful Truth*, his first major movie, where the Grant character received a crucial overhaul from director Leo McCarey.

Initially he wanted out of *The Awful Truth*. Dunne said that Grant was nervous for a while about McCarey's improvisational approach to directing, but eventually he achieved a kind of ultimate freedom in front of the camera, hemming and hawing verbally with Dunne, his second-best screen partner after Hepburn (and it's a close call). He lets Dunne sparkle brightly, setting her off, prancing and baring down on her sometimes but giving her the space to enchant him, to win his roving attention. In comic situations, he always does just enough while she goes just a little bit farther and wilder than he does facially and bodily. One comic set piece flows into another in *The Awful Truth* with seeming effortlessness, yet one flaw of emphasis or timing would screw them all up. Grant never puts a step wrong, nor does Dunne.

He had looked disgusted when Mae West told him to trust her because "hundreds have," whereas with Dunne he delights in teasing and creating a romantic space that they alone can share. Sex can be alluded to in *The Awful Truth* but never brought out into the open because it's too important. Unlike many other major stars, Grant is only at his best when stimulated by a romantic partner, and the flashier the better, and Dunne had only to smile brightly to prick up his interest. Their achievement in *The Awful Truth* is there to be enjoyed permanently—two people who belong together, on screen at least, retiring tenderly to a cabin upstate after their fun and games outside the bedroom have been thoroughly enjoyed.

It's hard to improve on perfection, but that's just what Grant did with his paleontologist David Huxley in Howard Hawks's *Bringing Up Baby* (1938), a screwball comedy in a darker, harsher key, based in frustration, sexual and otherwise, and the freedom of plans being ruined and unmade. Told by Hawks to think of silent comedian Harold Lloyd, Grant wears spectacles here until they are broken, so that Katharine Hepburn's Susan can tell him, "You're so good-looking without your glasses."

The film is filled with such gender reversals, which are only underlined by the sharp sexual ambiguity of Grant and Hepburn themselves, with their wholly made-up voices and accents and their making-it-up-as-we-go-along romantic lives, which were tormented in reality but blissfully free of all restraints on screen.

Susan takes David's clothes and his phallic brontosaurus bone away, leaving him to rush around her Connecticut farm in a frilly negligee until he's driven to announce, "I just went gay all of a sudden!" And David likes it, for his fury is his repressed sexuality rising to the surface. Grant fell down during Dunne's music recital in *The Awful Truth*, but in *Bringing Up Baby* he takes pratfalls throughout. Asked to make his own anger funny, Grant remembered a fellow he knew who used to whinny like a horse when he got mad, and this became one of his staple mannerisms, like an engine letting off steam. And so his anger became comic, and rather sweet, and rather sexy, too.

And then he even improved on that! In *Holiday* (1938) he was Johnny Case, a lovably boyish, rumpled, cuddly, sensitive, freewheeling guy who wants to find a "perfect playmate." Grant bounds into every scene with enormous energy here, spreading that energy cheerfully wherever he goes. "You know me, when I feel a worry coming on, you know what I do!" he says, right before flipping himself over like the acrobat he was. This is the movie and the performance where the fantasy figure called "Cary Grant" makes the deepest inroads, smiling and showing you the way to paradise, even making you believe in paradise, overriding all your sensible misgivings (and the real Grant had a lot of his own misgivings to override, so what he does in *Holiday* feels truly heroic).

Grant's characters share their internal monologue verbally, muttering to themselves and to others, starting a thought and then stopping it because they see the absurdity of everything. His clothes are baggy in *Holiday* because Johnny needs

Cary Grant's David Huxley, behind bars yet liberated in *Bringing Up Baby*.

to feel free in his movements. He wants to make a little money and then retire young for a while to have his fun. If the money runs out, it seems like he'll always know what to do to earn a little more, even if he has to go into music hall work like Grant did as a youth, for surely he has the charisma for that and for anything else at hand.

Not many stars can match those three films in a row, but Grant was just getting warmed up. He turned happily to boisterous adventure in *Gunga Din* (1939) and butched it up even further in Hawks's *Only Angels Have Wings* (1939), where he emphasized the dark, teasing side of his nihilistic flier, a cutely feckless deathtrap for the women he knows. But then in his third film from that year, a modest drama with Carole Lombard called *In Name Only*, he played a man unable to take control of his own personal life, and he was lusciously feminine and melting in his last scenes on his sickbed.

There was a physical change for *His Girl Friday*, back to the lean, mean, and angled manner of *Blonde Venus* but with all the streamlined skills of his mature style, and this was enough to knock the breath out of you. This time Hawks is back to the gender-fuckery of *Bringing Up Baby*, so much so that in *Notre Music* (2004), Jean-Luc Godard sets stills of Grant and Rosalind Russell in *His Girl Friday* next to each other and declares Hawks's inability to see "the difference between a woman and a man." And of course that's the area where Grant operates most dangerously.

The strident Russell plays at being female and Grant plays at being male and they animate these roles so fetchingly because each gender construct runs against their natural inclinations, and so their artifice is impressively detailed, challenging, comic, and a few other, darker things. Grant's Walter is a slightly dimmer man than he usually played, a man who laughs a bit at his own jokes—there is even, maybe, a bit of a movie studio head in this performance. And yet he's also extra-responsive here, full of unexpected little reactions of amusement.

"He sounds like a guy *I* ought to marry," Grant tells Russell in *His Girl Friday* when she is extolling the virtues of bland second banana Ralph Bellamy. Russell's Hildy keeps admonishing Grant's Walter to stop "hamming" and "acting," but she allows herself to be excited by his vulgar, double-talking, double-crossing, I-get-things-done style.

The speed of the film challenges Grant's physical and vocal inventiveness to the limit, and he shoots further and further with that speed until there can be nowhere else to go. It's one of the all-time great film performances, filled with little disgrace notes and comically large physical gestures of ruthless cunning. In the end he is so shamelessly butch, in a plastic, bendable, dance-like way, that he allows Russell to be openly feminine until the two of them transcend gender altogether. And that's what romance—or at least Platonic and borderless classic Hollywood screwball movie romance—is all about. *His Girl Friday* even allows Grant a final joke against his real self. Told by an official that he's through, Grant's Walter says, "The last man who said that to me was Archie Leach just before he cut his throat."

Leo McCarey was set to direct Grant and Irene Dunne in *My Favorite Wife* (1940) until he was in a bad automobile accident, so Garson Kanin took over. It's a good example of how much a director counts—a situation and stars that might have sparkled with McCarey falls rather flat under Kanin. Everything from the staging to the editing to the behavior feels off. Randolph Scott was utilized here as a stud who was stranded on an island with Dunne, and he plays an athletic marvel whose physique begins to obsess Grant, but even *this* perilous bit of casting has little resonance on screen, even when Grant is made to ask if Scott confines himself to "raw meat," or when Grant is caught modeling women's clothes and his sexuality comes under suspicion. It's all too on-the-nose for him and his bi-persona, and so his creativity just shuts down. He falls back on a little boy routine he was cultivating, his least interesting mode.

He was C. K. Dexter Haven, the ex-alcoholic ex-husband in *The Philadelphia Story* (1940), nursing grudges on the sidelines and telling off Katharine Hepburn until she was supposedly human enough for him. In the 1940s, he earned two Oscar nominations: for *Penny Serenade* (1941), a lengthy and heavily sincere weepie, and for *None But the Lonely Heart* (1944) a gloomy film dear to his heart, directed by Clifford Odets, where at 40 he was unable to quite get back in touch with Archie Leach, which was his intention.

He brings a nervous intensity to his Big Scene in *Penny Serenade* where he pleads to keep his adopted daughter, but this kind of punishment is not something most of us would want to see him try. When he's asked where he got the dimple in his chin in *Lonely Heart*, he smiles and says, "Present from me Pa," a painful and revealing moment, but also somehow false or beside the point. He had moved past that childhood pain in his screen persona, if not in his own life.

It was Alfred Hitchcock who allowed Grant to deepen his screen character even further in *Suspicion* (1941), where his immaculately groomed charm is revealed as brittle and irresponsible, hiding self-doubt and severe abuse, both self and otherwise, underneath. Famously, the studio would not allow Hitchcock to make Grant a murderer, so that he has to confess his own inadequacy at the end instead, and this wound up being even more disturbing than the original killer impulse indicated in the script. And then in the harrowing *Notorious* (1946), Grant's nihilism was brought to its limit.

As a secret agent named Devlin, Grant is not above punching a lady to keep her quiet, and he seems to know karate, too, but Devlin is no James Bond. He gets himself all tangled up emotionally with Ingrid Bergman's promiscuous Alicia, his eyes flashing with nearly murderous anger that he can just barely rein in as he allows her to seduce another man, the Nazi Sebastian (Claude Rains), to get information for his agency.

This is the darkest of all Grant's characters, a man who has been profoundly damaged and is profoundly suspicious, inflicting hurt on Alicia as he has been hurt. It's hard to forget the solitary and furious image of him sitting by himself in a cafe where he used to sit with Alicia while she is off carrying out her orders with Sebastian. It's a brief shot. Hitchcock doesn't linger over it or give Devlin any clarifying dialogue, but he doesn't need to. It's a shot that reveals the real loneliness of Cary Grant within his dream man/dream world mode.

He was a political malcontent stuck up in an attic in *The Talk of the Town* (1942) and a radio correspondent mixed up in the war in *Once Upon a Honeymoon* (1942), uneasy films that tried to Say Something while also aiming for hit comedy status (he does have a very nice poetic drunk scene with Ginger Rogers in *Honeymoon*). At the end of *Talk of the Town*, Jean Arthur chases him down a lobby until he says, "Stop following me or I'll call the police!" In a moment like that, filled with Grant's tense, contained movements of escape, he is clearly the greatest challenge for any woman and also the greatest prize, or at least the greatest excitement she will ever have, for good or ill. In *Mr. Lucky* (1943) he played a draft-dodging gambler who is made to learn how to knit, and they stuck him in a submarine in *Destination Tokyo* (1944).

When Grant is displeased with a project, as he clearly is with the slick and bogus Cole Porter biopic *Night and Day* (1946), he is never false or technical but slyly and even amusingly insincere, though sometimes given to film-haltingly angry glares. He is incapable of hiding his feelings, though he could get overly

A portrait of Cary Grant in the 1940s.

broad. He was way over the top for Frank Capra in *Arsenic and Old Lace*, filmed in 1941 but only let out in 1944; he whinnies and does double takes all over the place in that movie, like a cartoon version of himself gone berserk.

After the height of *Notorious*, his material deteriorated badly. *The Bachelor and the Bobby-Soxer* (1947), *The Bishop's Wife* (1947), *Mr. Blandings Builds His Dream House* (1948), and *Every Girl Should Be Married* (1948) feel like the situation TV comedy of the 1950s to come, and the last one in particular was very hard to take since it indulged his future wife Betsy Drake in all kinds of affectations only to have them nastily but accurately mocked by Grant on screen, hardly gallant or fair behavior.

Two more for Howard Hawks, *I Was a Male War Bride* (1949) and *Monkey Business* (1952), took the harsh flavor of their earlier films further into a kind of nauseating coarseness. In *War Bride* he is denied sex and emasculated for ever-grimmer laughs, while in *Monkey Business* he finds a fountain of youth for a while with a young Marilyn Monroe. He was more at home in the smart if overly solemn talk of *Crisis* (1950) and *People Will Talk* (1951), which he nearly saves by alternately underplaying and skeptically playing against Joseph L. Mankiewicz's would-be Shavian dialogue on death and medicine, and being a pursued male.

His looks and screen character were getting so distilled down to their essence that it almost felt like he didn't even need to be there anymore to do "Cary Grant," and maybe he was starting to get tired of it underneath, or the strain of it was too much for him. He was getting overly fussy on his sets, holding up production for hours if he objected to a doorknob or a cufflink. Times had changed, the luxury and fantasy and radicalism of 1930s comedy giving way to a softer, conformist, cozy style in the 1950s, which did not fit him well.

Hitchcock once again came to his rescue with *To Catch a Thief* (1955), where he is a kind of suntanned and spry uber–Grant, an ex-cat burglar and ex-Resistance fighter moving stylishly around the French Riviera. Asked how many men he killed in the war, Grant replies, "72!" with chilling aplomb. At 50, he was never more sumptuously sexy or sure of himself (when a waiter sees Grant in an outdoor restaurant, he excitedly pops the cork of the champagne bottle he's holding!).

Grant had one more fling with comic and then romantic muttering for Leo McCarey in *An Affair to Remember* (1957) with a game Deborah Kerr. In the last scene, when he realizes that Kerr's character has been crippled, the way Grant slowly closes his eyes might be corny if anyone else had done it, but he makes it land as a deeply felt gesture amidst all his other prickly impulses and by now rather grumpy playfulness.

Two years later, Tony Curtis mercilessly spoofed Grant's vocal mannerisms and screen character in a set piece in Billy Wilder's *Some Like It Hot* that suggested that new mores were starting to emerge to eclipse Grant's sublime sexual indirection. Curtis's Grant imitation claims that girls do nothing for him, so that Marilyn Monroe has to go into the most strenuous exertions to get his heterosexual libido back on track. As a rule in Grant's films, women pursued him and he acted like a moving target, but *Some Like It Hot* bluntly brings that dynamic out of the closet. Wilder always wanted Grant to be in one of his movies and Grant always avoided that, and when you see Curtis's imitation in *Some Like It Hot*, it's clear why he did.

But then, one more time for Hitchcock, he was Roger O. Thornhill, a Manhattan ad man mistaken for someone else, in *North by Northwest* (1959), Grant's real swan song. What does the "O" stand for? Nothing, though it does make for a nice monogram for him (ROT). Among other things, *North by Northwest* is very much a movie about Cary Grant, or "Cary Grant": identity problems, being beset by cryptically gay men (the James Mason and Martin Landau characters) and dealing with a domineering mother (Jessie Royce Landis, who was the same age as Grant). Thornhill is taken by force and made to drink the entire contents of a large bottle of bourbon by Landau and his associates, and then he is made to drive a car while he is blind drunk. The sexual implications for Grant and his whole persona are extremely suggestive here.

And then Hitchcock lets him off the hook in a clingingly sensual train encounter opposite coolly intelligent Eva Marie Saint. With his hair now as becomingly silver as his suits, Grant was severely tested here in an empty crop field, an auction room, and finally on Mount Rushmore, where Landau's villain steps hard on his hand. "I may go back to hating you, it was more fun," he tells Saint at one point, a last gesture towards the screwball comedy that made him. Best of all, when he surprises a sleeping blond in her room, she first says, "Stop!" in a censorious way until she sees that he's Cary Grant and then she says, "Stop" again, wistfully, as he wags a friendly finger at her. A moment like this expresses his screen character and what it meant to a whole generation better than just about anything else.

Dodging the issue of sex in his films started to seem grotesque around the time of *That Touch of Mink* (1962), where he tries to seduce Doris Day, seemingly a virgin at age 38. Talk about unreleased sexuality! Grant did one more diverting imitation-Hitchcock movie, *Charade* (1963), where he is very camp in a scene where he takes a shower with his suit on, before retiring from the screen in 1966, the year that movie censorship was being phased out and a return to sexual frankness was imminent.

He had 20 more years to go, and he spent them in his own way, doing as he liked, staying unshaven and in his pajamas if he wanted to. A big fan of Blaxploitation star Pam Grier, he would never miss one of her movies in the 1970s: "We must not be late for Miss Grier," he would say. He was not a contented or easy person, and he caused much strain and unhappiness for many of the people in his life, but they mainly seem to have forgiven him for that.

It was often said that stars of his time played themselves, or that they were "always the same," but that sameness was part of their accumulating character. Roger O. Thornhill is very different from David Huxley, just as Johnny Case couldn't be further away from C.K. Dexter Haven, but Grant was himself and the same, in a way, as all four of these different people, shifting constantly to evade detection, just as his singular Walter Burns gets himself out of any scrape and laughs as he does so. That's one way to do classic Hollywood screen acting. Just keep moving.

Very old and more than a bit senile, Katharine Hepburn was queried about Cary Grant, who had been dead for several years. She asked, "How's he doing?" I can't quite believe he's dead either, and that's because he isn't. He is still there, alive, in black and white or color (but oh, Grant in black and white), more sheer, dependable, life-embracing fun than any other film actor, because "fun" was the fantasy that could make up for the reality if you let it.

Charles Laughton
Leaning and Birthing

In the 1930s especially, Charles Laughton was known as a major actor, a difficult, unsparing performer who would not blush if you called him an artist. He compared his acting process to giving birth. To him, giving a performance was agony, and he often inflicted that agony on his less committed, more "professional" colleagues.

Laughton was homosexual, and tormented by that, and he funneled that torment, along with much else, into his creative process. He was a Method actor before his time, in a way, but also singular and of his moment. Unlike Cagney and Grant, he was a character actor from the English theater, and he was at his best when he could play as far away from himself as possible. Unlike the later performers from the Actors Studio from Brando onwards, he was not interested in the psychology or the why of a character, the motivation, the answer to behavior. He was interested, to an obsessive degree, in the behavior itself and what it might reveal about human nature.

There are certain hallmarks of a Laughton performance, but no circumscribed Laughton persona as such. He did the kind of acting that is usually not friendly to or conducive for the camera. It was part of his rare inner intensity, and seriousness, that he managed to get away with it. And maybe it was because he was laboring towards the essence of his characters rather than just their physical and vocal differences that his work began to seduce the camera, and the audience. It took great will, and great expressiveness, to get away with such blatantly conscious performances on screen. His aim was to show people what they were, in all its variety and beauty and ugliness, though the ugliness begins to predominate by the mid–1930s.

His work in films like *The Old Dark House, The Sign of the Cross, Island of Lost Souls* (all 1932), *The Private Life of Henry VIII* (1933), *The Barretts of Wimpole Street* (1934), *Ruggles of Red Gap, Les Misérables, Mutiny on the Bounty* (all 1935) and *Rembrandt* (1936) represents a still largely unparalleled stream of actor creativity, capped in 1939 by his greatest achievement as a performer, his portrayal of Quasimodo in *The Hunchback of Notre Dame*

(1939). After that final statement on human suffering, Laughton pulled back in the 1940s and began to coast. His full creative energies remained dormant until 1955, when he directed his only film, *The Night of the Hunter*. It failed financially, and Laughton did not direct again. He died in 1962, which is a shame. Imagine his delight if he could have experienced the loosening of sexual mores in the late 1960s. Imagine Laughton confronted with the screen presence of Joe Dallesandro.

The sensitive son of hoteliers, Laughton served a year in World War I at the age of 18. He killed some young German boys with a bayonet and got gassed, which caused health problems in later life. Laughton did promising work on stage and some short, experimental films before coming out to Hollywood in 1932. He is a slow, fastidious, imperious diner in his first feature from 1929, *Piccadilly,* where he is already demonstrating his conception of his character in his own somewhat laborious way. His style can look exceedingly odd or mistaken sometimes, even in his famous early movies, but there is no doubt that he is making an epic effort to raise the art of acting to new heights.

He was introduced in his first Hollywood movie, *Devil and the Deep* (1932), as "the eminent English character actor," as if the film wanted to alert audiences to pay attention to an Important (and Imported) British Thespian from the theater. In the big, gloating, portentous performance he gives as a psychotically jealous husband to Tallulah Bankhead, Laughton seems to be signaling that he is above this material but he is going to give you a fair measure of his talent anyway. The results are very weird, with all kinds of displays of self-pity and sadism and non-naturalistic instincts clanging discordantly together. But just try to look away from him.

Always there is a pure femininity in his manner that he alternately tries to hide and then blatantly flaunts, and there has never been anything quite like it on screen, either before or since. He obviously wanted to look like Gary Cooper and Cary Grant, the two leading men trying to save Bankhead in *Devil and the Deep*, and he also hated them, and he also secretly wanted to be ravished by them himself. "It must be a happy thing to look like you do," he tells Cooper, his hand kneading his own homely face. "I suppose women love you." His character hates himself so much that he wants to make his wife hate him, too, to prove his lack of worth.

Laughton was a character actor but a star character actor, and so his star parts were partly about his misery over not being a leading man, which in his hands seems like a vast cosmic and existential meditation on fate. Even those who dislike Laughton's early work must admit that it is fearsomely original, something rare, and still something new.

He had a reverence for sex, and a fear, too. When he calls Bankhead a "woman who cannot restrain herself" sexually in *Devil in the Deep*, the daring of his work is that he reveals the full longing for such a state underneath the repression and condemnation of it in a so-called "respectable" person. That type of repression doesn't exist much anymore, which is why it could be said that Laughton's major concerns as an artist have dated, and that could be so, but the expression of those concerns has not. There is an immense spirit behind his work that he unleashes in crucial moments. He lets it all hang out, and he has the emotional expressiveness and largeness of soul to get away with the biggest of choices.

Laughton is the fat misfit boy at school that everyone (even nice people) wanted to kick, mixed with a large slice of voluptuous, look-at-me female sexuality, and then sometimes this very tense Village Idiot thing emerges in his face when his eyes widen with innocent, blank neediness. It's a strange brew, but often an intoxicating one. He had very sexy lips stuck in the middle of his formless, fleshy face, and this was a further clue to his nature.

Even though his oft-expressed agony of creation in rehearsal often shows up on the screen, so does an enjoyment of acting for its own sake, mainly when his characters are doing very, very bad things. His vocal delivery could be John Barrymore–purple and of the theater of his time (this is what the impressionists imitated when they did his Captain Bligh from *Mutiny on the Bounty*), but it could also be very hushed and precise. It was as if he were licking his chops over his roles like they were meals to be consumed, and he didn't care if, as often happened, all that food made him sick.

He was larger-than-life as a laughing Yorkshire capitalist bringing a bit of albeit stagy and relative realism to James Whale's satirical *The Old Dark House*. In spite of, or perhaps because of, limited footage, he steals Cecil B. DeMille's *The Sign*

Charles Laughton's Nero, flanked by nude male slave George Bruggeman, in *The Sign of the Cross*.

of the Cross as an outright queeny Nero, an aesthete with a nude male slave by his side, a "monstrous perverse baby," as his biographer Simon Callow calls him, absurd but also truly odious, absolutely corrupted by absolute power. He repeated his stage success in *Payment Deferred* (1932), but the short takes of that movie tangibly upset the through-line of his work, and the result was a fragmented, incoherent performance.

He then made an atmospheric horror movie, *Island of Lost Souls*, where he was simultaneously campy and ominous. Laughton is never an easy screen presence. He puts all of his work up front and asks you to look at all of his strenuous choices, and in this way, he is much like a modern rhetorical character performer like Meryl Streep. Wearing a devilishly weird goatee and cracking a whip as he presides over his island of man-animal hybrids, Laughton is capable of playful behavior, as when he suddenly stretches himself out full length and lets his feet stick forward in a ridiculous position, or when he dissolves into naughty schoolboy grins as he contemplates his own daring and evil. At moments like these he is less like Streep and more like pure hambone Geraldine Page.

This initial colorful but minor work was just a warm-up for his star-making, bawdy performance in *The Private Life of Henry VIII*, which won him a richly deserved Academy Award for Best Actor. Lusty, authoritative, hedonistic, and just slightly vulnerable, Laughton's player card Henry is triumphantly heterosexual, a great gay actor stretching his imagination to the point of limitlessly hungry lady killing. His bearded face is somehow sharper, more defined, more confident, as if Laughton has willed it into being so, and being what you're not is part of the freeing fun of acting.

Laughton banishes all his "I'm ugly" self-pity, which mars a lot of his work, and makes his own fleshiness seem exuberantly sexy, so that you can see why the ladies are waiting to get into bed with him in spite of the risks involved. When his Henry laughs, he *laughs*, all out, mouth open and head thrown back and the sound coming and coming out of him. What had seemed pitiful and out of place laughter in his jealous husband in *Devil and the Deep* seems only right and just in a King, his laughter shooting out like staccato gunfire on all the masses he surveys. Like Streep at her spooky best, Laughton disappears and only Henry is there in his place.

When told his third wife has died in childbirth, Laughton's Henry takes a moment to genuinely mourn her but then moves right on in his ruthless and extra-human way. Laughton reserves his own softness for moments like that and then caps them with his imaginative grasp of this man's entitled lordliness. What is unclear, oddly enough for such a demonstrative actor, is whether Laughton is in sympathy with his King's attitude or not. He seems uncharacteristically neutral about that, which is perhaps what allowed him to have such a hit in the role. This is the rare major early Laughton performance with nothing truly nagging, uncomfortable or disturbing in it, and so of course it was his most popular.

In the famous eating scene, he burps and slurps and tears a capon apart with his bare hands. "All sauce and no substance!" he cries, chewing the meat with undisguised, enormous appetite and childishly tossing the bones away when he's done with them. "No delicacy nowadays, no consideration for others!" he announces as he bites and chews and violently tucks in to the fowl. "Refinement's a thing of the past! Manners are dead!" It's an easy joke, but Laughton makes it seem like the King is performing and enjoying his own easy joke with his court, making them enjoy how he takes such huge pleasure in it.

As the King declines, Laughton shows us the fading machismo gracefully, without underlining or judging it. When told his beloved fifth wife is cheating on him, his grief is an event, a slow-burning slide down to the opposite of his youthful laughter. In the last five minutes of the movie, he uncannily turns himself into a babyish and ill old man, licking what's left of the icing of life. This is an evergreen movie and performance, always there, always fresh.

Laughton was Horace Prin, a horny walrus type (he even has a walrus mustache) with a lust for shady lady Carole Lombard in the absurd and trifling *White Woman* (1933), where he puts together a deep, nasty, and original piece of work out of next to nothing, creating a villain who is insinuating, mysterious, and insidious, a horrible flypaper of a man. Even Cagney and Grant often stand or fall on their material and their director, but this was not true of Laughton in the 1930s. He is able to transform anything to his needs (and if *White Woman* isn't an "anything" item then nothing is), because he is far more solitary than they are. He doesn't really react or respond to the other actors as Cagney and Grant do. Laughton is above and apart from his fellow players, and this frees him but also limits him at times.

A Laughton performance is always partially a one-man show. A novelist creates a novel in a room, a painter in a studio, and Laughton creates his characters in the same isolated way, which was and still is very unusual when it comes to acting. But it is what he needed. This is also why he did some of his finest work in bad movies, and why he did not need a major director to thrive. Each performance he gave in this period was the result of long thought, research, and preparation. They are marinated with his study of human peculiarity and contradiction. Laughton would search and search for what he felt was "the key" to the man, and it could be anything: a painting, a piece of music. He was very difficult to work with until he found it, and then he might still need another key or two as he went forward with his creation.

He next gave three performances based around the idea that repression, sexual and otherwise, can lead to tyrannical behavior. The first and least of these was his incestuous religious fanatic in *The Barretts of Wimpole Street*, where he seems too young to be Norma Shearer's mutton-chopped father, and where he seems curiously unengaged by the villainous part he is playing. But it's not quite that. It's as if he's *gloating* over his lack of engagement, over his clammy stiffness, or something even more private and self-indulgent that does not express much of anything for the camera. In this performance, Laughton does anticipate the worst excesses of the 1950s-60s Actors Studio.

He was a blubbery-lipped, demented Javert in *Les Misérables* (1935), a man for whom the law is his whole life because it gives him some structure, without which he would fall directly into an abyss we can see all too clearly in his inward-looking eyes. His Javert wears his hair close cropped in wannabe jock fashion, and he struggles, often successfully, to make his face the very picture of anonymous conformity (quite a physical transformation for Laughton).

The originality of his work here comes from his emphasis on Javert's bottomless insecurity, from which all his behavior flows. The character seems to be torn out of him at intervals in massive, blunt, birthing heaves, and the result is amazing, unsettling. Laughton's conception of Javert is so vast and complete yet so volatile that it has the stamp of unruly life as few film performances do. Why do people become fanatics like Laughton's Javert? Because, as he shows you, they are scared to death of the alternative.

And then he was another martinet, the corrupt, ugly Captain Bligh, in *Mutiny on the Bounty*, threatening Mr. Christian (Clark Gable) and his mutineers that he would see them hanging "from the highest yard arm of the British fleet!" (a favorite line for Laughton impressionists, of which there were nearly as many as for Cagney and Grant). Gable was very annoyed that Laughton wouldn't look at him directly in their scenes together, giving him no chance to react.

In between these tyrants he fitted a comedy for Leo McCarey, *Ruggles of Red Gap*, where he played an English butler who gets won in a card game and sent to the American west. He gives a very weird performance in that, with habitual fidgets of mild panic and eye widenings until they are crossed, the Village Idiot taking over, except this time this Village Idiot seems to be female in character.

"Flamboyant" was a word often used to describe Laughton's performances, and this was often code for overtly or tacitly gay. His Ruggles is miscalculated work, as if he wants to be deadpan but can't help doing all kinds of superfluous business with his darting eyes. Very funny in *Island of Lost Souls* and as Henry VIII, in an outright comedy he is heavy-going, too emotional, which only suits his hushed recitation of the Gettysburg Address to a bar full of impressed cowboys.

Laughton brings another bar to a standstill when he talks romantically about women in *Rembrandt*, where he labored to find a new simplicity. Laborious simplicity is an odd thing to behold, but Laughton always had to take the long and rough way home. In this movie there is a kind of willing or even religious self-effacement in his work, as if he wanted to make his face stand in for everyone.

His imagination then crashed on the rocks of an unfinished project for Josef von Sternberg, *I, Claudius*. Sternberg carped in his memoirs, "Apparently he was attempting to imbue his characterizations with meanings that an actor should not attempt to express, intent on soaring into a rarefied air where he could pass Dali, Picasso, Kandinsky, and Chagall in full flight."

The surviving footage shows Laughton struggling to maintain a stutter *and* a limp, and it preserves his frustration, his doubts, his sense of failure in reaching as far as he wanted to. The struggle of the character is replaced by the struggle of the actor over-intellectualizing and struggling with that struggle, his imagination blocked, his talent expressing itself only in disordered fragments.

He had arrived at a crisis point in his work, and so he retreated for a bit, producing and also acting in three minor films in England, including a poor movie with Alfred Hitchcock, *Jamaica Inn* (1939). Like Sternberg, Hitchcock was nonplussed by Laughton's demands and need for control. "You can't direct a Laughton picture," he said. "The best you can hope for is to referee."

But he had one more major early performance in him, his Quasimodo in *The Hunchback of Notre Dame*. In the scene where Quasimodo is tied and beaten in the town square, Laughton reaches an effect of pure suffering agony that no other human actor has shown us on screen. The closest to what he achieved as Quasimodo is in the non-human reactions of the donkey in certain scenes of Robert Bresson's *Au Hasard Balthazar* (1966).

Laughton tore himself to shreds to get what he wanted here, and this was the last time he was willing to do that. In watching his Quasimodo, it is clear when he is showing us the character and very clear when he is superimposing his own feelings about himself onto him. That mixture is rich and upsetting and maybe even too much, sometimes. It makes an enormous mess that cannot be cleaned up or ordered or used by anyone. And it risks, as later mid-twentieth-century acting would do, being self-indulgent not for our sake but for the sake of the performer's truth only.

He had gone as far as he had wanted to go. The dynamic pressure that had made even his most undemanding 1930s roles so vital was gone now. Laughton gave up the agony of creation for steady work to "pay for ice for Father's piles," as he colorfully put it. He did a lot of movies in the 1940s, only one of which, Jean Renoir's *This Land Is Mine* (1943), contains some first-rate Laughton work based in cowardice and fear and fear of cowardice.

He makes some extremely unflattering physical choices in that Renoir movie; smoking a cigarette for the first time, his head nearly explodes (it should be funny, but it isn't). When Nazis come in to arrest him, he hurls his coffee cup down and the coffee itself dribbles disgustingly out of his mouth. They are memorable, striking choices, but distinctly unappetizing—even willfully grotesque.

In the last scene in court in *This Land Is Mine*, he talks and talks and talks, and then talks some more in his defense, in that soft, professor-like, didactic voice with which he was wont to deliver sections of the Bible and the Gettysburg Address on his reading tours (by the 1950s, when he appeared on the *Ed Sullivan Show*, he comically read out a national insurance form just as he read the Bible, with the same interminable, "this is good for you" good taste).

In *They Knew What They Wanted* (1940), based on a solid play by Sidney Howard and co-starring Carole Lombard, he is very far from the termite inventiveness of his Horace Prin in *White Woman* with the same actress. Basically uninspired, he does a Beeg Eye-Talian caricature, breezy and diverting but hardly human or touching. Even (or especially) humiliation was beyond him now, as in his segment of *Tales of Manhattan* (1942) where he plays a novice conductor laughed at by a huge audience when his jacket starts to come apart. Laughton simply mimes and indicates the man's distress.

Otherwise, he uncomplainingly worked twice with Deanna Durbin, played Captain Kidd, played Captain Kidd meeting Abbott and Costello, did another ill-conceived ogre for Hitchcock in *The Paradine Case* (1947), did a pale copy of his Henry VIII in *Young Bess* and a paler copy of his Nero as Herod in *Salome* (both 1953), and spent much time working with Bertolt Brecht on Brecht's play *Galileo*. When Brecht asked Laughton why he acted, or had acted, Laughton replied, "Because people don't know what they're like and I think I can show them."

But when he does try for some sort of characterization past 1940, 90 percent of the time the breath of life has left his work, to be replaced only by external mannerisms, which he cannot seem to quiet down. There is some mystery, sometimes, as to just *what* he is doing, and what he thinks he's doing, and what we are seeing, but that mystery came now from imprecision and eccentric, even trite choices and not creative wrestling and striving.

"When Laughton was sitting quietly in a chair, not speaking, he was doing too much," observed Peter Ustinov. It's a mistake that bad or amateur actors make, the gravest sin of all: reacting too much to something for no reason. And Laughton fell helplessly into it because he had never truly reacted at all. When he turned off all the lights, as he does in *The Suspect* (1944), some acclaimed his work as "subtle" when there is actually very little going on beneath the dutiful surface.

To keep working, he made himself seem harmless, genial, an "old ham" in early middle age. He gave big, obvious, crowd-pleasing performances in David Lean's *Hobson's Choice* (1954) and Billy Wilder's *Witness for the Prosecution* (1957) while a large group of younger actors and actresses were following his Method lead, on film and on stage. But he also turned to teaching some of those young Method actors, he did more dramatic readings, and he directed *The Night of the Hunter* in the mid-1950s, showing once and for all that he didn't need a great director to do great acting work because he had the instincts of a great director himself.

In a short interview on the essential Criterion Blu-ray DVD of *The Night of the Hunter*, Simon Callow, who wrote an extremely insightful critical biography of Laughton in 1987, marvels that the young actors he works with now don't know anything about Laughton as a performer, but they've all at least heard of *The Night of the Hunter*, and even those who haven't seen it might have seen at least a still photo of the words LOVE and HATE tattooed on Robert Mitchum's knuckles.

The Night of the Hunter is a movie made up entirely of poetic, uncanny moments, and it owes a large debt to James Agee, who wrote a lengthy screenplay out of Davis Grubb's source material, and to Stanley Cortez, that painter of light who had also photographed Orson Welles's *The Magnificent Ambersons* (1942), another movie stuffed with what can only be called uncanny tableaux and bits of behavior.

Confronted with a film as perfect and unsettling as *The Night of the Hunter*, it's natural to wonder just how it was created, and particularly what Laughton's contribution was. On the second disc of the Criterion Blu-ray is a revelatory feature called "Charles Laughton Directs," which collects more than two and a half hours of outtakes kept by Laughton's wife, Elsa Lanchester. This feature is a cardinal lesson in the patience it takes to give birth to a movie as fine as *Night*.

It's long been legend that Laughton couldn't stand the two kids at the center of *Night*, Billy Chapin and Sally Jane Bruce, and that star Robert Mitchum had to direct them himself, but these outtakes should put that story to rest once and for all. We never see much of Laughton in the outtakes, but we hear his gentle, drawling yet very commanding voice talking to his actors. He worked rather like a silent film director, keeping the camera running and attaining total control of his vision by speaking to his players in an incantatory way.

Chapin was a little pro who could rattle off his credits as an actor like a wind-up doll, and Laughton is impatient and cranky with the boy if he feels that Chapin isn't really listening to him. When Chapin has to feel a pain in the pit of his stomach as his on-screen father is captured by policemen, Laughton crouches off-camera and gives the boy light jabs to create just the right feeling of panic.

Shelley Winters gives a remarkably restrained, feeling performance in *Night* as Willa Harper, a vulnerable woman taken in by Mitchum's preacher, Harry Powell, and in the outtakes presented in "Charles Laughton Directs," it's clear that Laughton had to shape her work line by line and even word by word. In the scene where Willa addresses a religious revival meeting, Winters at first goes wildly over the top both vocally and visually, bugging her eyes and shouting at the top of her lungs, and Laughton stays with her until she has toned down this initial largeness into the scared, sensitive, smaller-scaled work that wound up in the finished film.

As a great actor himself, and one who took great pains with his own acting long before it was fashionable, Laughton was ideally suited to deal with a difficult-to-control Method actress like Winters. As Willa lies in bed, sensing the inevitability of her own murder by Powell, Laughton has Winters read a single line over and over again until it has exactly the right dream-like quality. Working with Lillian Gish in the second half of the film, Laughton has a much easier time of it. Gish offers him take after take with different readings and small adjustments, all of them good, all of them intelligent, and all of them usable. She's a dream actress for Laughton, ideal for the certainty of the film's Rachel Cooper, as ideal as Winters is for the lost Willa.

As a great actor who directed a great film, Laughton has few if any peers in this time. Gish herself directed a film, *Remodeling Her Husband* (1920), a vehicle for her sister, Dorothy, but it hasn't survived, and of course Chaplin directed himself for most of his life and career, but he is a special case. Ida Lupino directed some good second features that can't really compete with her own best work as an actress. James Cagney directed one unexceptional film, *Short Cut to Hell* (1957), and John Wayne's reputation is never going to rest on his direction of *The Alamo* (1960) or *The Green Berets* (1968). Surely

Laurence Olivier directed his films as occasions for his own acting, whatever the visual and conceptual merits of his two most famous efforts, *Henry V* (1944) and *Hamlet* (1948).

Marlon Brando and Peter Lorre are certainly on Laughton's high level as actors, and they both directed one film each. Lorre returned to Germany after World War II and directed and starred in *Der Verlorene* (1951), a grim, little-seen movie that has its problems but also many virtues, and the same can be said for Brando's *One-Eyed Jacks* (1961), which is notable for one of the most vicious beatings Brando ever endured on screen. In both cases, the presence of these actors at the center of the movies they're directing has a blurring effect, as if they can't focus on two things at the same time.

Laughton had wanted to play Harry Powell himself, but he was advised that the film wouldn't be bankable with only his name above the title, and so he chose Mitchum, who gave the performance of his life as the omnipresent preacher. In the *Night* outtakes, Mitchum is quite clear-cut in what he's attempting, and when he shakes himself out of the character he feels the need to laugh a bit, but his laughter isn't stemming from the famed mockery that he poured on his own profession in interviews. Instead, it looks like Mitchum's scared at how far out on a limb he's going for Laughton.

During filming, as they drove along a freeway, Laughton told Mitchum, "I don't know if you know, and I don't know if you care, and I don't care if you know, but there is a strong streak of homosexuality in me," to which Mitchum replied, "No shit!" and then "Stop the car!" to Laughton's torturously worded admission. This was a well-worn routine for Laughton, and Mitchum's joking reaction put Laughton finally at ease, a precious moment of understanding between two very different people. That's what art can be, too. Laughton liked to act as mentor to all of the performers in his orbit, and in Mitchum he found an unlikely conduit for his own dreams of bad but seductive fatherhood and diseased sexuality.

The Night of the Hunter is probably the most inspired one-off in movie history, and it stands alone as a piece of work that matches and even surpasses the acting career that first made Laughton's name as an artist. *The Night of the Hunter* could only have been made by a great actor because it partakes of the same sharp, insistent clinging to emotional truth and personal experience that the best performers fiercely guard against all outside, crass, commercial intrusion. It plays like a dream of escape, and it knows what prisons are. It is childlike and open-ended, a vision of grace transcending humiliation and fear. It shares both the bravery of the best acting and the coherence of vision of the best direction.

There was a noticeable and cheering spike in Laughton's acting work at the tail end of his life, which might partly have been due to a new freedom in his personal life. He had found a lover named Terry Jenkins who made him very happy, which Laughton's long-time wife Elsa Lanchester grudgingly accepted. Perhaps to impress Jenkins, or perhaps because new feelings had been released, he did lovely work as the wily old Roman senator Gracchus in *Spartacus* (1960), a little monument of worldliness and gratified sensuality and life-enhancing malice, like a ham cooked just to perfection in all of its juices (Laughton might also have been spurred by competition in scenes with one of his few acting peers, Laurence Olivier). He played King Lear at Stratford, doing a kind of demonstration of a role that had obsessed him his whole life, playing it small and then acting Lear's movement towards death "on a rising graph" instead of the usual descent downhill.

He is wonderful in an episode of a TV show called *Checkmate* from 1961 as an invigoratingly energetic old missionary filled with schoolboy enthusiasm for Chinese culture. You barely hear the words he says here because his conception of the character is so clear as to be blinding. It is pure behavior and spirit, as if he is working from a model, someone he knew who was dear to him. Most impressively, it is all a cunning mask, for the man he is playing is actually a malignant would-be killer, and the malignancy oozes out of his eyes when he is unmasked. Dazzling stuff.

Also dazzling was his final film performance as Senator Seab Cooley in Otto Preminger's *Advise & Consent* (1962), a conservative Southerner fighting the nomination of a liberal candidate (Henry Fonda). Laughton has fun with his accent (pronouncing "rendezvous" as "randy-voo") and with Seab's "benign" physicality. He sits there in the Senate and says he is just like "an old bullfrog sunnin' myself on a lily pad," as if he is just a human consciousness hanging on by a thread, but his "oldness" is a tactic, for he is really a snake ready to strike when he feels his moment come.

A dirty old man, a lover of ladies and moonshine, Seab shares some attributes with Laughton's Gracchus, but this is a more expansive and revealing performance. Laughton makes sure to show us that Seab cares surprisingly deeply what people think of him by letting us see his semi-guarded reaction to both applause for himself and applause for his opponents. This was a man and an artist who knew a lot about such vanity, and not many actors would want to show it, but Laughton in this brief Prospero phase will do so easily and even serenely, with no more cares and youthful worries about himself.

His work in *Spartacus* is cut up into pleasing moments, whereas Preminger lets Laughton build his character in long takes with minimal intervention. Laughton had lived just long enough to see a closeted gay character, Brig (Don Murray), dealt with dramatically on screen. Preminger moves his camera in on Laughton's face after Seab hears that Brig has killed himself, and Laughton shuts his eyes and allows all of his pain to blast down inside of himself, internally.

His was a checkered, difficult career as a screen actor because it had to be. The disturbances of his early work petered out in exhaustion, and pedestrian, oddball journeyman work took its place for a time, but his artistic quest ended on a note of grace, understanding, Buddha-like reflection, and quiet in the midst of the noisier forms of psychological Method acting that he had presaged.

Clark Gable
The King

"You know, this 'king' stuff is pure bullshit," said Clark Gable to an interviewer late in life, as the lights were coming down on old Hollywood. "I'm just a lucky slob from Ohio. I happened to be in the right place at the right time and I had a lot of smart guys helping me—that's all." But for a generation at the movies, he was the top of the heap, and no luck about it.

Up until 1940, at least, Gable smiled and his eyes squinted and he talked in "that wonderful crumbly voice," as his *Red Dust* (1932) co-star Mary Astor put it in her memoirs, and he made everybody feel better. Confident. Yes, his ears stuck out a mile, and why not? Gable made them want to be his girl, or his friend. He's what the word "virile" meant to just about everybody, if you didn't look too close or think it over too long.

Gable was not a complicated screen presence, and that was his charm. His greatest charm, though, was looking at complicated women with intricate appreciation. On screen, Gable liked all kinds of women: girls next door, older women (he was married to two older women in life), chorus girls, brassy girls like Jean Harlow (with whom he made five films), sensible, ironic Myrna Loy (with whom he made six films), even pretentious types, or roaring phonies. In fact, he seemed to be most tickled of all by phony women, affected women, women putting on a show in order to hide something, which is why he first made his special impact with Norma Shearer (three films with her) and he had a rapport at first, both off and on screen, with Joan Crawford (a full eight films with her).

Women on screen were like a show for Gable, and he watched them with a twinkle in his eye, even if he sometimes had to look askance at their antics. You didn't need to worry when he was in a movie, or watch out for anything, or gird yourself for a surprise. With Gable, you just get to sit back and sigh with pleasure. Joan Blondell told an interviewer:

> He was always a fine old teddy bear. He was a man that guys loved, women loved, and children loved. Somehow, he just made people grin ... he was able to see himself objectively, and he always did it tongue-in-cheek. It kind of amused him when the girls'

knees would cave in around him. He was flattered, of course, but mostly he was gentle and tender about it, and amused. It was like he was sitting aside, looking at someone else being worshipped by the pretty little girls.

His father tried to make an oil man out of him, but Gable disliked the hours and the strain of that work, much preferring the world of the theater instead. He didn't get much to eat on the road, and his teeth were bad, so that he later had to have most of them pulled (he would sometimes take out his dentures for a laugh on set). His first wife, Josephine Dillon, who was 14 years older than he was, taught him how to behave and was in essence his drama coach. He worked as an extra in films during the 1920s, waiting out the day of Valentino and John Gilbert.

On the New York stage, he caused a stir as the lover in Sophie Treadwell's play *Machinal* in 1928. He married again to an older woman, Ria Langham, who added polish and clothes-consciousness to his persona. Langham arranged for Gable to play *The Last Mile* on stage in Los Angeles, which got the attention of movie people. They needed actors who could talk, and Gable could certainly do that.

He was cast as an unshaven, snarly villain in a western, *The Painted Desert* (1931), because his simian look got him pegged as a heavy in his early days. He was in 12 released movies that first year, and by the end of it, he was a star, a sensation. His voice had a force and a harshness that made the same impact that Gilbert and Valentino once did with their eyes. Playing for the first time with Crawford as a gangster in *Dance, Fools, Dance* (1931), he stirred her so deeply that her knees buckled. "If he hadn't held me by both shoulders, I'd have dropped," she said. He lunges at her roughly in that movie, awkwardly, as if he can't spare time on niceties.

He was miscast as a Salvation Army man with Crawford in *Laughing Sinners* (1931) and played a few more gangsters. They tried to pin his ears back for *A Free Soul* (1931), but after a few days he let them spring back out: take him or leave him. That was the movie that really made him, a picture where Norma Shearer throws over wimpy Leslie Howard for Gable's primal brand of sex. He pushes her down on a couch not once but twice: "Ah sit down and take it and like it!" he snarls after the second time. There hadn't been a man who thrilled female audiences like this since Valentino, and this response came from the same source, the desire for a dominating male. If you look closely at Gable in this first year of movie work, it is possible to see his gaucheness, his nervousness, behind his simian Mr. Hyde look. He plays everything all on one bluff, hearty level because any other emotion scares him. Gable never thought of himself as an actor.

"I'm Nick, the chauffeur!" he growls at Barbara Stanwyck in *Night Nurse*

(1931) before punching her out and then getting his. A loan-out to Warners, *Night Nurse* was the darkest and nastiest he ever allowed himself to be in a movie. He scared Greta Garbo in *Susan Lenox: Her Fall and Rise* (1932), like a big Great Dane trying to curl up with a skittish deer, but he's far more good-natured in his first scenes here, offering glimpses of the Gable to come. He went back to initial form in *Possessed* (1931) with Crawford. "Only when the script calls for a snarl or for him to slap Miss Crawford in the face, to call her a 'little tramp' and to tell her to scram, did anything register on the Gable horizon," wrote *Variety*.

His initial impact might not have lasted if he hadn't met up with Jean Harlow for *Red Dust* (1932), the first really classic Gable-type part, where he added the key missing ingredient to his persona: humor. That humor, that air of enjoying himself, would shoot him right to the top and keep him there, and in Harlow he found his best partner, someone who didn't mind being crude and funny, unlike drama queens like Shearer and Crawford.

He pushes his own blustery virility a lot in a very conscious way in *Red Dust* that would seem unnecessary to Cagney or even Bogart. To modern eyes that pushing makes him seem a little insecure, but that was not noticed in his heyday. He was all at sea with Shearer in the Eugene O'Neill adaptation *Strange Interlude* (1932), and his subsequent pairings with Crawford were never quite comfortable, but with Harlow, and with Myrna Loy, he could relax and be silly if he wanted to. That silliness could shade into beefy, grinning fatuousness in some of his lesser movies, but audiences didn't mind.

Gable had found the secret to selling movie fantasy: acknowledging the pleasure he got out of it himself. That was all he needed, for a time. He worked with Carole Lombard in *No Man of Her Own* (1932), striking sexual sparks with her, and towards the end of the decade he married her. He tried his best to support Helen Hayes in *The White Sister* (1933) but was far happier mixing it up with Harlow again in *Hold Your Man* (1933), where he is nearly radioactive with his own sexy star assurance, like a big, friendly dog who wants to jump all over you. In *Dancing Lady* (1933), a large-scale confection for Joan Crawford, Gable is just along for the ride, for MGM was a woman's studio. The men there were expected to partner the women, either in a backstage musical or in Eugene O'Neill drama, it didn't matter much which.

And so he had to go to Columbia to star in the inaugural screwball romantic comedy, *It Happened One Night* (1934) for Frank Capra. "Make way for the King," joked his newsman buddies after Gable has pretended to tell off a newspaper editor who hung up on him. He wore a mustache now, a key final element for him visually, and he seemed far more comfortable, loved, and secure. Another key change here was that he played a wise ass man of the people who fought with his wits before resorting to his fists, and it was that adjustment that endeared him to just about everybody. In his goofing around with Claudette Colbert in *It Happened One Night*, there was double the humor of even his Harlow outings, and this humor added a touch of romance to him. Sex became something tacit, part of the game that might commence once the movie ended. When Gable smiled now, his dimples promised lively banter as well as sex.

Gable had improved a lot as a performer by the time of *It Happened One Night* compared to his 12 films of 1931. He is far more relaxed here, even gentle-eyed sometimes. The forcefulness is still there, but he doesn't need to brandish it crudely. It's just something he has, in reserve, and this is part of what makes him so immensely likable. "Your ego is absolutely colossal," says snooty heiress Colbert, to which he happily replies, "Yeah, not bad, how's yours?" He got her down off her high horse and then some, teaching her how to enjoy the simple things in life, like dunking donuts in coffee. The fantasy here still works, is still appealing. It probably always will be.

In the scene where Gable has to menace the meddling Shapeley (Roscoe Karns) in order to shut him up, part of the fun is that Gable is using his old menacing persona from 1931, but it is just one arrow in his quiver now. And he's sending it up. Watch the way Capra has him toughly spit after Shapeley and how the spit lands on his own shoulder.

Gable and Colbert set a screwball standard when they pretend to be a brawling young married couple in order to elude detection from her rich father's minions. They laugh at how elastic their personalities are, and Gable suggests that they should put on shows together. When she suggests *Cinderella*, he says, "Ah, that's too mushy," and she says, "I like mushy." They're just throwaway lines, rarely commented on, but they define what Gable meant in the movies.

A portrait of Clark Gable, king of all he surveyed as long as he kept his humor.

It was true, he basically didn't enjoy acting out romance, which is why he grew increasingly leery of Crawford, on screen and in life, though he did enjoy looking at and laughing at women, being entertained by them. In real life, he preferred to go hunting and fishing, and Lombard was happy to go with him, which is what made them such an ideal couple, for a time. At the end of *It Happened One Night*, he tells Colbert's father that she needs a guy who "will take a sock at her every day whether she has it coming to her or not." There aren't many excuses for a line like that anymore, though it comes out of the hurt feelings of his character at that point in the story.

He won the Oscar for *It Happened One Night*, and MGM rolled out the vehicles for him for the rest of the 1930s. He still had to squire Crawford through her paces, not to mention a tired-out Marion Davies, but he also got to be a naval man pitted against Charles Laughton in *Mutiny on the Bounty* (1935). He was holed up for a while on location with Loretta Young shooting *The Call of the Wild* (1935), and when she returned after a reported illness she brought with her a supposedly adopted baby girl, but the baby's big ears caused much comment as the years went by.

Gable tried to be a serious politician in *Parnell* (1937) and took a critical pasting for his hushed, tentative performance. No one wanted to see Gable looking unsure of himself or unconfident. He doubled down on his confidence for *Idiot's Delight* (1939), taking particular delight in doing a proudly dumb musical number with a chorus of girls behind him; he slams his feet decidedly on the floor and dares us not to call it dancing. Gable is naturally funny in that movie, which is all the more evident because his co-star Norma Shearer is trying so hard to be funny herself and never making it.

The height of his vogue, of course, was his Rhett Butler in *Gone with the Wind* (1939), in which all he had to do was look up at Vivien Leigh's Scarlett as if he knew what she looked like without her chemise and everybody but Scarlett herself would be excited. He pursued Scarlett for hours of screen time and even married her but never possessed her like he had all his other screen partners, and so he got fed up with all the game playing and finally carried her up the stairs of their house by force.

"You need kissing and often, and by someone who knows how," he tells her, and we know what "kissing" means. Again, if you look closely, you can see that Gable is just slightly impatient with Scarlett and Leigh, so that his mockery of her in certain scenes starts to seem more than a little contemptuous, but it could be said that that suits Rhett and his frustrations with Scarlett.

Finally, he told Scarlett he didn't give a damn, and that line and scene had the force in 1939 of the long-playing Frank Sinatra records of the 1950s, where male vulnerability to women was expressed in a soft, bendable way that Gable would have shrunk from. He has to cry in *GWTW* over his dead daughter, and he didn't want to do it (Gable Cries?), but if they wanted that mushy stuff, he'd make them take it and like it. He was a drinking man himself, and he knew that a drinking man falls into tears every now and again without being able to help it.

You can hardly move forward after *Gone with the Wind,* and Gable did not. When Lombard died in a place crash on her way home to him from a war bond rally, he was not consolable. He joined the army, and when he came back, he was still "Clark Gable" in voice and assumed attitude, but the man on the screen was not too happy to be there anymore, and his films were routine, especially his many pairings with Lana Turner.

He did a remake of *Red Dust* called *Mogambo* (1953) and still held his place opposite increasingly younger women, but he looked a little lost, distant. After 25 years and many millions made, Gable was not happy that MGM didn't give him so much as a farewell party when he left, and he made his last pictures resignedly. He lent his star power to Raoul Walsh's intriguing *Band of Angels* (1957) and then wound up with *The Misfits* (1961), opposite Marilyn Monroe, an unhappy movie in many ways where he was asked to play a long drunk scene and did it poorly. We didn't want him to act. We just wanted him to be sure of himself and transmit that pleasure to us. That was all, but that was still a helluva lot.

Spencer Tracy
Still Waters

Sometimes it's the unheralded programmers that reveal something about the major stars of the studio system. Take *Malaya* (1949), which is as minor as you can get, a quick thing about buying rubber somewhere and skullduggery and whatnot. James Stewart, who gets second billing, is responsible for handling the opening 20 minutes, and he does so in his familiar querulous fashion, with just a touch of darkness in the deeper set of his eyes post–World War II.

Stewart initially seems in charge of *Malaya*, in an absent-minded way, for he knows that this is just routine and not a special film. Or maybe it's because he knows Spencer Tracy is in the movie, and he's seen the rest of the script, and he knows things are hopeless for him. Whatever the situation, when Tracy comes on in his first scene and punches Stewart in the face as an opener, the movie springs to taut life in his presence. It's as if Tracy has flipped a switch, and he's "on," and when Spencer Tracy is on, anything might happen.

Where did Tracy get this authority? He is physically unprepossessing, a plain Irish potato of a man, and he had gotten awfully portly by 1950. James Curtis's exhaustive 2011 biography of Tracy traces a process whereby the actor's head got swelled by all the praise he received while he did, it seems, less and less to deserve such praise. And the book lays out in detail just what a precarious alcoholic Tracy was.

Tracy would go for years and not touch a drink, but if something set him off, he would have to buy cases of liquor and hole up in a hotel for weeks and not emerge until he was so broken down and sick with the stuff that he could go no further. Is *that* what the danger is in Tracy's performing style, that among other things? Tracy has that special, electric, soulful thing on screen that Stewart, for all his great skill and accomplishment in his finest movies, does not have.

He wipes the floor with Stewart in *Malaya*, taking scene after scene with flabbergasting ease, because he seems genuinely unpredictable and dangerous, and Stewart never did, no matter how much he pushed himself or let his own put-upon stubbornness be pushed. Not all parts or films need danger, of course. And Tracy was guilty in the second half of his career of just showing up and doing almost nothing because everyone said how great he was no matter what, so why bother? But when he bestirs himself, he is kin to Cagney in his overwhelming responsiveness.

If Tracy is listening to someone and decides to open his mouth and keep it open until they are done talking in order to hang on their every word, he doesn't care how silly this might look because he wants to be as fully "there" and present as possible. "I love your lies, because you believe in them," Valentina Cortese tells him in *Malaya*, and he just smiles at her, guarding his secrets.

When Tracy scratches himself, as he often does on screen, he "scratches," heightening the movement and making it seem like dance. He is not actually a naturalistic actor. Tracy is clearly conscious about every moment, shaping every gesture, sometimes lazily, but sometimes with such force that we seem to be watching something more than a man scratching or punching or walking across a room.

There are people in life who are heightened like that. That's why we watch them in a room and want them around for short periods to give us energy, but we need to beware of the point when they crash. Tracy is very pre–Method in that nothing he does ever seems private and he is always on stage. What happens to him in private is his affair. Based on what is revealed in Curtis's book, the private Tracy would need to be quickly turned away from, even shunned. No man got angry on screen quite the way that Tracy did, in that Irish devil way that had its roots in some blasted earth. In a rage on screen, he had to lay vindictive waste to everything in his path.

Like many other players of his time, he had a long apprenticeship on stage before signing up for talking pictures in 1930. He was trained by George M. Cohan, whom Cagney played so generously in *Yankee Doodle Dandy,* and scored big as a condemned prisoner in *The Last Mile* on Broadway. The author of that play, John Wexley, said of Tracy that "he was too much the 'actor'— effective, but playing to the audience a good deal of the time and to that extent, self-conscious." Wexley also called Tracy's playing "mannered." It would seem that he was already acting everything on a heightened plane, super-consciously. Cohan himself advised Tracy, "Whatever you do, kid, always serve it with a little dressing."

In his film debut for John Ford, a comic prison picture called *Up the River* (1930), Tracy played a convict with a distinctly contemptuous edge. He was typed as a low class, belligerent roughneck, in and out of the hoosegaw.

As a racketeer in Rowland Brown's oddly paced, cerebral *Quick Millions* (1931), Tracy serves up his part straight, with very little dressing. "It went out and grossed about a dollar and eighty cents," Tracy said of that picture, which was eighty-sixed by Cagney in *The Public Enemy*.

He was stuck on a treadmill at Fox studios until 1935 or so and made over 20 movies, many of which were so routine that he couldn't hide his restless discontent with them. If he had stopped making movies in 1935, Tracy might be remembered as an unusually obdurate and truculent leading man, harsh, often misogynistic, without charm or much relief. His chiselers of this era seem mean-minded and heavy-spirited, in marked contrast to the kaleidoscopic and joyful Cagney con men. But there were a handful of movies that hinted at what was to come.

It was Raoul Walsh who first brought out his essential qualities in *Me and My Gal* (1932), where Tracy is a cop sparring and wisecracking with hardboiled Joan Bennett. He is blunt here and rascally, and animated, just barely, by breezy Irish humor, though he is never really lighthearted on screen. On loan to Warners, he was a larger-than-life gangster with a liking for publicity acting too big for prison in *20,000 Years in Sing Sing* (1932), where he plays a slightly dimmer man than he usually did. Yet his performance is made up of strong, clear strokes and very legible choices.

There's something long-suffering but stoic and very male in Tracy's face and demeanor, with none of the feminine wildness or playfulness of Cagney or Grant. He was the salt of the earth, one of the people, but sorely lacking in ease or charm. Wiping his nose and scratching his hair are a kind of acting security blanket for him, an anchor for naturalism, or "naturalism." But then sometimes, when he is just sitting doing nothing and looking up, Tracy has a kind of moody grandeur that stops a film dead in its tracks.

He is at his best, even this early, when he is totally still and in the midst of some mysterious emotional upheaval, some resting spot of pure agony that somehow manages to look romantic on him, the same way that Eugene O'Neill has a blasted romantic look in his author photographs. Tracy was self-conscious about his looks, and that comes across particularly in his early Fox films, where he alternates between seeming obnoxiously confident with beautiful women and squirming in their company, as if he wants to re-arrange his own face or his body, which tended towards plumpness.

When asked to draw painful feelings out of himself, he does so methodically, digging into what looks like his own personal stock of guilt and torment. Unlike later Method actors, however, he always goes this route carefully, precisely, taking just the start of the emotion he needs and then hurrying out of that particular room, which is a very smart approach.

Tracy played a domineering railroad magnate at several different ages in *The Power and the Glory* (1933), which had an innovative Preston Sturges script told in flashbacks. It was a prestige movie, but not a financial success. At certain points in that picture, Tracy looks as solid as a rock and just about as expressive as one, except when his character lets out a little gloating smile when he's put one over on his business associates.

In Frank Borzage's erotic romance *Man's Castle* (1933), Tracy's lack of confidence in his own looks and appeal cause him to overemphasize his character's chauvinistic defensiveness and taciturn above-it-all stance towards Loretta Young's big-eyed devotion (to be fair, his part is written like that, with too many lines about how she's too skinny for him, how he should clobber her, etc.). But he has a really fascinating moment of realism here.

After he serves a subpoena to performer Glenda Farrell, who has been singing a song called, "Surprise," he tangles with some of her bodyguards in the wings and then winds up back on stage flat on his face. He looks up at the audience and says, "Surprise," quietly, like the end of some personal joke. It's wonderful because it feels like somebody caught in a home movie; there's nothing "acted" about it or sent out to the audience. Tracy was capable of that, and when people spoke of his underplaying, they meant the moments he did that were so naturalistic that they had a documentary flavor.

Through his years tied to Fox, Tracy was always disappearing on a bender, sometimes before shooting, sometimes in the middle of shooting, and there were moments when everyone thought he had thrown his career away. Though he was miscast in the role, his performance as blowhard Aubrey Piper in an MGM film of George Kelly's play *The Show-Off* (1934) was seen as a feature-length audition for the studio, which signed him in 1935 in spite of the trouble he had caused at Fox. They started him off supporting Jean Harlow and then Myrna Loy before he got the part of his life in Fritz Lang's *Fury* (1936). At MGM, there was a just perceptible lightening of his effects, as if he had gained in confidence at being signed by the biggest studio in town, and this made all the difference.

In his first scenes in *Fury*, Tracy is an everyman figure, amiable, maybe a little sulky, but a good, solid guy. The harshness of his Fox years had worn off, yet it is put to use in *Fury* when his character just barely escapes a lynch mob, a sequence that is sketched in pitiless detail by Lang. After this ordeal, he is a changed person, and suddenly Tracy's pessimism and uneasiness has a strong target. Watching him in the middle section of *Fury* is like seeing a fire hose get turned on.

There is an all-encompassing depth to his anger and vindictiveness here, something beyond the cares of one person. He seems to have tapped into some bottomless vein of rage, and it is a diabolic sight. This was a man deeply in touch with an almost overpowering sense of disgust, which partly came from his detestation of Lang, who worked everyone on the set hard and demanded multiple takes.

Tracy did not get his first Oscar nomination for *Fury* but for his priest in the hit film *San Francisco* (1936), a far more comforting and palatable fellow. *Fury* says that people, particularly in a group, are horrible, while *San Francisco* says that people, particularly in a group, are cheerful and full of can-do spirit, and so it's no wonder which one was more popular. To round out that year, Tracy was one of the stars in the farce *Libeled Lady* (1936), and he was also on the wagon. He knew this was his chance and he didn't want to blow it. He smiles in that movie like he knows he's a success, and for someone who had looked so steadily discouraged on screen, the effect was invigorating.

By this point he was a major star, given back-to-back lead Oscars in 1937 and 1938 for *Captains Courageous* and *Boys Town*. In *Captains Courageous*, Tracy is supposedly a Portuguese fisherman with curly hair. "I researched the accent for *Captains Courageous* and thought I'd worked up a real beaut until they brought a *real* Portuguese-American fisherman to me," said Tracy. "We sat down in the director's office and I tried out my exotic new accent on him. I said, 'Now, would you say 'leetle feesh?' and he said, 'No, I'd say little fish.' So in the film, I probably had the most un–Portuguese accent in history."

Tracy is rarely interested in realism. He knew "leetle feesh" would sound more fun, and so he went with that. He liked the *idea* of "leetle feesh," and that was the key he needed. Those two movies that he won his awards for are hard to take too seriously at this point, especially the second one, but they made Tracy an institution, respected, one of the greats, and the very sentimental *Captains Courageous* is maybe still an irresistible tearjerker if you're in the right mood for it.

He had developed a trick where he would speed up the words he was saying and lower his volume, which sounded impressively life-like until you noticed how often he did it, so that it became one of his routines, like the overlapping dialogue that the Lunts did on stage, which Tracy much admired. A lot of practice and repetition and technique go into such displays of actorly spontaneity, but Tracy would just say in interviews that he would learn his lines and not bump into the furniture. He wanted it to look easy. And it still does with him, most of the time. You can't imitate Tracy the way you can Cagney, Grant, Laughton, and Gable. That's part of why he was so admired, his seeming lack of idiosyncrasy and signature sounds and moves.

He played second banana to Clark Gable two more times, supported

Joan Crawford in *Mannequin* (1938), and then met the more fulfilling task of being the head of Rogers' Rangers in King Vidor's adventure *Northwest Passage* (1940). Trying to be both *Dr. Jekyll and Mr. Hyde* (1941) made him uneasy, and not in a productive way. He had wanted to play Mr. Hyde without any extreme make-up, but his instinct and reputation for underplaying seems to be holding him down in the Hyde scenes. When writer Somerset Maugham visited the set, he was heard to murmur, "Which one is he now?"

With *Woman of the Year* (1942), Tracy began his long-running partnership, both on screen and off, in a way, with Katharine Hepburn, in nine films that ran all the way until his death in 1967. There are moments in that first movie where he seems as stirred by a woman as he ever would be on screen, particularly in the early scenes, and he has funny moments, like his little curtsey on stage when he leaves a feminist meeting she's been addressing.

He throws away a lot of his lines in a quiet voice in *Woman of the Year*, and this makes Hepburn get all hushed herself. There are a few scenes where he seems smugly closed off from her and from everything else. But when she brings home a refugee kid that she has adopted without asking him, his silent reaction is correspondingly large. He widens his eyes as if to say, "You know, I'm an easygoing guy, but you've got to be *kidding* me with this." He's very Irish and very male.

He usually lets Hepburn do the histrionic heavy lifting in their movies together, in both comedy and drama, and so sometimes she looks like she is doing a little too much in response to his granitic solidity. He seemed to make her nervous, and Hepburn had so many nerves anyway that the result could be a little uncomfortable, yet they were acclaimed as one of the major screen teams.

Tracy takes more of a lead in *Keeper of the Flame* (1943) while she retreats a bit, and in *Adam's Rib* (1949) he is so comfortable with Hepburn and with his part that he takes some delightful chances, hemming and hawing at her like Alfred Lunt used to do with Lynn Fontanne, and willingly sacrificing his physical dignity for a laugh. His Noo Yawk sports promoter in *Pat and Mike* (1952) is a beautifully constructed, relaxed creation, and much fun, particularly when he looks at Hepburn walking away and says, "Not much meat on her, but what's there is cherce"—the "cherce" being this guy's way of saying "choice." Tracy looks personally delighted with his own choice as he bends down to drink some water from a fountain after he says it.

But that relaxation could lead to torpor in some of his less interesting assignments at MGM. He's at his best in *The Seventh Cross* (1944), stimulated by the challenge of carrying long sections of screen time with no dialogue (he liked to toss words away, and so maybe he liked doing away with them entirely). His work in Elia Kazan's *Sea of Grass* (1947) with Hepburn, however, is contemptuously bored and boring, like a man sleepwalking. "He's only giving a tenth of what he's got," said Kazan. "I never could get him to stretch himself."

He was at his best, funny and scary, as the *Father of the Bride* (1950) for Vincente Minnelli, in full charge of all manner of comic business but always ready to reveal the nightmare that lurks just underneath the suburban milieu of the film. Tracy has moments in that movie where he registers a distinctively sour comic dismay. In the scene where he drinks as he is talking to his prospective in-laws, a hole seems to open up in his performing style, and we begin to stare at something out of Samuel Beckett, some Irish and morbid and merry unrest.

A portrait of Spencer Tracy, who usually served things up with a little dressing.

The Actress (1953), directed by George Cukor, is filled with long takes that are set up to give Tracy very challenging showcases for his skill, but a curious thing happens in that movie. In a scene study class, a teacher will often have a novice actor work with props so that they will lose their self-consciousness. If you give them something to *do*, packing a suitcase or making tea or whatever, they suddenly start behaving and reacting in a more natural way; it works almost every time.

Yet when the highly experienced Tracy is given "business" like this by Cukor in *The Actress*, like eating or fiddling with something around the room, he immediately gets artificial and fussy, stagy. It's as if the wellspring of his talent comes from a deep kind of concentration that can only really kick in when he is physically still. He did thrive on the violence of *Bad Day at Black Rock* (1955), one of his best later films, but only as a respite from talking and behaving. He didn't like to rehearse and would do a scene in one take if he could. In the 1950s, he started drinking again, with dire effects to his looks and his health.

The last scene he ever shot, his concluding monologue in *Guess Who's Coming to Dinner* (1967), is moving in spite of the personal exploitation of his perceived off-screen life with Hepburn because illness has diminished him physically, and so he has to stay stock still as he delivers this final speech. Those grim last few movies he did for Stanley Kramer in the 1960s were painful to watch for many reasons, not least of which was Tracy's physical deterioration. He had his demons, and whatever they were, he kept them to himself.

Tracy was a byword for fine acting in his day, an actor's actor, but his actual record is tricky, or unfinished somehow. He could not face playing James Tyrone with Hepburn in *Long Day's Journey Into Night* because he was beyond such tasks by then, and because he said that the low salary, $25,000, was far too small for him. The feeling remains that Hepburn pushed herself too much as an actress while Tracy pushed himself too little, maybe because he was basically afraid of acting and what it might reveal about himself. He is one of those men of his time who felt a bit ashamed or defensive about being an actor, and so he shuts himself down sometimes. Whereas in *Fury*, or in *Father of the Bride*, he shows us what he is capable of and what he is capable of suggesting.

Humphrey Bogart
The Stuff That Dreams Are Made Of

By the time he played Dixon Steele (don't think about that name for too long), an alcoholic screenwriter with a violent streak in Nicholas Ray's *In a Lonely Place* (1950), Humphrey Bogart had already attained a kind of legendary status after much knocking around and paying his dues in his youth. Movies like *Casablanca* (1942) and *To Have and Have Not* (1944) had enshrined him as the hard-drinking outsider with a secret streak of nobility, a persona that he learned to play gradually in the less flashy movies he made in between.

He had a very low-pitched, resonant voice with a sibilant "s" that made it sound like he had gotten punched a few too many times at 3AM somewhere, and his laugh was as outright nasty as his deep, dark eyes, which could glow with self-pity, as they do in *Casablanca*, or with animal-like malevolence, as they do in *In a Lonely Place*, where he gives his finest and most disturbing performance.

In her essay "Humphrey and Bogey," Louise Brooks wrote, "Before inertia set in, he played one fascinatingly complex character, craftily directed by Nicholas Ray, in a film whose title perfectly defined Humphrey's own isolation among people. *In a Lonely Place* gave him a role that he could play with complexity because the film character's, the screenwriter's, pride in his art, his selfishness, his drunkenness, his lack of energy stabbed with lightning strokes of violence, were shared equally by the real Bogart." His best late parts, Dixon Steele, Fred C. Dobbs in John Huston's *The Treasure of the Sierra Madre* (1948) ("Nobody puts anything over on Fred C. Dobbs!") and Captain Queeg in *The Caine Mutiny* (1954) are all built around the emotion of paranoia and how paranoids are sometimes right, until they aren't, until they go too far with it.

The greatness of his performance in *In a Lonely Place* comes from the depth of Bogart's disgust with the world, so that his resort to violence is classically inevitable. In many of his other 1940s movies, that disgust was treated lightly, even comically, until it could be put aside by the call to an older code of honor. Bogart may himself have believed in such honor, but he let go of it in his best work. The thing that really stings about his performance in *In a Lonely Place* is how Ray frames it in the usual Bogart way and makes you see the world through Bogart's eyes and then gradually pulls away from him until you see that his reaction to life is not in scale to the petty indignities of his profession but pathologically extreme, the reaction of a scorned egomaniac, with the emphasis on "maniac."

His Dix is smart and in the right, but his rightness is sick, too much, cruel, gloating, maybe murderous, adolescent. He can't help it, but why can't he? Ray very kindly and indulgently romanticized James Dean's teenager in *Rebel Without a Cause* (1955), creating an image for him that still has potency, yet he exposes Bogart's image in the most far-reaching and pitiless fashion. The "coolness" of Bogart is revealed as maybe homicidal, or close to sociopathy. When Gloria Grahame's Laurel tells a police chief that she finds his face "interesting," what she means is teasingly ambiguous, and maybe masochistic in that she likes dangerous men.

The mature Bogart of the 1940s had a very sour humor that might have seemed bitchy if he had had anything of the feminine in his character, which he did not, not by a long shot. He believed in his own bullshit, most of the time, while continually calling out the bullshit of others, a bit of hypocrisy that made him go over very well with the rebellious American students of the 1960s. It seemed like he stood for something, but just what that something was could be a little vague.

Just what he was so upset about, deep down, can also seem a little vague, or drunkenly fuzzy. He was "cool" only if you don't question him too much, for if you do, as Ray does, you're looking at something that might be studied or taken apart by a psychoanalyst. *In a Lonely Place* shows how sick and ingrowing his brand of romanticism really is, and how exciting. That's what is really killer about that movie and about Bogart in that movie, how his brand of romanticism is questioned and ruined but still gets up at the end to seem attractive. Some lies are unkillable. Dynamite: it explodes sometimes, and then you re-build until you can lay hands on it again.

He was born on Christmas Day in 1899. Bogart's parents were well to do, and his mother was an illustrator and vocal women's suffragist, like Katharine Hepburn's mother, who used him as a model for a baby food ad, dressing him up like Little Lord Fauntleroy. "I was brought up very unsentimentally but very straightforwardly," he told an interviewer. "A kiss, in our family, was an event. Our mother and father didn't glug over my two sisters and me." He briefly joined the navy and somehow got a scar on his lip (the source of this scar has been long disputed) before coming back to New York and working in the theater in the 1920s, where he would come on in pressed white clothes and ask, "Tennis anyone?" He liked the late theater hours and attention and drank very heavily at speakeasies.

All his life he supposedly carried around a notice of one of his early performances on stage from the poison-penned critic Alexander Woollcott that said, "The young man who embodies the sprig is what is usually and mercifully described as inadequate." He felt self-loathing for his profession at first, thinking it was a sissy thing for a man to be doing—a big problem for all the men coming into acting at this time. "I was born to be indolent and this was the softest of rackets," he claimed.

When he came to Hollywood in 1930, he didn't make much of an impression. He's nice-looking, well mannered, and fairly green in John Ford's *Up the River* (1930), and he does a lot of smiling in *The Bad Sister* (1931). He was far more assured as a natty gangster in *Three on a Match* (1932), taking his time and holding the screen with his slightly exaggerated, whiny voice and definite, stylized movements. But that first attempt on Hollywood ended in a retreat back to the theater.

Thanks to co-star Leslie Howard, Bogart repeated his stage success in *The Petrified Forest* (1936) as killer Duke Mantee, but it didn't change his status at Warner Brothers. It's a pretty embarrassing performance, filled with studied movement and artificially prolonged line readings: "Talkin' to an *old man like dat*," he whines, when he objects to egghead Howard talking tough to Charley Grapewin. It's the sort of work that looks like it has been embalmed from a stage performance given far too many times.

Between 1936 and 1939, Bogart was in 25 movies for Warner Brothers, six or seven a year, mostly in small gangster parts, where he shot off guns and got shot himself. This sometimes worked out very badly for him. He's embarrassing again in *The Roaring Twenties* (1939) when he has to beg James Cagney for his life, like an amateur forced to do something he doesn't want to do.

It was clear that Bogart wanted to be the hero himself, but he was made to feel like a jerk, a villain, a guy who could only get a girl by force. He got a good lead in the muckraking *Black Legion* (1937), where he convincingly plays a not-very-bright incipient bigot who joins a Ku Klux Klan–like organization. Bogart doesn't flinch from the fear, cowardice or loathsomeness involved in this part, even when it gets very ugly (his laughing drunkenness after burning down the farm of a rival and running him out of town is truly nasty).

But socially conscious movies were never his thing. There are times when he is just going through the motions in *Black Legion*, making faces, not connecting to the emotions he's supposed to be feeling. Though he is somewhat improved as the gangster in *Dead End* (1937), something was still not clicking for him. He moved through his parts as if he didn't quite believe them, or himself in them. "I can't get in a mild discussion without turning it into an argument," he said. "There must be something in my tone of voice, or this arrogant face—something that antagonizes everybody. Nobody likes me on sight. I suppose that's why I'm cast as the heavy." He wanted to be liked on sight, or at least after a while, but he kept that hidden for now.

He was a big complainer on the Warner lot, taking suspensions from salary to avoid even worse roles, but putting in his time in movie after movie. He provided a shoulder for Bette Davis to cry on in *Marked Woman* (1937) and *Dark Victory* (1939), in which he attempts an Irish brogue. He's really not so bad in that movie, in spite of the accent. When a part like that called for romantic intensity and bad blood disappointment, he could summon these emotions very quickly, but most of his other parts did not call for these favorite things of his.

The lowest points on his Warner treadmill were *King of the Underworld* (1939) a low-budget movie with on-the-skids Kay Francis, and *The Return of Doctor X* (1939), a horror movie where he played an evil man with a white skunk stripe in his hair, spectacles on his face, and a white bunny in his hands to stroke. His life off screen was even worse as he battled it out nightly with wife Mayo Methot, a tough broad actress who got him drunk and kept him drunk.

Bogart said that every time Methot would start to sing "Embraceable You" he knew that she was ready to get a gun or a knife and come after him. And yet this marriage lasted for years. He was a needler, delighting in putting people on the spot and sending them up. The press liked him because he had a big mouth about movies and movie stars he didn't like. Most of his friends were writers and screenwriters, so he probably knew one or two like Dixon Steele.

Yet again it was Raoul Walsh who finally brought out a star's full character. Walsh bolstered and expertly framed Bogart in *High Sierra* (1941), a movie in which Bogart's escaped convict Roy "Mad Dog" Earle has grey in his hair and a quiet, fatalistic attitude towards life. All the elements of the later Bogart are here, including his foolish romanticism, for Earle prefers the wholesome-seeming but selfish Velma (Joan Leslie) over the loyalty of Ida Lupino's Marie.

The release of John Huston's sleeper hit *The Maltese Falcon* in that same year represented a one-two punch for Bogart. It's always surprising to go back to that famous movie and see how campy it is, how it surrounds Bogart's private eye Sam Spade with a variety of gay and gay-ish characters for him to react to with fear and disgust. Spade is a homophobe in the classic sense, so afraid of homosexuality that he sees it everywhere, even when it isn't present (it's one thing to be leery of Peter Lorre's Joel Cairo, but why on earth is he suspicious of cop Ward Bond and his partner Barton MacLane?). Bogart gets the drinking-at-4PM rot of Spade, the crumminess and the hypocritical sense of honor, all by instinct.

"When you're slapped, you'll take it and like it!" he tells Cairo after smacking him around a bit, a takeoff on what Clark Gable told Norma Shearer in *A Free Soul*, which lets us know that masculinity has come under some threat in 10 years time. Bogart makes a show of being amused by people and their foibles, but it's a sneering sort of amusement. His reactions are generally unexpected in *The Maltese Falcon* and seem to bounce off of some core of cynicism. It's impossible to imagine this jeering fellow as a young juvenile on the stage, or as a young anything.

Bogart needed to be well and truly middle-aged before he came into his own, not only as a star but as an actor. He needed to be marinated by enough booze and disbelief before he was ready, before he had earned that basso gallows voice of his. There's a self-parodying or camp aspect to *The Maltese Falcon* that he seems to understand only slightly, or inexactly, but it was enough to make his Spade one of the most troubling of movie heroes, the first antihero, even.

Cagney actually was a working class guy from the streets, a street fighter, even, and he always relates to life in an open, super-quick way and is willing to try things for fun. Bogart, on the other hand, is someone who wasn't from the streets but for most of his life on screen pretended that he was, and that pretense made him a more limited actor and presence, a man who was somehow closed-down, even when he was trying to be hip or with-it.

Bogart is a conservative figure, whatever else he might signal, whereas Cagney is liberal and even radical. Bogart would never risk being as feminine as Cagney or Grant or even Gary Cooper could be. He's too pre-occupied with sustaining his own rickety street smarts masquerade, and this always involved, ironically, sneering at more obvious pretenders. It was an uneasy position, to say the least (maybe that's why he was always wincing), but a rich one for a central figure in the wartime movies of the 1940s.

If there is a moment when he really became a star, it is when he first sees Ingrid Bergman in *Casablanca* and his dark eyes register hurt, bitter love for her. This was the most emotional he had let himself be on screen, and it made him seem fully human and dimensional finally, a man of character and feeling underneath the wisecracks and cute evasions. This was a new persona for a man. The whole of Frank Sinatra's career as a torch singer in the 1950s might be traced back to the way Bogart unexpectedly sees Bergman again after having lost her, which makes the four hours of torch carrying done by Gable's Rhett Butler seem protected and quaint by comparison. Yes, men could feel pain over women, and it could be even more painful because it needed to be hidden away, just between a guy and a bottle of liquor.

In his scenes with Bergman, Bogart lets her glowing charisma take the lead and do the heavy lifting for him. "I didn't do anything I've never done before, but when the camera moves in on that Bergman face, and she's saying she loves you, it would make anybody feel romantic," he said. Duty and desire are pitted against each other in *Casablanca*, and duty wins. By the 1970s, desire in the movies would be winning that fight and then leading us on to self-destruction, sometimes because the forces of duty, now called "the establishment," were ready to punish us.

Humphrey Bogart smokes a cigarette during his 1940s star period.

Bogart reached his zenith for Howard Hawks with his future wife, 19-year-old Lauren Bacall, in two dreamlike films, *To Have and Have Not* and especially *The Big Sleep* (1946), which is a very funny, sexy, sophisticated commentary on watching movies like *The Big Sleep* while also being one of those movies itself. Tricky Bogart seems to instinctively understand both levels of that film, so that he is genuinely funny, and hip, the storm clouds of his Mayo Methot years breaking up like a bad nightmare.

It was as if through some stroke of luck his secret fantasy of himself had been vindicated, and it was all the sweeter for him because he had to wait for it for so long. What happened to his life and career when he met Bacall seems a little like a movie now, in the best and most satisfying way. He overtook Cagney at the box office and set up his own production company in order to have more control over his work, and this led to *In a Lonely Place*, which was not fully appreciated in its time.

From his first close-up in *The Treasure of the Sierra Madre*, it is clear that Bogart has foregone the sometimes uneasy fantasy version of himself for down-at-heel reality. His Fred C. Dobbs is just a crummy guy who hasn't eaten in a while, angry, beaten down, like some animal ready to make one final bite or slash with a claw at the world. As Dobbs goes on an expedition to look for gold with two other partners, Bogart steadily and impressively charts his mental deterioration into paranoia, though he does have his forced and obvious moments towards the end.

They gave him an Oscar for his river rat Charlie Allnut, a Canadian talked into taking his old boat down rough water by Katharine Hepburn's spinster Rose Sayer in *The African Queen* (1951). He gives a performance that is full of charm and relaxed invention, if a little broad sometimes (see especially his wide-eyed reaction at the boiler after he kisses Rose for the first time). Huston and Bogart were the only two members of the production not to get dysentery because they weren't drinking water. "All I ate was baked beans, canned asparagus, and Scotch whiskey," he said. "Whenever a fly bit Huston or me, it dropped dead."

After that recognition, he got sort of surly and out-of-touch with his own movies, particularly in Billy Wilder's *Sabrina* (1954), where he steadfastly, almost perversely refuses to be charmed by Audrey Hepburn (not his kind of woman, of course) and in Huston's campy *Beat the Devil* (1954), where it is clear, sometimes to an embarrassing degree, that he doesn't get the hip, deconstructive tone. This from the guy who laughed his way through *The Big Sleep*!

Then again, *The Big Sleep* is a deeply heterosexual fantasy whereas *Beat the Devil*, written by Truman Capote, is far-out in a garish way that probably offended Bogart. It's like a film written and made for Joel Cairo, and Bogart reacted like Sam Spade would have. "Only the phonies think it's funny, it's a mess," he said, convinced, apparently, of his own lack of phoniness. "Bogart's a hell of a nice guy until around 11:30PM," said Hollywood restaurateur Dave Chasen. "After that, he thinks he's Bogart."

But he also didn't seem happy with all the sour talk of Joseph L. Mankiewicz's *The Barefoot Contessa* (1954), which should have suited him perfectly, so it seems he had reached a point where there was just no pleasing him. Yet he did go all out in *The Caine Mutiny* as Captain Queeg, a pathetic twerp of a man whose darting eyes broadcast his insecurities and his unfitness for the job of commanding a ship. His Captain Queeg is a highly controlled, striking, three-dimensional performance, a far cry from the more callow work he did in something like *Black Legion*. His most potent vein on screen was always deep paranoia, maybe because he was always afraid of being found out by others, or even by himself.

His movies after that are minor, and marked by his illness with lung cancer off screen. In spite of everything, in spite of all the small films and the missteps of his early years and even the mistakes in his star period, Bogart is a deeply reassuring star presence if you just enjoy his surface, if you enjoy the lowest voice in show business, the nighttime sang-froid, the leader of the pack laugh, if you don't think about him too long in the light of the morning, outside the movie house. John Cassavetes was very much a successor to the Bogart spirit, but he took the unruliness of his own male character to ruder and scarier conclusions.

For almost 60 years after his death, the imperial yet insecure Bacall was still around suggesting, in her equally low voice, that Bogart was just as he was in the movies, and that their life together was much like *The Big Sleep*, though some people in their circle remembered some fights between them when he was drinking that were hopefully far removed from his battles with Methot and with the passive Laurel in *In a Lonely Place*. ("Bogie fell in love with the character Bacall played, so she had to keep playing it the rest of her life," Howard Hawks observed.) Bacall is not around to haughtily growl about his superiority anymore, but her assertions have their print-the-legend potency.

Marlon Brando
Before and After

Women have always been more comfortable with acting, but particularly in the period I'm describing (Barbara Stanwyck isn't included here only because I did a whole book on her). Some of the major male stars in the classic Hollywood period like Gary Cooper, James Stewart, and Henry Fonda did very fine work in their time, but they are examples now on screen of what men were comfortable expressing and what they were not, or not able to.

All three represented a version of what America wanted to think about itself, and they all hid far more than they dared to express. Cooper is outstanding and touching in Frank Borzage's *A Farewell to Arms* (1932), especially in the final scene where he is in despair over his lover's illness, and he was taciturn and sexy enough to drive Dietrich crazy in *Morocco* (1930). He had a beautiful face and a beautifully proportioned body and a disarmingly bashful way of moving, like a moving target, and this was very seductive. It's hard to believe in his flawlessly heroic and honorable characters now, though Cooper apparently did. He was better when he didn't talk, and he knew that, too.

It was often said by other players that when they acted with Cooper on the set they would think he wasn't doing anything and then they'd see him on screen and everything that needed to be there would be there. And that's fine, up to a point, or up to about 1936, when he played *Mr. Deeds Goes to Town* for Frank Capra. In that film, and the many that followed, worry, self-doubt, self-pity, self-satisfaction, and dogged mannerism set in, not so much naturalistic as busy and tricky and weirdly groveling. His face aged in a harrowed way, well enough for the abandoned sheriff in *High Noon* (1952), and for Anthony Mann's *Man of the West* (1958), where he has to stand by as Julie London is ordered to strip by a gunman—one of the ugliest scenes in film.

Stewart gave one of the all-time best film performances as the defense lawyer in Otto Preminger's *Anatomy of a Murder* (1959) by turning the expected ingredients of his old "aw shucks" screen persona on their head; he showed how this persona was in fact a tactic to be deployed. He is everything he needs to be in Alfred Hitchcock's stone masterpieces *Rear Window* (1954) and *Vertigo* (1958), crabby, querulous, lecherous, in distress. But his earlier characters could seem slow-witted in the midst of their charming of more sophisticated women. His style could be "artless" yet sometimes overdone, a very bad combination, but he had an air of great likability that got him through, and talent, too, just enough. His weakness was always a tendency towards over-emphasis in moments of upset, or even in ordinary moments, where he was just trying, probably, to be funny.

In *Navy Blue and Gold* (1937), Stewart has a Big Scene where he has to plead with officials, and he builds it with a nice and palpable intensity, but you can feel his effort, his need to do it well, and you shouldn't feel things like that. He could be distinctively ardent, as he is when wooing Katharine Hepburn with some very florid language after too much champagne in *The Philadelphia Story* (1940), which won him a Best Actor Oscar that was widely considered a consolation prize for not winning for his Jefferson Smith in Capra's *Mr. Smith Goes to Washington* (1939). But the drunk scene he plays with Cary Grant in *The Philadelphia Story* is slightly self-indulgent, and inexact. He's no match for Grant's own unerring sense of timing and attack.

"Why do we have to have all these kids?" he asks wife Donna Reed in a particularly low moment in Capra's *It's a Wonderful Life* (1946), but the movie lets Stewart admit that level of despair and disconnection only to bring him back to life with an eleventh hour lesson in love thy neighbor. His series of westerns for Anthony Mann dispelled any lingering hope about the goodness of men, yet Stewart himself sailed on into being an institution as if basically untouched by such lessons.

In many ways Fonda is the most intriguing of the three because of fugitive glimpses of stubbornness and perversity in his character. He is the only one of them to play an out-and-out villain, his blue-eyed child killer in Sergio Leone's *Once Upon a Time in the West* (1969), as ice cold a murderer as has ever been seen on screen. His best work came 20 years apart, as the hunted convict in Fritz Lang's *You Only Live Once* (1937), where his anger is monolithically fierce, and Alfred Hitchcock's *The Wrong Man* (1957), where he is a man falsely accused of a crime and religiously resigned to it. Fonda's image was that of a decent man up against societal injustice, and he made many questionable films with John Ford on that basis.

The legend of John Wayne lives on for many. He is an axiom of the cinema and a distinctive walker across prairies who toiled in low-budget Westerns through the 1930s until John Ford made him a star in one dolly shot in *Stagecoach* (1939), the camera catching a look of purity and sweetness on his face. This is followed by a shot in which Wayne looks tough and hard, a shot from behind in tight jeans where he walks forward that establishes his sexiness and physical grace, and then a shot where he looks extremely tough as he speaks to the people on the stagecoach.

Like the greatest stars, Wayne had a way of talking that was entirely his own where he lingered over words and gave them unexpected emphases. He was usually open and listening and reacting, at his worst on screen when he was small-minded and crabby and at his best when he was tender with others and with his own strength. Unlike other stars in his preferred genres (westerns and war movies), Wayne clearly loves women and is always sparked by them, and this is a major plus that makes up for many of his debits.

It's hard to imagine Wayne's Ethan Edwards in Ford's *The Searchers* (1956) without the impact that Marlon Brando had made on movie acting six years before. If you want to talk about profound screen acting, watch the moment when Ford dollies in on Wayne's face in *The Searchers* as he reacts to the sight of a room full of maddened and ruined women. The sting of the moment comes from its air of personal revelation, for Wayne's Ethan confronts an abyss outside of himself and also clearly recognizes it *within* himself.

Someone like Robert Mitchum, with his full sort of nothingness, gets closer to what Brando would be doing in movies, but Mitchum's screen motto is "Baby, I don't care" and Brando cared immensely even when he was making an angry show of not caring. (It could also be said that cool Mitchum is the opposite of coiled Cary Grant, which shows just how singular Mitchum is.) In *The Story of G.I Joe* (1945), which was the first film where he was really noticed, Mitchum has a sensitive face but a deep, tough voice, and this contrast is also what made Wayne a star in *Stagecoach*, but there are key differences between them. Mitchum was both a tower of impregnable masculinity and a satirist, with large doses of the teaser, the loafer, and even the hipster. (Imagine him in a film with Marlene Dietrich.) He was a large man with a barrel chest who was capable of brute force or emotional daintiness, a proto-Beat who had once been a wild boy of the road during the Depression.

Mitchum eyes Katharine Hepburn skeptically in *Undercurrent* (1946), and she professed to be offended by his seeming lack of enthusiasm and his louche attitude. A series of noir films established Mitchum as a "wait and see" presence on screen, and this led to three major performances in the 1950s: *The Lusty Men* (1952), *Angel Face* (1952), where he offers a complete and very unsettling portrait of moral inertia, and *The Night of the Hunter*.

Mitchum often doesn't seem to be doing anything unless you pay very close attention to the way he listens to others, the way he will lightly emphasize a word, the vagrant expressions on his face that barely last. In Mitchum's best work, there is a mysterious sadness about him that he seems embarrassed about, and that quality is very pre–Brando, as they say. Brando and his followers would brandish their own sadness like a weapon.

The limitation of so many of the screen men of the classic Hollywood period is their sense that a man should not be acting at all, should not be pretending, should not be showing off, and though Brando busted those feelings right open on screen, he suffered from them himself off screen. Brando's main impact was brief: from 1950 to 1954.

His debut, *The Men* (1950), is a well-meaning movie about paraplegics, and the overall falseness of the film throws Brando's sensitive, uncompromising, imaginative work into relief. Sometimes he will completely empty his face out in *The Men*, which people often do in life but seldom do on screen because it is so physically unflattering. Brando was in his mid-twenties in 1950, but his emotional energy is adolescent, his anger the first limited yet limitless anger of a teenager. What he brought to acting was a revolution in some obvious ways but also a regression in other, less obvious ways.

In *A Streetcar Named Desire* (1951), Brando seems to be just existing, not acting. He is a sexy, slobby beast caught unawares, and a lot of skill went into that impression. He doesn't seem to be controlling or shaping anything, but of course he is, we know he is, yet still the surprise of it remains intact. His choices don't seem like choices at all because he never underlines them, which is a dangerous thing to do, and far different from mere underplaying. It's the way most people are in life, the way he behaves in *Streetcar*. Nothing is pushed out to us, shown, or trumpeted.

It's no surprise that as he aged Brando took to not memorizing his lines but had them read to him in an earpiece, or written all over the set. His logic was that people don't know what they're going to say before they say it, and if he knew the words beforehand they wouldn't seem as radically natural as he wanted them to be.

Marlon Brando as Stanley in *A Streetcar Named Desire*.

There was no fantasy in what Brando did—no stylization of himself. He was never mannered, for he looked on manners and mannerisms as a kind of disease to be avoided at all cost. When he first met his very mannered co-star of *Streetcar*, Vivien Leigh, he asked her why she used perfume. "I like to smell nice, don't you?" she asked. Brando said he didn't take baths. "I just throw a gob of spit in the air and run under it," he joked.

His slurry, muddy diction seemed like it came from the streets, not the stage, though he had trained extensively with acting teacher Stella Adler and had worked in the theater with Katharine Cornell and Tallulah Bankhead, old school theater stars. (Adler's version of the Method was based around research and imagination, and her teaching stood in opposition to Lee Strasberg's devotion to the supposedly real emotions of his actors.) Brando sounded like he had been punched in the head one too many times. Everyone had to get used to the way he talked, so that it was mocked and then imitated and then passed into legend. He was a palooka who was so beautiful that he hinted he had the soul of a poet, but maybe it was just a hint, a ruse, a put-on like any of his other put-ons. Moody, a sullen brooder, he was not a joiner, he was against everything, and so of course he was against the mostly bad or at least stodgy movies he was in, too.

He was at his volatile, lunging, trust-no-one best in *Viva Zapata!* (1952), physically poetic and verbally inarticulate, but his Marc Antony in *Julius Caesar* (1953) can only be judged a success on the level of painstaking effort, and he had made his name on seeming effortlessness. Whereas John Gielgud and James Mason in that movie are connected to emotion, intellectual intention, and the Shakespearean verse itself, Brando is basically disconnected from all three but laboring visibly to catch up and forcing most of his vocal effects (words were never friends to him).

He led with his rapidly expanding lower body in *The Wild One* (1953), heading up a motorcycle gang and strutting around in the tightest jeans that could be found. That looks like a ludicrous movie now, but Brando still has his sexual charge in it, his lazy authority, his animal magnetism, the softness of his face, voice, and flesh putting the lie to any charges of hooliganism. Off screen he was unstoppably self-indulgent when it came to women and food, indulging his fondness for each with little discrimination and eventually scattering the globe with around 20 or more children.

He won his first Oscar for *On the Waterfront* (1954), where he exposed the delicacy and fine feelings of a betrayed and then redeemed ex-boxer (Bette Davis gave him his award). The moment when he picks up Eva Marie Saint's glove and puts it on, an improvisation, has been eulogized many times, but it does not have the sexy jolt of tender curiosity that Cagney brings to the moment when he holds Joan Blondell's underwear to himself in *Blonde Crazy*. It feels, instead, wheedling and slightly aggressive. Cagney's characters loved and wanted women, even if they got physically rough. The same cannot be said, alas, for Brando's screen persona.

After *On the Waterfront*, Brando was increasingly arbitrary and removed in projects that were chosen or forced on him as a kind of contemptuous cashing in, things like *Désirée* (1954), *Guys and Dolls* (1955), where he is hardly a natural song and dance man, and *Sayonara* (1957). And there were many more pedestrian or worse films like that to come in the 1960s before he made his decisive second impact in *The Godfather* (1972) and *Last Tango in Paris* (1973) and presided over a new generation of actors that he had prepared the way for.

Easily bored, Brando liked to put things on his head and put on accents just to entertain himself, following his whims to such a degree that he blurred the line between eccentric and unbalanced. He was our resident genius, lost to reason and swiftly lost to us. Brando was always getting beaten up on screen as if to pay for his own and maybe all our sins. He is beaten in *The Wild One* and in *On the Waterfront*, whipped in *One-Eyed Jacks* (1961), which he directed, and punched to a bloody pulp in *The Chase* (1966). He is a figure who still inspires awe and trembling, a force for tremendous rejection and negativity. Maybe that's what we deserve.

There were some new screen women in the 1950s, too, usually somewhat limited or somewhat neurotic. James Harvey takes care of two of them with one sharp stone of a single line in his 2001 book *Movie Love in the Fifties*: "if (Grace) Kelly often reminded you of a triumphant hostess, Kim Novak seemed more like the unwanted guest." Judy Holliday brought her odd clockwork timing to a small series of films where she played dumb blonde heroines who were wide-eyed and vaguely dissatisfied, and not that far short of outright mental disability.

Audrey Hepburn was a special case, with her charming singsong Dutch cadences and purity of expression. She is pure pleasure for those who respond to her, but very hard to analyze. Hepburn did sculpted line readings, basically, all artifice, very far from the Method, and she might have made her full impact in an earlier era.

Trained as a dancer, Hepburn is at her best, as in the last scene in the back of a cab in *Breakfast at Tiffany's* (1961), when she can express herself with her body. Just watch the way she puts on her clothes in the back of that cab, all contained, angry energy, clean lines, definite. There was nothing ambiguous or complex about her. She was made for fairy tales, and she said, "I love you" to her leading men, often much older, with vulnerable abandon. As Roland Barthes wrote, her face was an event, whereas Garbo's was an idea.

Film audiences accepted the changeover in movie men with Montgomery Clift, Brando, and James Dean, but Method women like Julie Harris, Kim Stanley, and Geraldine Page were barely tolerated and mainly worked in the theater. The palmy days of Davis, Hepburn and Stanwyck were almost over, and the comediennes like Irene Dunne, Jean Arthur, and Myrna Loy were also basically finished. The real new players, both women and men, were at the Actors Studio, working on stage and in class and on all kinds of live TV where they changed the way things were done. A few key figures can stand in for this change, this bridge that would lead to a whole different world of acting in the 1970s and after.

Montgomery Clift
Fallen Aristocrat

Before Montgomery Clift, there had been leading men in the movies who were soft and feminine, pretty boys like David Manners and Douglass Montgomery, but they generally weren't headliners and were meant to prop up the more macho female stars like Katharine Hepburn and Margaret Sullavan. (Gary Cooper was beautiful in a very feminine way in his youth, but his laconic air of pre-occupation usually neutralized the beauty.)

On the other side of the divide were the big male stars: Clark Gable, Spencer Tracy, Humphrey Bogart, all men of the old school, drinkers, hunters, brawlers. Clift was revolutionary because he fused these two archetypes into a bewildering new male personality, pared down as these other stars were but inflected with a new kind of sophisticated neuroticism. He made only 17 movies, a precious eight of them before his life smashing car accident in 1956 at age 36. Those eight movies changed male acting on screen in ways that we are still coming to terms with.

Clift was brought up in Europe by his very demanding mother, Sunny Clift. Though she was often strapped for cash, no museum was left unvisited and no string quartet was left unheard by her children under Sunny's tutelage. A note Clift wrote to Sunny as a small boy was found among his papers after he died. It read: "I love you. Why not?"

Clift had a twin sister named Ethel, with whom he had his own private language, and he was raised by Sunny, who was obsessed with her ancestry, to be a little prince. Clift started acting on the Broadway stage as a kid, and many remarked on his exceptional poise and technique. A friend of his as a teenager, Ed Foote, who was suffering from acne, caught Clift staring at his own perfectly formed face in a mirror one day. Looking away from his reflection, Clift glanced at Foote and said, "My God, you're ugly." He was very aware of things like that, and brutally candid about it.

Patricia Collinge, who acted with Clift in a play called *Dame Nature*, observed Clift and his mother together. "I found her bewitching and charming but a killer too," Collinge said. "She stifled and repressed Monty." A reviewer of Clift in that play called him "too neurotic for comfort," and Collinge reported that he was "a terrible flirt. He had a way of looking at you with those gorgeous eyes of his and you'd feel faint." Clift worked out daily at a gym, unusual for those days. "He was conceited as hell because he was such a great beauty," said his friend Bill Le Massena.

Clift got a role with Alfred Lunt and Lynn Fontanne in *There Shall Be No Night*, and the fabled Lunts helped him bring his talent to fruition, working with him on subtext and cultivating an inner life for his character, counseling him to use aspects of his own life for his part. Clift, like Lunt, was never an actor to hide behind accents or wigs or externals to make a difference. He presented himself as he was and brought everything up from the inside. It was a new way of working, and it could get startling, and convincingly naturalistic, results.

This method could also lead, if you were not careful, to self-indulgence and repetition. But Clift never worked enough that he fell prey to any of that. He worked sparingly, as if to hold on to the special status his mother had claimed for him. He wanted to be the greatest actor in the world, and he eyed that goal intently, obsessively. He was a tactile person in his private life, cuddly, always reaching out to hug and kiss and caress the people around him, never wanting to let them go.

He played with Tallulah Bankhead on stage in Thornton Wilder's *The Skin of Our Teeth* under the direction of Elia Kazan, and he steered clear of the long-term Hollywood contracts that were offered him. He idolized Margaret Sullavan's acting, her secret voice, her fresh and eccentric feelings. He found an acting coach in Mira Rostova, a small, intensely focused woman who had once acted in the German theater and who taught acting classes at the New School in New York during the mid-1940s. Clift also worked with Bobby Lewis, one of the founders of the Group Theatre.

This was the start of a time when actors began to talk and think about their work a lot, sometimes to excess, and sometimes there would even be actors who did almost all their work in class. Acting was becoming a lifestyle choice as well as a profession, and psychoanalysis was beginning to make strong inroads into this world of actors and their theories and their scene study work. Improvisation and movement exercises were starting to come into play, and the emotional truth of the actor was starting to become more important, to some of its practitioners, than the emotions set down as written in the roles they were playing. Clift, along with Brando, became the figurehead of this new way of doing things.

Clift made his movie debut in *The Search* (1948), a modest film about a soldier and a refugee boy that he enriched with various improvisations off the conventional script (the producer of the film kept threatening him with legal action for these interventions). Unlike screen actors of the 1930s and '40s, Clift does not heighten his own behavior, or stand at a distance from it, or comment on it in any way.

He works in a mode of damped-down naturalism, and perhaps part of this was his arrogance about his own appearance, for he knew that people would read things into his looks, and so he gets away with very spare work. There are even times when he blurs his behavior here for an even more naturalistic effect, deliberately disconnecting himself from cause-and-effect choices so that he seems like a limited man caught unawares. "In movies you *see* first and *hear* second," he told his older brother Brooks. "Words aren't as important as visual images."

His disarmingly casual vocal delivery was something he learned from Alfred Lunt, but Lunt in his only leading screen role, *The Guardsman* (1931), lets the seams of his trickery show a bit underneath the chatty vocal mannerisms he had developed with his wife Lynn Fontanne. Clift at his best lets his own technique disappear, especially when he talks. His voice is deep and clotted, blocked, with a mild kind of retard to the way the words come out. This idiosyncrasy of his became a kind of Method trademark, beginning here in *The Search* and moving on to Brando's notorious mumble until by the mid–1960s you reach the full demented vocal hesitations of Sandy Dennis.

Clift taught actors that they didn't need to learn how to talk in a heightened way for the camera in the fashion of Cary Grant or James Cagney, with his playfully over-articulated consonants. Instead, Clift gave permission to use and even flaunt all your vocal faults because that meant that your work was more real, more true. And yet this too could be imitated, as a whole generation who imitated Brando showed us. Even the trickier Clift could be imitated, as proved by Martin Short's hilarious send-up of Clift's looks and voice in "I Married Monty," a sketch from a 1985 TV comedy special.

The more eccentric you were, to the 1950s Method actors, the more "real" you were, so that behavior once reserved for character actors, usually comic in nature, became acceptable for leading men on screen and leading women on stage. Clift reserves any points he wants to make in *The Search* for moments of stillness where he uses his staring eyes under heavy brows to signal his rather stunned sensitivity to others. He displays his slender body proudly and then twists it into all kinds of pretzel-like shapes, as if heeding some inner music, some bebop, maybe. The sum total of all this work is still beguiling. He made being a mess seem romantic, a proper response to life. That dark trend has ebbed with time, but it was going strong mid-twentieth century, and Clift began it all.

When he first came on screen in Howard Hawks's *Red River* (1948), Clift resembled those girlish boys of the 1930s who spent most of their time looking in mirrors, but there were crucial differences. He was alien and strange, an avenging angel if necessary, and even a little macho, too. And also pretty gay. When faced with John Ireland's humpy gunslinger Cherry Valance, Clift's Matt is as amused and turned-on as any slim gay boy reacting to a particularly aggressive admirer when the two of them whip out their guns for a classic dick-measuring contest. Clift seems dazed by Ireland here, and there are times when his work has a druggy effect.

In his first scene in *Red River*, as he stands in the middle of John Wayne and Walter Brennan, who have most of the dialogue, Clift seems to be doing nothing, maybe even coasting on his looks, or smartly underplaying his hand while the seasoned movie men do their stuff. But look closer and you will see that his "nothing" is actually filled with all kinds of things, all sorts of thoughts that he is having that he is just barely sharing with us.

This would become another staple of the Method of this time: an extraordinary amount of work being done only so that one percent of it can be shown to the audience. Clift spearheaded a cerebral kind of style, thinking, thinking, thinking away, chewing on things privately and endlessly, so that when he takes pauses seemingly for no reason during his lines we have learned not to question them, for if it makes sense to him, that's all that is supposed to matter. When his Matt meets Tess (Joanne Dru) in *Red River* and she gives him some comfort, Clift offers a little exploding galaxy of tiny thoughts and emotions running over his face, showing us that he likes what she's saying in a split-second reaction of pleasure.

It must have taken enormous thought and technique to achieve this little complex mess of a close-up, and it proves that stylistic decadence can be as expressive at its height as the clean lines of Grant, Cagney, and Clift's co-star Wayne. Clift was always most touching on screen when considering the would-be safe harbor of a romantic love, and funny, too, as when he runs a hand over Dru's face and then shoots us a sidelong, very campy, "Well, fellas, what ya gonna do?" look. When he's being gay like that on screen, he is free to not be so torturously subtle and hidden.

Clift delights in being sexually provocative in *Red River*, shifting his tight little butt in his tight little pants with a line of bullets running along the top of them as a kind of accessory, and shamelessly giving head to a piece of straw. He knew what a looker he was, and he drew on that entitlement. In *Red River*, Clift even risked some blatant double entendre with Wayne, the symbol of old-school American masculinity. "You're going to wind up branding every rump in the state of Texas except mine," he quips, as Wayne's insecurity visibly grew. The Duke was never the same after hearing that, and neither were we.

When Clift's Matt finally realizes he has to stand up to Wayne's Tom for the sake of the men on their cattle drive, he is appealingly doubtful, almost bashful. But firm. When Wayne comes at him in the end with a gun, Clift just stands there staring, a cowboy St. Sebastian. "Won't anything make a man of ya?" the Duke snarled. The answer was "no," even if Clift did a standard fistfight with him for the conclusion, which took a lot of coaching from Hawks. The message seems to be that if you stand up to a bully the bully will back down. And that's the kind of thing happy endings are made of.

Elizabeth Taylor, who could have any man she wanted and generally did, flipped out over Clift. They connected both in life and in the sumptuous close-ups they shared in *A Place in the Sun* (1951), in which she memorably implored him to, "Tell Mama all." Taylor was even more beautiful than he was, but she knew that there had always been girls like her, whereas there had never been a man like Clift, at least not in the movies. His shrinking vulnerability and twitchy anxieties provided a cover for his serene confidence and downright stubborn insistence in living his life his own way and being who he was. When Ireland tells him that his heart is too soft and he might suffer for it in *Red River,* he just says, "Could be, but I wouldn't count on it." Well before James Dean, Clift was the real Mutant King.

Clift's characters were always joining the army or the priesthood, some institution where they could feel the security of rules and a structure. Acting was Clift's real-life institution and, like his movie prisons, it did not provide comfort and ultimately alienated him and made him resentful. There are lines of sensual duplicity that can be clearly traced through all his early film roles.

After finishing his first two movies, Clift attended classes and worked on scenes at the Actors Studio, where he was in unspoken competition with Marlon Brando. The new opacity he was bringing to the screen was beautifully used in William Wyler's *The Heiress* (1949), where Clift is Morris Townsend, a seductive, wolfish fortune hunter going after Olivia de Havilland's plain Catherine and her family funds.

Clift wanted the challenge of period clothes and no contractions in his dialogue and no room for odd pauses in *The Heiress*. He's so winning here, so deeply charming, and so attentive to de Havilland's Catherine that even if we have seen the movie 10 times we still can't be sure that he doesn't mean what he says to her (his Scarlett O'Hara waistline in tailored jackets and his big handsome head help this effect considerably). Acting is always partly about being a virtuoso of lying, and being a closeted gay actor gives you lots of time to practice that. Clift's Morris is mercenary but also, somehow, truly ardent as well. Or so it seems.

He was not happy with de Havilland and would make up his own dialogue for her instead of truly listening to her "because she isn't giving me what I need to respond," he told his friend Kevin McCarthy. He thought Miriam Hopkins was trying to hog scenes (he was right about that) and was put out by English theater pro Ralph Richardson's ability to do the same scene 30 times in exactly the same way. "Can't that man make any mistakes?" he wondered.

It was in mistakes and mess that Clift found his reality. *The Heiress* is fascinating partly because of the way Wyler meshes the very different styles of Clift, Richardson, Hopkins, and de Havilland. Richardson hits every nuance, and more besides, with his unerring theatrical instinct. Hopkins doesn't appear to be giving any thought to her role beyond its opportunity for showing off, yet she is very effective in it anyway, and her bluster works well in scenes with Clift because Morris is supposed to be impatient with her Aunt Penniman. De Havilland is as obvious and clear-cut as possible in her showy role, and up against Clift's scrupulous and disturbing un-obviousness.

Clift carried on a secret gay life while putting off enormous press attention, and this took its toll. He began taking all kinds of pills indiscriminately and sought out analysis partly because he didn't want to become "totally queer." He managed to take Garbo on a date and kissed her good night. "Her lips are chapped," he complained. He had a long-term and very unhealthy relationship with the older torch singer Libby Holman, who indulged him in every vice he had. "He wanted to love women, but he was attracted to men, and he crucified himself for it," observed Deborah Kerr.

He was having trouble getting any sleep at night. He started drinking very heavily (before 1949, he mainly drank milk). He was a soldier again in the weakest movie of his early period, *The Big Lift* (1950), where he tried to be a regular guy. Always in the background was his coach Mira Rostova, the lady he called his "artistic conscience." When Clift did a take, he would look to Rostova to nod or disapprove, and if she disapproved they did another take, regardless of what anyone else thought.

But then came *A Place in the Sun*, his signature film and performance in which he is a beautiful and lost man on a highway searching to belong, to join the aristocracy of money that he has been barred from by class, and to love, or at least be loved by, Elizabeth Taylor. (What did his mother Sunny make of this film?) Being outside looking in suited him, and so did a sense of impending doom.

A Place in the Sun is a slow, morbid movie, dependent on the poetry of Clift's face and its furtive responsiveness. He often touches his face, cupping it in his hand, because it is his fortune and he knows it. His boyish George is keen to escape his religious mother's hold on him, and he is seemingly dying of loneliness. He is desperate and selfish, or absorbed only in himself and his desires. And this was our hero, our identification point. There are times when he is a recessive pawn in that movie's scheme, a sacrificial lamb continually assailed by guilt and doubts. The faults of Clift's George in this movie are not wholly his but the faults of the system, man. Personal responsibility was a thing of the past, of the 1930s.

And of course the film helps Clift be sympathetic by making George's victim, played by Shelley Winters, as whiny and unappealing as possible, and Raymond Burr so absurdly aggressive as the showboating attorney browbeating Clift to the chair. (To his credit, Clift was very much against the way Winters played her part.) In all the scenes in the second half of the movie, where George is riding the waves of his worry and upset, Clift is constantly working up inner emotion, and the effort really shows, but it was that very effort that would lead to such acclaim by his fellow actors and by segments of the public. Here was process. Look at all this acting. Here was serious work, and so much of it.

He had become a huge romantic star. Women wanted to take care of him, mother him. They had not wanted to mother Cary Grant or Clark Gable, and Cagney could take care of himself. Clift made being vulnerable seem deeply attractive. But vulnerability like his could not last for long. And that's what retrospective cults are built out of. If Cary Grant was a cat and James Cagney a bantam rooster, then Clift was a needy puppy dog who needed 24/7 affection and attention.

In Alfred Hitchcock's *I Confess* (1953), Clift thinks and thinks and thinks opaquely as the compromised priest, exhaustingly, but it's hard to forget a close-up he has towards the end. Forced to hide his contempt for his victimizer, the murderous Otto Keller (O.E. Hasse), he makes his face into a mask, yet he can't keep his rage from radiating up out of his eyes, his mouth, even his nose. On screen and in life, Clift was at his most movingly tormented when he had to hide something.

He was a soldier a third time as Prewitt in *From Here to Eternity* (1953), his second signature role, where his face was a still and tragic mask with tears flowing down it as he played taps on a bugle for a fallen friend. These were real tears, no doubt—not Ingrid Bergman's glycerin. Prewitt was a boxer who did not want to fight anymore, and once again Clift was sacrificed. The dialogue keeps telling us that Prewitt is a loner, a rebel, a lone wolf, etc. And so Clift plays that, stubbornly. Nothing subtle in this movie, except the workings behind his eyes. With the prostitute Lorene (Donna Reed, with dark hair), he acts like a spoiled little kid who never wants to be away from his mother. It all seemed fresh at the time, far less so now. Everything in this movie seems sanitized, and everything has to be spelled out in block letters.

Clift is focused and at his best as Jennifer Jones's Italian lover in Vittorio De Sica's blighted *Indiscretion of an American Wife* (1954), and intensely male as he presses her to stay with him. Then, as they make up in a deserted railway car, Clift travels to the opposite end of the male spectrum and dares yet again to be soft, helpless, and ravishable. It is here that his neediness begins to seem ever-so-slightly creepy, or at least unreasonable. When he finally says goodbye to Jones, he falls off of her train onto the platform and makes an agonized face as he pulls himself up.

After his near-fatal car accident in 1956, which ruined his looks, he was difficult to watch on screen because his control and his confidence had deserted him. One side of his face was paralyzed, and his broken nose had destroyed his doll-like beauty. He was in excruciating pain, which no pills could really dent. His vanity obliterated, Clift even took down the mirrors that had once hung all over his New York brownstone.

His film roles after that were purely painful. *Raintree County* (1957) alternates between pre-accident and post-accident footage, often within the same scene. At the premiere of *The Young Lions* (1958), a woman in the audience screamed and fainted when she saw the first close-up of his face, and Clift was there to hear that reaction. After that personal disaster he flinched through several others, doing work that was too much in terms of physical tics and not enough in terms of strong, expressive choices. He was cradled by Lee Remick in *Wild River* (1960), was horribly exploited by Stanley Kramer as a man broken by Nazis in *Judgment at Nuremberg* (1961), and tended once again to Elizabeth Taylor in Tennessee Williams's *Suddenly, Last Summer* (1959).

"My face is fine, all healed up, as good as new," he tells his unseen mother on the phone in *The Misfits*

Montgomery Clift is both beseeching and demanding in *Indiscretion of an American Wife*.

(1961), where he plays a punchy rodeo rider. Clark Gable looks indulgently at him, while Marilyn Monroe seems lost in her own chemical ether, as needy and baby-like as he is. It was impossible to cast or believe him now as anything but what he was, a broken person in a state of constant disorder and pain. A big part of his problem, too, was that he was closing in on 40 but was still acting like a much younger man. His life off screen became a series of squalid episodes, embarrassing, humiliating, damning and damned.

In an interview she did with John Kobal in the early 1970s, Loretta Young, a beauty and a journeyman player of the 1930s and '40s, made a fairly brutal assessment of Clift and what happened to him. "The effect that you have is not only your acting but it's also your looks," she said. "Before his accident when his face was all destroyed, he was considered one of the most attractive, marvelous actors, one of the greats, because his face was so gorgeous and so romantic, and everything he did, if you just looked at him, oh, you just died! Then he had the accident. Now, he was the same actor, saying the same dialogue exactly as before, but now you just thought, 'What is he doing?'" It was not as simple as that, but Young's pragmatic verdict on Clift is worth pondering. To have so much and to have it taken entirely away from you is tragic, and the definition of tragedy is in its inevitability, its portentousness. That was all there with Clift from the start.

Clift died in 1966, and though he has been written about fairly often and still has his fans, he is not the icon that his less elegant bastard children, Marlon Brando and Dean, have become. Clift is buried not in Paris, Rome or Los Angeles but in Prospect Park, Brooklyn, in a Quaker cemetery owned by the Religious Society of Friends. Clift's mother Sunny had insisted he be buried there. It is not open to the public.

Kim Stanley
Private Moments

Anyone who saw Kim Stanley on stage during her 10-year Broadway heyday from William Inge's *Picnic* in 1953 to Inge's *Natural Affection* in 1963 marveled at her frayed immediacy and her predilection for unearthing the most painful emotions. She did not work for the camera too much, but her influence was so extreme that she can stand in, as example and cautionary tale, for what was happening in acting for women at this time.

Stanley was the queen of the Actors Studio and a prized pupil of Lee Strasberg. She went as far as she could with his most dangerous acting technique, affective memory, the substitution of an actor's real life emotions for the feelings of the character they are playing. Stanley was a Jeanne Eagels for the Freudian 1950s, and she seems to have viewed her profession as some kind of adjunct to psychotherapy. An acquaintance noticed something in her "like a high C held too long."

Such intensity exacted a high price, and Stanley seems to have paid it willingly, even gloatingly. In Jon Krampner's valuable 2006 biography of the actress, *Female Brando*, he answers a lot of questions about what went wrong with her career and her life. After a disastrous London production of Chekhov's *Three Sisters*, Stanley retreated from the stage permanently, and there was little word about what had happened to her, other than that she'd had a nervous breakdown, or several nervous breakdowns. Krampner digs to the bottom of her mystery and what he reveals is as upsetting and suggestive as the tales of the remaining few who remember her work on stage.

Stanley was born in New Mexico. She was one of those people who spun tall tales about their past, and she usually insisted that she was from Texas. With her tiny eyes, large nose, and heavy jaw, she was far from pretty, but she turned this into an asset, even emphasizing her physical flaws in her search for raw truth. She did a lot of live television along with her plays, focusing particularly on the work of Horton Foote and Inge, who gave her her biggest theatrical hit, *Bus Stop*. Stanley received nearly nothing but raves from the critics for everything she did on stage. Her personal life was messy and she liked it that way—it seems clear that she created pain and chaos for herself in order to channel it into her performances. Actress Anne Jackson observed, "Unless she went into a frenzy of emotion, she didn't think she was giving it her all."

Because of the nerve-scraping way she worked, Stanley missed many performances and could only tolerate short runs, and she left successful plays when the strain got to be too much for her. She did an unusually long run in Eugene O'Neill's *A Touch of the Poet* in 1958, where she shared the stage with an abusive Eric Portman and an above-it-all Helen Hayes. After Stanley's departure, old pro Hayes reflected, "Kim would have tried the patience of a saint with her striving for an opening-night level of performance—even on rainy Thursdays."

In 1961, when she played a patient of Freud himself on stage in *A Far Country*, Stanley was flaming out. In order to do a primal scream at the end of Act II, she used the memory of her brother's death for a while to get the effect she wanted. Several firsthand witnesses testify in Krampner's book to this moment's unnerving power, but whether it seemed specific to the character she was playing is another matter. What isn't up for debate is that such Strasberg methods began to destroy Stanley, and that her drinking, which was always heavy, began to take over her life.

By the time of Strasberg's production of *Three Sisters*, Stanley had put on considerable weight, and this reflected her plunge into unbridled self-indulgence. In a recording of the production, Stanley gives a self-centered, pre-occupied performance, playing Masha as if she were mentally ill or disturbed. Unmoved by Chekhov's words, she often improvised some of her own. Kevin McCarthy, who played Vershinin, picked up Stanley's script one day and saw that for every one of his lines she had struck out "Vershinin" and written, "Father." This substitution makes little sense for the character, but it made perfect sense for Stanley, who spent a lifetime in loathing resentment of her daddy, a man who paid no attention to her. Opening under poor circumstances in London, Stanley and the Actors Studio company were booed. This was a sort of last straw for her.

Many of her friends reported that Stanley couldn't tell the difference, finally, between off stage and on. Anyone who has utilized substitutions and affective memory knows that they can have a devastating effect on a performer, especially if they're using traumas on stage night after night, as Stanley did. Most acting coaches advise their students to only use substitutions as a last resort, and then but carefully and briefly. Stanley made a whole career out of them and they ruined her life.

As always when it came to women on film, looks and sexual viability played a part in who got screen work and who didn't. Harry Cohn, the Columbia executive who had humiliated Louise Brooks in the 1930s when she turned him down sexually, made sure that Stanley didn't play the Donna Reed part in *From Here to Eternity* that Fred Zinnemann wanted her for. "Why are you bringing me this girlie?" Cohn asked Zinnemann, staring straight at Stanley. "She's not even pretty." Stanley called Cohn a pig and left. "I mean, I *knew* I wasn't pretty," she said later to interviewer John Kobal. "But I wasn't ready for that kind of artillery at that close a range!" She could not be naked like Brooks on screen, or naked and needy like Marilyn Monroe. She would need to prove herself by acting, and acting for her meant hysteria, push, and aggressively expressed unhappiness.

Stanley only starred in two features, *The Goddess* (1958) and *Séance on a Wet Afternoon* (1964). To her credit, she was unhappy with her performance in *The Goddess*, where she's playing a sort of Marilyn Monroe figure re-cast in her own image. A producer says here that Stanley's Rita Shawn will be popular because she is "not particularly pretty" but has a quality of "availability" that will please a male audience.

Stanley was thrown by the way films are shot out of sequence, and she is very self-consciously aware of the camera in *The Goddess* and forced to do too many crying jags towards the end, all at an immense level of emotional breakdown. We are a long way from Gish's True Heart Susie hiding her feelings of sorrow from the boy she loves at his engagement party, or Hepburn's Alice Adams brightly chattering through disaster. In Stanley's time, giving in to your worst emotional impulses was seen by some as a badge of honesty and honor.

Kim Stanley screams, "There ain't no God!" in *The Goddess*.

In the non-breakdown scenes in *The Goddess*, Stanley sometimes gets by on technique and seems somewhat disconnected from what she's doing, or trying to do, but Paddy Chayefsky's screenplay is so self-important, moralizing, and blunt that it leaves her with few other options. James Cromwell, the son of director John Cromwell, has said that his father was forced to piece together *The Goddess* from out-takes after Chayefsky had tried to edit the film himself and had destroyed most of the preferred takes. And so this movie debut for Stanley was in many ways cursed.

Stanley's movements can be very abruptly diva theatrical in *The Goddess*, more Bette Davis than Marilyn, and her eyes are as hooded and inexpressive as another stage star, Tallulah Bankhead, who made only a few films. Her high voice falls into mannered repetitions, particularly an overused laugh on an exhalation of breath meant to release tension. She'll stumble over words sometimes for a naturalistic effect (or because this was the only take available), but there's a basic unreality to her performance in *The Goddess* that she was well aware of.

In his 1991 book *Method Actors*, Steve Vineberg is unsparing in his criticism of Stanley's work: "She's too pre-occupied with her own feelings to pay attention to the relationship between dialogue and action, action and motivation, character and context (of all kinds—settings, situations, the other characters) ... the separation between cause and effect is too much a constant in her acting."

As *Séance*'s half-crazy medium, Stanley is far more controlled than she is in *The Goddess*, but so lost in her own fantasy world that she doesn't share any of it with the audience. Her scenes play like inward, cut-off acting exercises for Strasberg, and she could not or would not match shots to be in the same place twice. At one point her director, Bryan Forbes, had the camera moving across a kitchen with her when she stopped unexpectedly. He called cut and asked her what she was doing. "I was relating to the oranges," she told him.

In the séance that ends the film, she goes all out, in her way. "This sequence is a catalogue of weird Stanley mannerisms," writes Vineberg. "The insistent distractedness; the ritualistic singsong dissociations; the cry of release on a sharp intake of breath; and the buzzing, closed-off tantrum (as if she heard some inner hum and was pulling in all her energies to track it down)."

Stanley fares better in surviving live TV dramas like Horton Foote's *A Young Lady of Property* (1953), where her channeling of fear and nostalgia has a spooky kind of enclosure, and *The Traveling Lady* (1957), where she's touching because her character is clearly fighting against extreme upset, True

Heart Susie–like, rather than giving in to it. "She could use stillness, she could use quiet," Foote said. "She could not say anything, and yet there was this compelling thing about her. She changed the whole style of acting in that period for young women. They weren't always good imitations, but she had an enormous influence."

In *Tomorrow* (1960), a TV adaptation of a William Faulkner story, Stanley plays most of her scenes in bed, and she brings an immediacy to everything she says and does, diving down into the depths and immersing herself in every feeling she is summoning, which is why Stanley was at her best on live TV and in the theater, and also why she was so tormented.

That torment is especially visible in a two-part *Ben Casey* TV episode from 1963 called "A Cardinal Act of Mercy," for which she won her first Emmy. As a smart, mean-mouthed junkie lawyer, Stanley's delivery is Bette Davis–like in its imperiousness, and when she goes through withdrawal, every moment feels fresh, intuitive yet precise. No stopping to relate to the oranges here, or getting neurotically lost in every little moment. This is a performance that defines the term "riveting" and helps explain Stanley's reputation. Right before she fell apart, she proved she could have Davis's authority, but she lacked Davis's sense of fight and professionalism.

The quality of her performance on that show was at least partly due to some direction from Sydney Pollack, who told her that her work was "full of little pearls that are beautiful in themselves, but it needs an overall bit of connection, something to string the pearls together." Stanley was hurt by his criticism, but it very much helped her, and she needed that help and guidance. It might be said that like Clift in *Judgment at Nuremberg* Stanley is a mess being a mess on this show, but there is just enough technique visible here to lift her out of that mire.

There were only a few more credits before she capsized. She narrated *To Kill a Mockingbird* (1962) and refused screen credit. In a filmed Tennessee Williams one-act from 1970 called *I Can't Imagine Tomorrow*, Stanley is clearly diminished physically and emotionally, barely holding herself together. She has entered a zone where she has no control over even her lack of control, and the results are highly unsettling, tied to grimacing alcoholic half-impulses, hyperventilating, and foggy ideas. She gropes around in the dark, in chaos, the inverse of what Lillian Gish was doing at the dawn of the twentieth century. Stanley could barely remember lines at this point, and she reads them from off camera, as Brando was doing, and blurs every one of them. At the end of the play she gets upset and yells a bit, as if to remind us, and herself, who she is.

Tony Richardson hired her to play Claire in the film of Edward Albee's

A Delicate Balance in 1973. When the cast gathered for a first reading, Stanley went off script. "She began to improvise on Edward's text," Richardson said. "She crawled on the floor, she sputtered, she cried. Looked on one way it was a parody of the stereotypical view of Method acting ... it had the ugliness, the truth, the understanding of great art. But it was clear that Kim's truth was at the expense of everything else—the other performers, the text of the play, and the exigencies of the production." After this reading, the film's star Katharine Hepburn said she was withdrawing from the production. Stanley tried to meet to talk with Hepburn but was refused. Stanley was fired, and Hepburn rejoined the cast. After that, Stanley disappeared to do her serious drinking.

Flat broke, Stanley got work as an acting teacher in New Mexico and directed her biggest stage triumph, *Bus Stop*, for students. Later she moved to New York for a time and gave legendary acting classes that started at 7PM and sometimes lasted until dawn. Such marathon sessions would alternate with weeks of dedicated boozing. One day, two students saw her struggling with groceries on the street and ran to help her. She didn't recognize them but turned to one and said mysteriously, "You—I kill. And I don't kill many." Then she went upstairs to drink, a once important actress playing out an extended psychodrama to the four walls of her filthy, bare apartment in Soho.

She continued to exercise her art, but in isolation. In the late 1970s, she told an inquisitive reporter that she was still "working quietly—from within." Though Stanley is often compared to Brando, the real point of comparison would seem to be Charles Laughton, another tormented actor who viewed acting as an art much like writing or painting. It's hard not to think that Stanley continued to perform, even if her performance was generally "great actress fallen on hard times." She didn't feel finally that she needed an audience. If those walls in Soho could talk, we might have an actress equivalent to Joyce's *Finnegans Wake*.

In the early 1980s, Stanley re-surfaced for three films, doing a cameo in *The Right Stuff* (1983), winning another Emmy as a boisterous, shrill Big Mama in a made-for-cable *Cat on a Hot Tin Roof* (1984), and giving herself over to *Frances* (1982), where she's excellent as a touchy, disappointed, and finally vengeful mother to Jessica Lange's embattled movie star. Her most vivid moment here is when her baleful features are flooded by outright evil as she sits at the bottom of a staircase after a huge confrontation with her daughter and then says, "You have really done it, little sister." She is nearly unmoving but alive inside with malice, as if Stanley is channeling something demonic.

She was after the truth, and the truth to her could be extremely ugly. In all three of her major feature film performances, Stanley played miserable neurotics who longed for fame. The real woman rejected fame and went on a quixotic search for truth by herself. She gave some more acting classes in the mid–1980s, but after about 1988 she became a recluse who rarely left her home. She died in 2001.

Unlike Laurette Taylor, another major and alcoholic star of the theater, Stanley never emerged for one more hurrah, as Taylor did on stage in the original production of Tennessee Williams's *The Glass Menagerie* in 1944. But her retreat seems to have been an elaborate, modernist, and stinging gesture of defiance from a woman who had had enough of the world and who had the guts and the perversity to continue practicing her art in squalid, Beckett-like isolation.

James Dean
Cause and Effect

James Dean, who died in a car crash at age 24, has outstripped even Brando in iconographical status because he was a world-class exhibitionist who, in the last few years of his life, was almost always in front of a camera. It is in still photos that the Dean legend is most potent and most understandable, and he has this in common with Marilyn Monroe and Elvis Presley. His cool vibe still works in photo books and on T-shirts, on mugs and posters.

In his first lead feature role, Elia Kazan's *East of Eden* (1955), he's doing a Brando take off deepened by his own aggressive need to charm every man, woman, child, and dog around him. Dean even tries to charm plants. Hoping to raise a bean crop to help his financially ruined father (Raymond Massey), Dean does a dance around the crops and talks to them as if they were a lover. His miming of vulnerability is hair-raisingly calculated.

Dean's unhappy Indiana childhood and teen years have been raked over again and again and have become clearer with time: the loss of his mother, his distant relationship with his unloving father, his mentorship with an older man, a certain Reverend DeWeerd, who initiated an inappropriate sexual relationship with the troubled teenager. This was followed by the self-loathing sexual ambiguity that led to whoring himself out to male Hollywood executives who might help his ambition to become an actor, the most important of whom was Rogers Brackett, who let Dean live with him in exchange for sexual favors.

In New York, Dean played the Apostle John in his first credited appearance on TV, "Hill Number One" (1951), where he spoke in a lowered voice due to a bad cold. Back in Hollywood, he had uncredited bits in Samuel Fuller's *Fixed Bayonets* (1951) and as a soda jerk in Douglas Sirk's *Has Anybody Seen My Gal* (1952).

He worked a lot more on live TV in New York, mainly as lowlifes and crooks. In 1952, Dean used a minuscule bellhop role to briefly steal focus from John Forsythe in "Ten Thousand Horses Singing" and he was a snivelingly abject soldier pardoned by Abraham Lincoln (Robert Pastene) for *Studio*

One. He did 16 short television episodes in 1953, playing Bob Ford in "The Capture of Jesse James," a bespectacled assistant to Rod Steiger in "The Evil Within," and a convincingly dumb and sweet ex-convict unjustly accused of murder in "Sentence of Death," where his every gesture and movement feels very fresh, very original, very direct.

As a thief redeemed by love in "Something for an Empty Briefcase," there's something prodigious and Mozartian about Dean's sensual and sometimes downright goofy series of physical gestures, his dancer-like little epiphanies, the pure and very adolescent immediacy of his emotions, particularly those that are based in shame and surprise. He could look almost ugly sometimes but could turn on a dime and appear to be one of the best-looking men who had ever lived—a freak and a prince, a lower class sinner and saint. He was the liberating, all-seeing, all-sensitive, tender, uninhibited person everyone longs to meet as a friend or a lover or both.

Dean was a shirtless laborer in "The Bells of Cockaigne," an advertisement for his sexiness, and he played Dorothy Gish's restless son in "Harvest." He created an extraordinary sense of intimacy with Natalie Wood in the final scene of "I'm a Fool" (1954), a Sherwood Anderson adaptation that is otherwise given over to a lot of narration from Eddie Albert, supposedly Dean as an older man (as if!).

He was a hepcat criminal tormenting Ronald Reagan in "The Dark, Dark Hours" (1954), where when the tables turn Dean whines, "Hit me, why don't you hit me?" He played with Mary Astor in "The Thief" (1955), and she later wrote, "Jimmy was six feet away from me in one scene and I could barely hear what he was saying, and what I could hear seemed to have very little to do with the script." But she recognized that she was being too rigid in her strict professionalism after Dean got all the notice, and the notices, with his unorthodox approach on their show.

He played on Broadway as a homosexual Arab boy seducer in an adaptation of André Gide's *The Immoralist* and made quite an impression, but he left the play soon after it opened to be in *East of Eden*. He crouches in that movie, slouches, throws himself to the ground, and throws his head back in agony or ecstasy. Radioactively sexy, Dean is also a grotesque, a weird mixture of Frankenstein's monster and the prettiest of pouting pretty boys (as a kid he once dressed up as Karloff's creature for a school play, and this Karloff influence seems key).

But whenever he talks in *East of Eden*, he's doing his very mannered idea of Brando: taking pauses for no clear reason, hesitating over words, repeating words, scratching himself, pulling his ear, mumbling. He burrows into himself and suggests a sly and private interior life, something closed-off, and this was a seductive thing for many people watching him. At times his body language seems so presentational yet shrinking that the effect is deeply submissive and seems intensely sexual. Brando outright displays his body like this too, but in a drastically different, sexually dominant way.

Meant to be naturalistic, Dean's performance is highly self-conscious, even in the famous moment when he tries to give his father money and explodes in frightening, far-out grief. In Lillian Gish's scenes with her father in *Broken Blossoms*, she has such control over her most extreme visual effects that they are lucid for us even at their highest pitch of emotion. Dean gives in to his extreme emotions and makes a colorful, difficult-to-parse mess, impressive but basically non-functional, un-useful for anyone else but himself. Gish's work stands in for all suffering children. Dean's work stands not even for his character Cal but for himself, and it won't do to say that millions identified with him, and still do. It was more that they had fallen in love with him. And that love is a morbid thing.

Dean is so lost in his own acted-out neuroses that he forces Julie Harris, his gifted, lyrical leading lady, to mop up his excess in scene after scene, which she does successfully, especially in their lengthy jaunt through an amusement park. When he kisses her on top of a Ferris wheel, he leans in submissively like some newborn creature, and the intense and liquid quality of his slow movements transfix the camera just as Eleonora Duse's did in her film *Ashes* from 1916. What Dean was adding, in ways that would have surprised and even offended Duse and Lillian Gish, were touches of the neurotic and the sexual, the hip and the disordered, the romantic and the self-destructive.

Gish might have been delighted with the work of Julie Harris, Eva Marie Saint (who played the sweet Thelma with her on TV and Broadway in *A Trip to Bountiful*), and Kim Hunter, the sane and even saintly Method women of

James Dean looks for love from Julie Harris in *East of Eden*.

this time. But just imagine her frown of disapproval and bewilderment at the work of Kim Stanley (who played the shrewish Jessie Mae with her in a tour of *A Trip to Bountiful*), Geraldine Page, Sandy Dennis, Shirley Knight, and Shelley Winters, with whom she does not share a scene in *The Night of the Hunter*.

Then again, Gish might have viewed Dean, as she does her charges in *The Night of the Hunter*, with a stern but indulgent smile. She knew more about sexual display and withholding than Brando and Dean combined, but she worked in that area by instinct. These new actors blasted away her hypocrisy and the stylized distance of the classic Hollywood players and made all behavior unknowable yet fully conscious, so conscious that it led to self-love and self-loathing until the individual self seems sick, untenable, in desperate need of others.

Dean's scenes with Raymond Massey in *East of Eden* play out like a less inspired version of Kazan's Vivien Leigh/Brando dichotomy in *Streetcar*. Kazan sets up the older performer (Massey and Leigh) as the hollow, fussy standard bearer, while his young rebels (Brando and Dean) wear tight clothes and deploy an arsenal of Method tactics in order to sexily sneer at the establishment. It all finally seems to have more to do with acting than with anything else the movies are supposed to be about. In *East of Eden*, the deck is stacked in another way in that Richard Davalos, who plays Dean's brother and rival Aaron, is a limited actor and no competition for Dean on any level.

"I don't want any kind of love," Dean finally tells Massey. "It doesn't pay off," he mumbles, walking away, and this mumble is actually very close to the way Cary Grant would sometimes talk to himself. Even the most representative classic Hollywood stars like Grant and Katharine Hepburn had their private moments, or private thoughts, running commentaries, there for those who might notice them and take them to heart. But they were special gifts, tucked away inside so much else.

Dean played a Korean war vet in an undistinguished TV drama, "The Unlighted Road" (1955), and then he took his great film role, Jim Stark in Nicholas Ray's romantic, despairing *Rebel Without a Cause* (1955), a self-contained portrait of three isolated teenagers. You'd think that *Rebel* would date more than Dean's first film *East of Eden*, and it's true that some of its details and performances don't ring true now, especially the cartoonish portrayals of the parents of the teenagers at its center. At revival houses, the scenes with the parents tend to get unwanted laughs, and they are flawed, but only on the surface. The Oedipal attitudes of *East of Eden* are dated and broad but the poetic longing for connection in *Rebel* can never really date.

Dean isn't fussy in *Rebel*, as he is in his agonized Brando-esque contortions in *East of Eden*. He's emotionally direct, tenderly seductive, protective of others, and blessed with courtly humor, mercurial, enjoying his own unexpected reactions, like a jazz musician improvising and setting the tone. Dean's Jim Stark is clearly laboring under a burden of heightened sensitivity, which is why the 1950s complacency of his parents and their milieu is, in his words, tearing him apart.

Jim doesn't want to be called a chicken by his peers, but he realizes that the tests of manhood he is forced to endure by the thugs at school are bullshit, as false in their way as the world of his parents. So, in the most magical section of the film, Jim and his friends Judy (Natalie Wood) and Plato (Sal Mineo) take over a deserted mansion and try to make a family for themselves. This primal, Frank Borzage–like sequence doesn't last long, but it has made a major impact on anybody who has seen it.

Stewart Stern's screenplay can be didactic, but Ray and his young trio of actors transcend this limitation. Ray emphasizes the reds and blues in his widescreen frame for a sexily neurotic effect, and he showcases savant-like Dean as gently as Jim Stark takes care of Plato. Ray seems to understand the self-dramatizations and exaggerated melancholy of adolescence, but he portrays these qualities with deep affection, respect, and insight.

The most complicated aspect of *Rebel*, and the thing that makes it seem daring even today, is its sexuality. Ray was bisexual and he was sleeping with both Wood and Mineo while they shot the film. He brings Wood's beauty into full flowering and gets a simple, touching performance from her (though she is overwrought in her first scene). With Mineo, Ray craftily put together a portrait of a tormented gay teenager. Stern's script tells us that Plato is searching for a father figure in Jim Stark, and Plato's locker photo of Alan Ladd shows that he wants a Shane-type father, not a lover, but the way Mineo looks at Dean leaves no modern audience in doubt as to what his real feelings are.

The teenagers' idyll in the deserted mansion is ended by the intrusion of school thugs (one of them a young Dennis Hopper). Plato, confused and unbalanced, starts firing a gun he took from his mother's room. He finds refuge in a planetarium, and Jim goes in to get him, talking him outside and surreptitiously taking the bullets from the gun. But Plato gets scared and runs, the cops see the gun, and they shoot him.

When Plato is shot, Ray has Jim and Judy in the frame with him and Ray tilts the camera with the impact of the bullet, one of the most visceral shots in film history because it visually annihilates the rapport the three teenagers have built up in an instant. Jim and Judy go off together, but Ray underlines the film's sense of loss by saving the last close-up for the only other person who loved Plato, his family maid (Marietta Canty). As everyone drives away, it is Ray himself who enters the planetarium at the break of day, a romantic film director surveying the blank slate left after Jim, Judy, and Plato's wishful, improved civilization is wiped out in a flash of gunfire.

The thing about Dean that was and still is so powerfully attractive is the feeling that he has a better idea about how to live than we do. In his best work, he is paternal in a new kind of embracing, accepting way. Which is why it's such a shame that he never lived to come into his own in the 1960s. Surely he might have been a leader in that time, instead of a deceased and longed-for mutant king. On the other hand, there are moments in his films when he suggests that he might have become a self-indulgent tyrant, making others wait on his every tormented pause.

Giant (1956), the last and least of Dean's three movies, is a lengthy, earnest, arbitrary Texas soap opera, and Dean is not in all that much of it (director George Stevens disliked him and thwarted his attempts at improvisation). As Jett Rink, an outsider who strikes oil, Dean is usually shot in shadow in cowboy hat and tight blue jeans, and he has only two good scenes. His Jett touchingly tries to make Elizabeth Taylor's Leslie feel at home by making her tea in his little house, and when he comes covered in Texas crude to her ranch to announce that he has struck oil, Dean's Jett is filled with his own crude animal vitality.

Otherwise, the only thing worth remembering for Dean fans is the way he dances weirdly across the prairie every now and again, still trying to charm the land as he does in *East of Eden*. He really does mumble a lot in *Giant* and stays resolutely inside himself, to an excessive degree. It was a kind of final retreat, this performance, and it set a bad example, alas. Lofty and obscure self-pity crept into many of our screen actors, and it has been a hard thing to wash away.

With Gish, with Cagney and Stanwyck and Grant and Hepburn, acting was a way of finding the right look for an emotion, a thought, a state of mind. It could be extreme, or subtle. It was meant to communicate. It had other people in mind. With Brando and Dean and the other Method actors of the 1950s, communication is in the back of their mind, but it gets blurred and dim in the swamp of their own needs and selves and pre-occupations. They are creeping away from us all the time, and that creeping was sexy, seductive. But some sex is a dead end. And some sex is a miraculous communication.

When he was told Dean had died by his lover Libby Holman, Montgomery Clift instantly threw up all over her white satin sheets. A cult sprang up after Dean's premature death the likes of which has seldom been seen. For decades there were documentaries, books, and pilgrimages to the site of

Cary Grant and Katharine Hepburn in *Bringing Up Baby*.

Dean's grave in his hometown of Fairmount, Indiana, the headstone of which was always covered with lipstick traces. The few people who knew him became Dean lifers: his teacher Adeline Nall, his best friend Bill Bast, his Actors Studio scene partner Christine White, his dancer girlfriend Dizzy Sheridan, all of whom went over and over again the short time they knew him.

We've had Dean for a long time now, and his influence can still be felt. He divides acting on screen in the twentieth century right down the middle. The men who came after him and Brando would make a new way of doing things in the 1970s, a very neurotic time, a time where failure was a given. For me, I generally prefer to dwell in the time before that dissolution, in the time when Cary Grant was moving at an angle, when James Cagney was dancing on the sides of his legs, when Bette Davis was flashing her eyes and telling people off, and when Katharine Hepburn's Susan Vance was saying "Everything is going to be all right" through every possible disaster.

Bibliography

Affron, Charles. *Lillian Gish: Her Legend, Her Life*. University of California Press, 2002.
Affron, Charles. *Star Acting: Gish, Garbo, Davis*. E.P. Dutton, 1977.
Agee, James. *Agee on Film*. Modern Library, 2000.
Astor, Mary. *My Life on Film*. Delacorte, 1971.
Bacall, Lauren. *Lauren Bacall: By Myself*. Knopf, 1978.
Bach, Steven. *Marlene Dietrich*. William Morrow, 1992.
Bachardy, Don. *Stars in My Eyes*. University of Wisconsin Press, 2000.
Bast, Bill. *Surviving James Dean*. Barricade Books, 2006.
Bergman, Ingrid, with Alan Burgess. *Ingrid Bergman: My Story*. Delacorte Press, 1980.
Blake, Michael, F. *Lon Chaney: The Man Behind the Thousand Faces*. Vestal Press, 1997.
Bosworth, Patricia. *Montgomery Clift*. Harcourt, 1978.
Brooks, Louise. *Lulu in Hollywood*. Knopf, 1982.
Brownlow, Kevin. *Mary Pickford Rediscovered*. Abrams, 1999.
Callow, Simon. *Charles Laughton: A Difficult Actor*. Methuen, 1987.
Capra, Frank. *Frank Capra: The Name Above the Title*. Macmillan, 1971.
Considine, Shaun. *Bette and Joan: The Divine Feud*. Dutton, 1989.
Crawford, Christina. *Mommie Dearest*. William Morrow, 1978.
Crawford, Joan. *My Way of Life*. Simon & Schuster, 1971.
Crawford, Joan, with Jane Kesner Ardmore. *A Portrait of Joan*. Doubleday, 1962.
Croce, Arlene. *The Fred Astaire and Ginger Rogers Book*. Dutton, 1972.
Curcio, Vincent. *Suicide Blonde: The Life of Gloria Grahame*. Morrow, 1989.
Curtis, James. *Spencer Tracy: A Biography*. Knopf, 2011.
Dalton, David. *James Dean: The Mutant King*. St. Martin's Press, 1974.
Davis, Bette. *The Lonely Life*. Putnam's, 1962.
Deschner, Donald. *Complete Films of Cary Grant*. Citadel, 1983.
Dickens, Homer. *The Films of Katharine Hepburn*. Citadel, 1971.
Dietrich, Marlene. *Marlene*. Avon, 1987.
Dietrich, Marlene. *Marlene Dietrich's ABC*. Ungar, 1961.
Donati, William. *Ida Lupino: A Biography*. University Press of Kentucky, 2000.
Epstein, Edward Z. *Portrait of Jennifer: A Biography of Jennifer Jones*. Simon & Schuster, 1995.
Eyman, Scott. *Mary Pickford: America's Sweetheart*. Dutton, 1990.
Gallagher, Tag. *The Adventures of Roberto Rossellini*. Da Capo Press, 1998.
Gish, Lillian, with Ann Pinchot. *The Movies, Mr. Griffith, and Me*. Prentice Hall, 1969.
Harvey, James. *Movie Love in the Fifties*. Knopf, 2001.
Harvey, James. *Romantic Comedy*. Knopf, 1987.
Hayward, Brooke. *Haywire*. Knopf, 1977.
Hepburn, Katharine. *Me*. Knopf, 1991.
Hyman, B.D. *My Mother's Keeper*. William Morrow, 1985.
Kael, Pauline. *5001 Nights at the Movies*. Holt, Rinehart and Winston, 1982.
Kazan, Elia. *A Life*. Knopf, 1988.
Kear, Lynn, with John Rossman. *Kay Francis: A Passionate Life and Career*. McFarland, 2006.
Kobal, John. *People Will Talk*. Knopf, 1985.
Krampner, Jon. *Female Brando: The Legend of Kim Stanley*. Back Stage Books, 2006.
Lambert, Gavin. *Norma Shearer: A Biography*. Knopf, 1990.

Lambert, Gavin. *On Cukor.* G.P. Putnam's, 1972.
Loy, Myrna, with James Kotsilibas-Davis. *Being and Becoming.* Knopf, 1987.
Mann, William J. *Kate: The Woman Who Was Hepburn.* Henry Holt, 2006.
McCabe, John. *Cagney.* Random House, 1997.
Morley, Sheridan. *James Mason: Odd Man Out.* HarperCollins, 1989.
Morrison, Michael A. *John Barrymore: Shakespearian Actor.* Cambridge University Press, 1999.
Newquist, Roy. *Conversations with Joan Crawford.* Citadel Press, 1980.
O'Brien, Scott. *Kay Francis: I Can't Wait to Be Forgotten: Her Life on Film and Stage.* BearManor Media, 2007.
Oderman, Stuart. *Lillian Gish: A Life on Stage and Screen.* McFarland, 2009.
Oller, John. *Jean Arthur: The Actress Nobody Knew.* Limelight, 1997.
Ott, Frederick. *The Films of Carole Lombard.* Lyle Stuart, 1984.
Paris, Barry. *Garbo.* Knopf, 1994.
Paris, Barry. *Louise Brooks.* Knopf, 1989.
Pickford, Mary. *Sunshine and Shadow.* Doubleday, 1955.
Quirk, Lawrence J. *Fasten Your Seatbelts: The Passionate Life of Bette Davis.* Morrow, 1990.
Quirk, Lawrence J. *The Films of Gloria Swanson.* Citadel Press, 1984.
Quirk, Lawrence, with William Schoell. *Joan Crawford: The Essential Biography.* University Press of Kentucky, 2002.
Riva, Maria. *Marlene Dietrich.* Ballantine Books, 1992.
Rogers, Ginger. *My Story.* HarperCollins, 1991.
Rooney, Mickey. *Life Is Too Short.* Villard Books, 1991.
Royce, Bill. *Cary Grant: The Wizard of Beverly Grove.* Cool Titles, 2006.
Skal, David J, with Jessica Rains. *Claude Rains: An Actor's Voice.* University Press of Kentucky, 2009.
Stenn, David. *Bombshell: The Life and Death of Jean Harlow.* Doubleday, 1993.
Stenn, David. *Clara Bow: Runnin' Wild.* Doubleday, 1988.
Sternberg, Josef von. *Fun in a Chinese Laundry.* Macmillan, 1965.
Stine, Whitney. *"I'd Love to Kiss You...": Conversations with Bette Davis.* Pocket Books, 1990.
Stine, Whitney, with Bette Davis. *Mother Goddam.* Berkeley, 1974.
Swanson, Gloria. *Swanson on Swanson*, Random House, 1980.
Swindell, Larry. *Charles Boyer: The Reluctant Lover.* Doubleday, 1983.
Thomas, Bob. *Joan Crawford.* Simon & Schuster, 1978.
Thomson, David. *A Biographical Dictionary of Film.* Knopf, 2014.
Vanderbeets, Richard. *George Sanders: An Exhausted Life.* Madison Books, 1993.
Vineberg, Steve. *Method Actors: Three Generations of an American Acting Style.* Schirmer Trade Books, 1991.
Youngkin, Stephen, D. *The Lost One: A Life of Peter Lorre.* University Press of Kentucky, 2005.

Index

Abbott and Costello 164
The Actress (1953) 182
Adam's Rib (1949) 104, 181
Adler, Stella 196
Adrian 52, 118
Advise & Consent (1962) 168
An Affair to Remember (1957) 154
Affron, Charles 50
The African Queen 104, 105, 190
Agee, James 165
Aherne, Brian 75
Airport 1975 (1974) 28
Albee, Edward 109, 212
Aldrich, Robert 88, 90, 123, 124
Alice Adams (1935) 99
All About Eve (1950) 87
All This, and Heaven Too (1940) 81, 82
Altman, Robert 19
Anastasia (1956) 135
Anatomy of a Murder (1959) 192
Anderson, Lindsay 5
Angel Face (1952) 194
Angels with Dirty Faces (1938) 140
Anna Christie (1930) 50, 53
Anna Karenina (1935) 53
Arch of Triumph (1948) 130
Arlen, Harold 75
Arlen, Richard 36, 37
Arliss, George 77, 138
Arsenic and Old Lace 154
Arthur, Jean 72, 129, 153, 198
Arzner, Dorothy 96
As You Desire Me (1932) 51
As You Like It 104
Astaire, Fred 118
Astor, Mary 33, 170, 216
Atwill, Lionel 70
Au Hasard Balthazar (1966) 163
Autumn Leaves (1956) 123
Autumn Sonata (1978) 135, 136
The Awful Truth (1937) 149, 150
Ayres, Lew 48

Bacall, Lauren 19, 189, 191

Bach, Steven 58
Bacharach, Burt 73
Bachardy, Don 45
The Bachelor and the Bobby-Soxer (1947) 154
Bad Day at Black Rock (1955) 183
The Bad Sister (1931) 77, 91, 186
Ball, Lucille 124
Balzac, Honoré de 56, 76
Band of Angels (1957) 175
Bankhead, Tallulah 94, 158, 196, 200, 211
Banton, Travis 66
Barr, Jeanne 108
The Barretts of Wimpole Street (1934) 157, 162
Barrie, J.M. 98, 100
Barry, Philip 95
Barrymore, Drew 33
Barrymore, Ethel 33, 34
Barrymore, John 29-34, 48, 50, 95, 116, 140, 159
Barrymore, Lionel 17, 25, 33, 52, 54, 117
Barthelmess, Richard 11, 75
Barthes, Roland 46, 197
Baryshnikov, Mikhail 75
Bast, Bill 221
The Battle of Elderbush Gulch (1913) 7
Baxter, Anne 31
Beat the Devil (1954) 190
Beatty, Warren 111
Beau Brummel (1924) 33
Beery, Wallace 22, 116
Beggars of Life (1928) 36
Bellamy, Ralph 151
Belle de Jour (1967) 41
The Bells of St. Mary's 130
The Beloved Rogue (1927) 31
Benchley, Robert 107
Benderson, Bruce 125
Bening, Annette 111
Bennett, Constance 149
Bennett, Joan 148, 178
Berg, Scott 111
Bergman, Ingmar 135, 136

225

Index

Bergman, Ingrid 127–136, 146, 153, 188, 189, 205
Bernhardt, Sarah 1–2
Berserk (1968) 120
The Best of Everything (1959) 124
Beyond the Forest (1949) 81, 86
Beyond the Rocks (1922) 23
Bickford, Charles 51
Big Brown Eyes (1936) 148
The Big Lift (1950) 204
The Big Parade (1924) 13
The Big Sleep (1946) 189, 191
A Bill of Divorcement (1932) 32, 95, 96
The Birds (1963) 15
The Birth of a Nation (1915) 7
The Bishop's Wife (1947) 154
Black Legion (1937) 186, 190
Blonde Crazy (1931) 138, 139, 140, 197
Blonde Venus (1932) 67, 68, 145, 146, 151
Blondell, Joan 106, 138, 139, 143, 170, 197
Blood on the Sun (1945) 142
The Blue Angel (1930) 38, 59, 60, 61, 62, 65
Blyth, Ann 119
Bogart, Humphrey 104, 105, 184–191, 199
La Bohème 13, 20, 43, 55, 83
Booth, Edwin 29
Borden, Lizzie 16
Bordertown (1935) 80, 82
Borzage, Frank 71, 113, 179, 192, 219
Boy Meets Girl (1938) 140
Boyer, Charles 19, 48, 98, 135
Boys Town (1938) 180
Brando, Marlon 1–2, 31, 34, 134, 135, 167, 192–198, 201, 207, 212, 216, 220, 221
Brazzi, Rossano 106
Break of Hearts (1934) 98, 99
Breakfast at Tiffany's (1961) 197
Brecht, Bertolt 164
Brennan, Walter 202
Brent, George 77
Bresson, Robert 163
The Bride Came C.O.D. (1941) 81
The Bride Wore Red (1937) 118
Bringing Up Baby (1938) 2, 101, 149, 150, 151
Broken Blossoms (1919) 10, 14, 217
Brook, Clive 66
Brooks, Louise 9, 35–45, 49, 58, 62, 94, 114, 129, 184, 210
Brooks, Richard 88
The Brothers Karamazov 11
Brown, Clarence 50, 53
Brown, Rowland 178
Brownlow, Kevin 37
Bruggeman, George 159
Brynner, Yul 75
Bunny O'Hare (1971) 90, 109

Buñuel, Luis 41, 65
Burke, Billie 17, 96
Burnett, Carol 21
Burr, Raymond 205
Byron, Walter 26

The Cabin in the Cotton (1932) 77, 78
Café Electric (1927) 59
Cagney (book, 1997) 139
Cagney, James 1–2, 32, 43, 78, 95, 137–143, 146, 161, 166, 177, 186, 188, 196, 201, 202, 220, 221
The Caine Mutiny (1954) 184, 190
The Call of the Wild (1935) 174
Callow, Simon 160, 165
Camille (1936) 54, 83
The Canary Murder Case (1929) 38, 41
Canty, Marietta 220
Capote, Truman 190
Capra, Frank 88, 154, 172, 192, 193
Captains Courageous (1937) 180
Card, James 44
Carroll, Nancy 147
Casablanca (1942) 129, 184, 188
Cassavetes, John 191
Castle, William 124
The Catered Affair (1956) 87, 88
Catherine Was Great 69
Cavett, Dick 93
Cenere (Ashes) (1915) 3, 217
Chaney, Lon 114, 137
Charade (1963) 155
The Chase (1966) 197
Chatterton, Ruth 77
Chayefsky, Paddy 211
Checkmate 168
Chekhov, Anton 16, 208
Cherrill, Virginia 147
Chevalier, Maurice 64, 75
Christopher Strong (1933) 96, 100
The Circle (1925) 113
City for Conquest (1940) 141
Clair, René 42
Clarke, Mae 137
Clift, Montgomery 27, 198, 199–207, 212, 220
Clift, Sunny 199, 207
Clive, Colin 96, 100
The Coast of Folly (1924) 24
Coburn, Charles 85
The Cobweb (1955) 19
Coco (1969) 109
Cocteau, Jean 135
Cohan, George M. 141, 177
Cohen, Larry 91
Cohn, Harry 43, 210

Index

Colbert, Claudette 129, 173
Collier, Constance 95, 107
Collinge, Patricia 199
Colman, Ronald 13, 75
Commandos Strike at Dawn (1942) 17
Connecting Rooms (1970) 90
Conquest (1937) 56
Cooper, Gary 63, 71, 158, 192, 199
Cooper, Gladys 86
Cooper, Jackie 118
Coquette (1929) 26
Corey, Wendell 106
The Corn Is Green (1945) 86
Cornell, Katharine 196
Cortese, Valentina 177
Cortez, Stanley 165
Costello, Dolores 33
Cotton, Joseph 86
Counsellor at Law (1933) 34
Cousin Bette 76
Coward, Noel 145
Cowie, Peter 35
Crawford, Christina 112, 120, 125, 126
Crawford, Christopher 120
Crawford, Joan 25, 33, 52, 88, 89, 91, 95, 103, 110, 112–126, 129, 170, 171, 172, 181
Crisis (1950) 154
Crisp, Donald 10
Cromwell, James 211
Cromwell, John 211
Cukor, George 27, 32, 33, 54, 96, 100, 107, 110, 119, 129, 130, 144, 148, 182
Curtis, James 176
Curtis, Tony 155
Curtiz, Michael 78

Daisy Kenyon (1947) 120
Dallesandro, Joe 158
Dance, Fools, Dance (1931) 116, 170
Dancing Lady (1933) 118, 172
The Danger Girl (1916) 22
Dangerous (1935) 80, 81, 82
Daniell, Henry 55
Dark Victory (1939) 83, 187
Davies, Marion 16, 23, 45, 174
Davis, Bette 1–2, 5, 14, 19, 76–92, 41, 93, 94, 96, 100, 101, 102, 103, 110, 124, 126, 129, 187, 196, 198, 211, 221
Day, Doris 142, 155
Dean, James 185, 198, 203, 207, 215–222
Deception (1946) 86
de Havilland, Olivia 203
A Delicate Balance (1973) 109, 110, 213
Delsarte 6
DeMille, Cecil B. 22, 159
Deneuve, Catherine 41, 65

Dennis, Sandy 201, 218
De Sica, Vittorio 206
Desire (1936) 71
Désirée (1954) 197
Desk Set (1957) 106
Destination Tokyo (1944) 153
Destry Rides Again (1939) 71
Devil and the Deep (1932) 158, 159, 160
The Devil Is a Woman (1934) 69, 70
Diary of a Lost Girl (1929) 41, 42
Diessl, Gustav 40
Dieterle, William 59, 72
Dietrich, Marlene 38, 44, 56, 57, 58–75, 91, 111, 121, 129, 132, 146, 192, 194
Dinner at Eight (1933) 33
The Disappearance of Aimee (1976) 90
Dishonored (1931) 64, 68, 72
Dr. Jekyll and Mr. Hyde (1920) 31
Dr. Jekyll and Mr. Hyde (1941) 128, 181
A Doll's House 118
Don Juan (1926) 31
Donaldson, Maureen 146
Don't Change Your Husband (1919) 22
Dostoyevsky, Fyodor 11
Douglas, Kirk 75
Drake, Betsy 146, 154
Dresser, Louise 68
Dressler, Marie 31, 51
Dru, Joanne 202
Duchesse de Langeais 56
Duel in the Sun (1946) 17
Duell, Charles 18
Dunaway, Faye 120, 125
Duncan, Isadora 17
Dunne, Irene 129, 148, 149, 152, 198
Durbin, Deanna 164
Duse, Eleonora 1, 3, 6, 51, 217
Dwan, Allan 24

Eagels, Jeanne 25, 208
The Eagle and the Hawk (1933) 148
East of Eden (1955) 215, 217, 220
Eder, Shirley 122
Ekman, Gosta 128
Eliot, George 13
Empty Saddles (1936) 43
Eternal Love (1929) 31
Euripides 109
Europa '51 (1952) 127, 132, 134
Every Girl Should Be Married (1948) 154
Ex-Lady (1933) 78, 88

Fairbanks, Douglas 115
Fairbanks, Douglas Jr. 75, 115
Family Reunion (1981) 90
A Farewell to Arms (1932) 192

Farrell, Glenda 179
Fashions of 1934 78
Father of the Bride (1950) 182, 183
Father Takes a Wife (1941) 26
Fay, Frank 43
Fear (1954) 134
Female on the Beach (1955) 123
Feud: Bette and Joan 126
Fields, W.C. 37
The Fighting 69th (1940) 140
Fine Manners (1926) 25
Fitzgerald, F. Scott 44, 118
Fixed Bayonets (1951) 215
Flamingo Road (1949) 121
Flesh and the Devil (1926) 49
Fog Over Frisco (1934) 78
Fonda, Henry 82, 110, 168, 192, 193
Fontanne, Lynn 181, 200, 201
Foote, Horton 17, 208, 211,
Footlight Parade (1933) 140
For Whom the Bell Tolls (1943) 129
Forbes, Bryan 211
Ford, John 100, 178, 186, 193, 194
A Foreign Affair (1948) 72
Four Walls (1928) 114
Fox, Sidney 77
Frances (1982) 213
Francis, Kay 187
A Free Soul (1931) 171, 188
From Here to Eternity (1953) 205, 210
Front Page Woman (1935) 80
Fuller, Samuel 215
Fun in a Chinese Laundry (1965) 69
Fury (1936) 179, 183

Gabin, Jean 72, 75
Gable, Clark 116, 162, 170–175, 180, 188, 189, 199, 205, 207
Garbo, Greta 2, 30, 33, 44, 46–57, 67, 71, 73, 83, 91, 129, 172, 204
The Garden of Allah (1936) 71
Garfield, John 120
Gaslight (1944) 129
Genina, Augusto 42
Giant (1956) 220
Gielgud, John 16, 29, 30, 196
Gilbert, John 13, 48, 49, 52, 53, 56, 75, 114, 170
A Girl in Every Port (1928) 37
Gish, Dorothy 6, 9, 12, 166, 216
Gish, Lillian 2–3, 5–20, 24, 35, 41, 43, 44, 48, 51, 55, 62, 83, 91, 96, 103, 129, 131, 166, 210, 212, 217, 220
The Glass Menagerie (1973) 110
Glyn, Elinor 24
Godard, Jean-Luc 127, 151

The Goddess (1958) 210, 211
The Godfather (1972) 197
God's Gift to Women (1931) 43
Gone with the Wind (1939) 174, 175
Gordon, Ruth 97, 110
Goulding, Edmund 25, 114
Grace Quigley (1984) 111
Graham, Martha 37, 77
Grahame, Gloria 19, 121, 185
Grand Hotel (1932) 30, 33, 47, 50, 52, 55, 56, 116, 123
Grant, Cary 1–2, 94, 95, 101, 102, 130, 143, 144–156, 158, 161, 193, 194, 201, 202, 205, 218, 220, 221
The Great Moment (1921) 24
The Great Profile (1940) 31
The Greatest Question (1919) 11
The Greatest Thing in Life (1918) 9
Green, Sam 57
Grier, Pam 156
Griffith, D.W. 6–20, 49
Grubb, Davis 165
The Guardsman (1931) 201
Guess Who's Coming to Dinner (1967) 109, 183
Gunga Din (1939) 151
Guys and Dolls (1955) 197

Haines, William 114
Hamlet 34
Hamlet (1948) 167
Hanson, Lars 14, 15, 47, 49
Hard to Handle (1933) 140
Harding, Laura 95, 96
Harlow, Jean 43, 149, 170, 172
Harriet Craig (1950) 121
Harrington, Curtis 28
Harris, Julie 198, 217
Harris, Radie 118
Harron, Bobby 9
Harvey, Anthony 109
Harvey, James 197
Has Anybody Seen My Gal (1952) 215
Hawks, Howard 30, 37, 101, 144, 149, 151, 154, 189, 191, 202
Hayden, Sterling 122
Hayes, Helen 29, 172, 209
Hayward, Leland 95
Hearts of the World (1918) 8
Heflin, Van 120
The Heiress (1949) 203
Hellman, Lillian 85
Hemingway, Ernest 75
Henry V (1944) 167
Henry VI 29
Hepburn, Audrey 35, 129, 146, 197

Index

Hepburn, Katharine 1–2, 14, 32, 33, 71, 84, 93–111, 126, 129, 140, 146, 148, 150, 152, 156, 181, 183, 185, 190, 194, 198, 199, 210, 213, 218, 220, 221
High Noon (1952) 192
High Sierra (1941) 187
His Double Life (1933) 17
His Girl Friday (1940) 144, 151, 152
His Greatest Bluff (1927) 59
Hitchcock, Alfred 15, 66, 72, 130, 136, 144, 152, 154, 155, 163, 164, 193, 205
Hitler, Adolf 57
Hobson's Choice (1953) 165
Hold Your Man (1933) 172
Holden, William 21, 27
Holiday (1938) 101, 150
Holiday (play) 95
Hollander, Friedrich 72
Holliday, Judy 197
The Hollywood Revue of 1929 115
Holm, Celeste 88
Holman, Libby 204, 220
Hopkins, Miriam 83, 129, 204
Hopper, Dennis 219
Horn, Camilla 31
Hot Saturday (1932) 146, 147
A House Divided (1931) 77
Houseboat (1958) 146
Houseman, John 16
Housewife (1934) 80
Howard, Leslie 79, 171, 186
Howard, Sidney 164
Hughes, Howard 95
The Human Voice (1966) 135
Humoresque (1946) 120
The Hunchback of Notre Dame (1939) 157, 163
Hunter, Kim 217
Huppert, Isabelle 55
Hush ... Hush, Sweet Charlotte (1964) 89, 90
Huston, John 19, 81, 187
Huston, Walter 117, 141
Huysmans, J.K. 57

I, Claudius (1936) 163
I Confess (1953) 205
I Kiss Your Hand, Madame (1929) 59
I Saw What You Did (1965) 124
I Was a Male War Bride (1949) 154
Ibsen, Henrik 76, 118
I'm No Angel (1933) 148
In a Lonely Place (1950) 184, 185, 189
In Name Only 152
In This Our Life (1942) 81, 85, 88
Indiscreet (1931) 26

Indiscretion of an American Wife (1954) 206
Inge, William 208
Innocent Eyes 113
Intermezzo (1936) 127
Intermezzo (1939) 128
Intolerance (1916) 8
Inspiration (1931) 51
Ireland, John 202
Irving, Henry 29
Island of Lost Souls (1932) 157, 160, 163
It Happened One Night (1934) 172, 173, 174
It Pays to Advertise (1931) 43
It's a Wonderful Life (1946) 193
It's in the Air 59
It's the Old Army Game (1926) 37

Jaffe, Sam 68
Jamaica Inn (1939) 163
Jannings, Emil 60, 61, 62
Jenkins, Terry 168
Jezebel (1938) 81, 91
Jimmy the Gent (1934) 78
Joan Crawford: The Essential Biography (2002) 113
Joan of Arc (1948) 130
Joan of Arc at the Stake (1954) 133
Johnny Come Lately (1943) 140
Johnny Guitar (1954) 122, 123
Johnson, Edwin C. 131
Jolson, Al 122, 138
Jones, Jennifer 17, 129, 206
The Joyless Street (1924) 47
Juarez 83
Judgment at Nuremberg (1961) 206, 212
Julius Caesar (1953) 196
June Bride (1948) 81

Kanin, Garson 152
Karlin, Fred 90
Karloff, Boris 90
Kate: The Woman Who Was Hepburn (2006) 95
Kazan, Elia 182, 200, 215, 218
Kelly, Grace 146, 197
Kennedy, Arthur 61
Kennedy, Joseph 26
Kerr, Deborah 154, 204
Killer Bees (1974) 28
Kismet (1944) 72
The Kiss (1929) 50
Knight, Shirley 218
Knight Without Armor (1937) 71
Knox, Alexander 133
Kobal, John 130, 207, 210
Kortner, Fritz 38

Index

Kramer, Stanley 183, 206
Krampner, Jon 208

Ladd, Alan 219
The Lady Eve (1941) 103
Lady of the Night (1925) 113
Laemmle, Junior 77
The Lake 98, 107
Lamarr, Hedy 128
Lanchester, Elsa 165, 168
Landau, Martin 155
Landis, Jessie Royce 155
Lang, Fritz 61, 179, 193
Langdon, Harry 114
Lange, Jessica 126, 213
Langlois, Henri 44
La Rue, Jack 148
The Last Laugh (1924) 62
The Last Mile 171, 177
Last Tango in Paris (1972) 33, 197
Laughton, Charles 17, 157–169, 174, 213
Laurents, Arthur 105
Leacock, Richard 36, 41
Lean, David 105, 165
Lederer, Pepi 45
Leigh, Vivien 174, 196, 218
Lemmon, Jack 2
Leone, Sergio 193
The Letter (1929) 25
The Letter (1940) 1, 84, 87, 100
Letty Lynton (1932) 117
Levant, Oscar 19
Lewis, Bobby 200
Libeled Lady (1936) 180
Lion, Margo 59
The Lion in Winter (1968) 109
Listen to Me Marlon (2015) 2
Little, Rich 143
The Little Foxes (1941) 85
The Little Minister (1934) 98
The Little Napoleon (1923) 59
Little Women (1933) 97
Lloyd, Harold 150
Lodge, John 68
Lombard, Carole 129, 161, 164, 172, 175
London, Julie 192
The Lonely Life (1962) 76, 81
Long Day's Journey Into Night (1962) 107, 108, 183
Loren, Sophia 146
Lorre, Peter 167, 188
Louise, Anita 82
Love (1927) 49
Love, Montagu 15
Love Affair (1994) 111
Love Among the Ruins (1975) 110

Love 'Em and Leave 'Em (1926) 37, 129
Love Me or Leave Me (1955) 142
The Love of Sunya (1927) 25
Love Tragedy (1923) 59
Lubitsch, Ernst 71
Lulu in Berlin (1974) 36, 39
Lumet, Sidney 107
Lunt, Alfred 181, 200, 201
Lupino, Ida 166, 187
The Lusty Men (1952) 194
Loy, Myrna 33, 122, 129, 170, 198
Lulu in Hollywood 36

MacMurray, Fred 99
Maddin, Guy 127
Magnani, Anna 132, 135
The Magnificent Ambersons (1942) 165
Malaya (1949) 176, 177
Male and Female (1919) 23
The Maltese Falcon (1941) 187, 188
Mamoulian, Rouben 52
Man by the Roadside (1923) 59
Man of a Thousand Faces (1957) 137
Man of the West (1958) 192
The Man Who Came to Dinner (1942) 81
The Man Who Played God (1932) 77
Manhandled (1924) 24
Mankiewicz, Joseph 87, 154, 190
Mann, Anthony 192, 193
Mann, William 95
Manners, David 96, 100, 199
Man's Castle (1933) 179
Mansfield, Richard 29
March, Fredric 48
Mari, Febo 3
Marked Woman (1937) 81, 82, 84, 187
Marlene (1984) 62, 64, 73, 74
Marlene Dietrich's ABC (1961) 62
Marshall, George 38, 43
Marshall, Herbert 85
Marshall, Tully 26
Martin Roumagnac (1946) 72
Marx, Harpo 68
Mary of Scotland (1936) 100
Mason, James 56, 155, 196
Massey, Raymond 215, 218
Mata Hari (1931) 52
Matlock 57
A Matter of Time (1976) 135
Maugham, Somerset 79, 181
Mayer, Louis B. 48, 63
McCabe, John 139
McCarey, Leo 130, 136, 144, 149, 152, 154, 162
McCarthy, Kevin 204, 209
McDowall, Roddy 45

Index

Me and My Gal (1932) 178
Meir, Golda 136
The Men (1950) 1, 195
The Merchant of Venice 104
Method Actors (1991) 211
Methot, Mayo 187, 189
A Midsummer Night's Dream (1935) 140
Mildred Pierce (1945) 119
Milestone, Lewis 117
Millay, Edna St. Vincent 45
Miller, Walter 7
The Millionaire (1931) 138
The Millionairess 104
Mineo, Sal 219
Minnelli, Vincente 19, 104, 135, 182
Miranda, Isa 105
Les Misérables (1935) 157, 162
The Misfits (1961) 175, 206
Mr. Blandings Builds His Dream House (1948) 154
Mr. Deeds Goes to Town (1936) 192
Mr. Lucky (1943) 153
Mister Roberts (1955) 142
Mr. Skeffington (1944) 81
Mr. Smith Goes to Washington (1939) 193
Mistinguett 113
Mitchum, Robert 18, 165, 166, 167, 194
Mogambo (1953) 175
Mommie Dearest (book, 1978) 112
Mommie Dearest (film, 1981) 120, 125
Monkey Business (1952) 154
Monroe, Marilyn 62, 154, 155, 175, 207, 210, 215
Moore, Colleen 13
Morning Glory (1933) 97
Morocco (1930) 63, 64, 68, 192
The Mothering Heart (1913) 7
Movie Love in the Fifties (2001) 197
The Movies, Mr. Griffith, and Me 5
Murder on the Orient Express (1974) 135
Murnau, F.W. 62
Murray, Don 169
Murrow, Edward R. 75
Music in the Air (1934) 26
The Musketeers of Pig Alley (1912) 7
Mutiny on the Bounty (1935) 157, 159, 162, 174
My Dad Is 100 Years Old (2005) 127, 132
My Favorite Wife (1940) 152
My Mother's Keeper (1985) 91
My Voyage to Italy (1999) 127
My Way of Life (1971) 124
The Mysterious Lady (1928) 49

Naldi, Nita 32
Nall, Adeline 221
The Nanny (1966) 90
Nathan, George Jean 18
Navy Blue and Gold (1937) 193
Newman, Paul 145, 146
Nielsen, Asta 47
Night and Day (1946) 153
Night Nurse (1931) 171
The Night of the Hunter (1955) 17–20, 158, 165, 167, 194, 218
Ninotchka (1939) 55, 56, 71
No Man of Her Own (1932) 172
No More Ladies (1935) 118
None But the Lonely Heart (1944) 152
North by Northwest (1959) 155
Notorious (1946) 130, 134, 152
Notre Music (2004) 151
Novak, Kim 197
Novarro, Ramon 48, 52
Now, Voyager (1942) 77, 85, 86

Oberon, Merle 139
O'Brien, Pat 140
O'Casey, Sean 16
Odets, Clifford 120, 152
Of Human Bondage (1934) 79
Old Clothes (1925) 113
The Old Dark House (1932) 157
The Old Maid 83
Olivier, Laurence 26, 29, 30, 167, 168
On Golden Pond (1981) 110
On the Waterfront (1954) 196, 197
Once Upon a Honeymoon (1942) 153
Once Upon a Time in the West (1969) 193
One-Eyed Jacks (1961) 167, 197
One Romantic Night (1930) 16
One, Two, Three (1961) 142
O'Neill, Eugene 50, 107, 172, 178, 209
Only Angels Have Wings (1939) 151
Ophuls, Max 56
Orphans of the Storm (1921) 12
Orry-Kelly 145
Other Men's Women (1931) 138
Our Blushing Brides (1930) 115
Our Dancing Daughters (1928) 114, 115, 121
Overland Stage Raiders (1938) 43
Owsley, Monroe 78

Pabst, G.W. 35, 38, 41, 42, 45, 47
Page, Geraldine 17, 106, 160, 198, 218
Paid (1930) 115
The Painted Desert (1931) 170
Paisan (1946) 127
Palance, Jack 121
Paley, William 44
Pallette, Eugene 80
Pandora's Box (1929) 35, 38, 39, 40

Parachute Jumper (1933) 88
The Paradine Case (1947) 164
Paris, Barry 35, 46
Parker, Dorothy 98
Pat and Mike (1952) 105, 181
The Patsy (1928) 16
Payment Deferred (1932) 160
Penny Serenade (1941) 152
People Will Talk (1951) 154
A Perfect Understanding (1933) 26
Peter the Tramp (1922) 47
The Petrified Forest (1936) 81, 110, 186
The Philadelphia Story (1940) 1, 71, 102, 103, 152, 193
Piaf, Edith 75
A Piano for Mrs. Cimino (1982) 91
Piccadilly (1929) 158
Pickford, Mary 6, 24, 26, 35, 49, 115
Picture Snatcher (1933) 138
Pirandello, Luigi 22
Pitts, ZaSu 17, 113
Pittsburgh (1942) 62
A Place in the Sun (1951) 203, 204
Playmates (1941) 34
Plummer, Christopher 30
Pocketful of Miracles (1961) 88
Pollack, Sydney 212
Ponti, Carlo 146
Porter, Cole 153
Portman, Eric 209
Portrait of Jennie (1948) 17
A Portrait of Joan (1962)
Possessed (1931) 116, 117
Possessed (1947) 120
The Power and the Glory (1933) 179
Preminger, Otto 120, 168, 192
Presley, Elvis 215
Pretty Ladies (1925) 113
The Pride and the Passion (1957) 146
Prideaux, James 95
The Private Life of Henry VIII (1933) 157, 160
The Private Lives of Elizabeth and Essex 83
Prix de Beauté (1930) 42, 44
The Public Enemy (1931) 43, 137, 138, 139

Quality Street (1937) 100
Queen Bee (1955) 123
Queen Christina (1933) 52, 53
Queen Elizabeth (1912) 3
Queen Kelly (1929) 26
Quick Millions (1931) 178
Quirk, Lawrence J. 113

Ragtime (1981) 142
Rain (1932) 117

The Rainmaker (1956) 106
Rains, Claude 83, 90, 153
Raintree County (1957) 206
Rancho Notorious (1952) 61
Rapf, Harry 113
Rapper, Irving 86
Rasputin and the Empress (1932) 33
Rathbone, Basil 53
Ray, Nicholas 122, 142, 184, 218, 219
Reagan, Ronald 216
Rear Window (1954) 193
Rebel Without a Cause (1955) 185, 218, 219
Red Dust (1932) 170, 172
Red River (1948) 202
Reed, Donna 193, 205, 210
Reflections in a Golden Eye (1967) 31
Remarque, Erich Maria 75
Rembrandt (1936) 157, 163
Remick, Lee 206
Remodeling Her Husband (1920) 166
Renoir, Jean 164
Reynolds, Debbie 122
Rice, Elmer 34
Richardson, Ralph 204
Richardson, Tony 212, 213
Riva, Maria 58, 67, 74, 111
Rivette, Jacques 127
Roberts, Alice 39
Robertson, Cliff 123
Robinson, Edward G. 138
Rogers, Ginger 101, 129, 153
Rohmer, Eric 127
Romance (1930) 51, 52
A Romance of Happy Valley (1919) 9
Rome, Open City (1945) 127, 131
Romeo and Juliet (1936) 30
Romero, Cesar 70
Romola (1924) 13
Rooney, Mickey 140
Rooster Cogburn 110
Rossellini, Isabella 127, 132
Rossellini, Roberto 127, 131, 132, 133, 134, 136
Rostova, Mira 200, 204
Rowlands, Gena 90
Royce, Bill 146
Ruggles of Red Gap (1935) 157, 162
Run for Cover (1955) 142
Russell, Rosalind 2, 151

Sabrina (1954) 190
Sadie Thompson (1928) 25
The Saga of Gosta Berling (1924) 47, 48
Saint, Eva Marie 155, 196, 217
St. Denis, Ruth 35
The St. Louis Kid (1934) 140

Sally, Irene and Mary (1925) 114
Salome (1953) 164
San Francisco (1936) 180
Sanders, George 133
Saratoga Trunk (1945) 129, 130
Sayonara (1957) 197
The Scapegoat (1959) 88
The Scarlet Empress (1934) 68
The Scarlet Letter (1926) 13, 16, 20
Schell, Maximilian 73, 74
Schopenhauer, Arthur 36
Schulberg, B.P. 38
The Scientific Cardplayer (1972) 90
Scofield, Paul 110
Scott, Randolph 146, 147, 152
The Sea Beast (1926) 33
Sea of Grass (1947) 182
Séance on a Wet Afternoon (1964) 210, 211
The Search (1948) 200, 201
The Searchers (1956) 194
Seed (1931) 77
Selznick, David 17, 95, 129
Sennett, Mack 22
Seven Sinners (1940) 71
Seymour, Clarine 10
Shakespeare, William 16, 118
Shall, Theo 51
Shanghai Express (1932) 66
Shawn, Ted 35
She Done Him Wrong (1933) 147
Shearer, Norma 99, 113, 119, 162, 170, 171, 172, 174, 188
Sheridan, Ann 141
Sheridan, Dizzy 221
Sherman, Vincent 86
Short, Martin 201
Short Cut to Hell (1957) 166
The Show of Shows (1929) 29
The Show-Off (1926) 37
Show People (1928) 23
Sieber, Rudi 59
Siegmann, George 7
Sidney, Sylvia 142, 148
The Sign of the Cross (1932) 157, 159
Sills, Milton 24
Sinatra, Frank 75, 175, 189
Singin' in the Rain (1952) 31
Sinners' Holiday (1930) 138
Sirk, Douglas 215
Sjöström, Victor 14, 15, 18
The Skin of Our Teeth 200
Smart Money (1931) 138
Smith, Ludlow Ogden 94
So Big! (1932) 77
Some Like It Hot (1959) 155
Something to Sing About (1937) 140

Sondheim, Stephen 45
Spartacus (1960) 168
Special Agent (1935) 80
Spellbound (1945) 130
Spitfire (1934) 98, 110
Spring Fever (1927) 114
Stage Door (1937) 95, 100, 107
Stage Fright (1950) 66, 72
Stage Struck (1924) 24
Stagecoach (1939) 193
Stahl, John M. 77
Stanislavski 2
Stanley, Kim 2, 198, 208–214, 218
Stanwyck, Barbara 77, 81, 84, 94, 101, 102, 103, 110, 116, 122, 126, 171, 192, 198, 220
The Star (1952) 87, 88
State of the Union (1948) 104, 106
Steele, Alfred 123, 124, 125
Steiger, Rod 216
Steiner, Max 82, 90
Sternberg, Josef von 38, 45, 58–75, 132, 145, 163
Stevens, George 220
Stevens, Ruthelma 69
Stevenson, Adlai 75
Stewart, James 75, 176, 192
Stiller, Mauritz 47
Stine, Whitney 90
Stockwell, Dean 108
Storm Center (1956) 88
Story of O 6
Strait-Jacket (1964) 120
Strange Interlude (1932) 172
Strangers: The Story of a Mother and Daughter (1979) 90
Strasberg, Lee 120, 196, 208, 209
Strauss, Richard 28
The Strawberry Blonde (1941) 141
Streep, Meryl 160
A Streetcar Named Desire (1951) 1, 195
Stroheim, Erich von 26
Stromboli (1950) 131, 132, 134
Sturges, Preston 104, 148
Sudden Fear (1952) 121
Suddenly, Last Summer (1959) 106, 108, 206
Sullavan, Margaret 146, 199
Summertime (1955) 105, 106, 111
Summerville, Slim 77
Sunset Boulevard (1950) 21, 27, 28
Susan and God (1940) 119
Susan Lenox: Her Fall and Rise (1931) 51, 171
The Suspect (1944) 165
Suspicion (1941) 152
Suzy (1936) 149
Svengali (1931) 33

Swanson, Gloria 21–28, 35
Swanson on Swanson (1980) 26
Sylvia Scarlett (1936) 100, 148

Tales of Manhattan (1942) 164
The Talk of the Town (1942) 153
Tallichet, Margaret 83
The Taming of the Shrew 104
Taxi! (1932) 140
Taylor, Elizabeth 203, 204, 206, 220
Taylor, Kent 148
Taylor, Laurette 214
Taylor, Robert 48, 54, 55
Teddy at the Throttle (1917) 22
Tempest (1928) 31, 32
The Temptress (1926) 48
Terrible Joe Moran (1984) 142
Thalberg, Irving 13, 54, 55
That Touch of Mink (1962) 155
That's Entertainment III (1994) 122
They Knew What They Wanted (1940) 164
Thirty Day Princess (1934) 148
This Is the Night (1932) 145
This Land Is Mine (1943) 164
The Time of the Cuckoo 105
The Time of Your Life (1948) 140
To Catch a Thief (1955) 154
To Have and Have Not (1944) 184, 189
To Kill a Mockingbird (1962) 212
Tone, Franchot 80, 118
Tonight or Never (1931) 26
Topaze (1933) 33
Topper (1937) 149
Torch Song (1953) 121, 122
Tosca 3
Touch of Evil (1958) 65
Tracy, Lee 33
Tracy, Spencer 78, 103, 104, 106, 109, 176–183, 199
Tramp, Tramp, Tramp (1926) 114
Treadwell, Sophie 170
The Treasure of the Sierra Madre (1948) 184, 189
The Trespasser (1929) 22, 26
The Trip to Bountiful (1953) 17
Tristana (1970) 65
Trog (1970) 109, 124
The Trojan Women (1971) 109
True Heart Susie (1919) 9, 14, 51
Truffaut, François 127
The Turn of the Screw (1959) 135
Turner, Lana 175
Twelfth Night 104
Twentieth Century (1934) 30
20,000 Years in Sing Sing (1932) 78, 178

Two-Faced Woman (1941) 56
Tynan, Kenneth 35, 46, 60

Ullmann, Liv 135
Under Capricorn (1949) 130, 131, 134, 135
Under the Lash (1921) 24
Undercurrent (1946) 104, 194
The Unforgiven (1960) 19
The Unknown (1927) 114, 121
The Unseen Enemy (1912) 7
Untamed (1929) 115
Up the River (1930) 178, 186
Ustinov, Peter 165

Valentino, Rudolph 23, 170
Velez, Lupe 34
Der Verlorene (1951)
Vertigo (1958) 193
Vidal, Gore 83
Vidor, King 13, 16, 17, 18, 23, 81, 87, 181
Vineberg, Steve 211
The Virgin Queen (1955) 87
Visconti, Luchino 134
Viva Zapata! (1952) 196
Voyage in Italy (1954) 133

Wallis, Hal 110
Walsh, Raoul 25, 141, 175, 178, 187
Walthall, Henry B. 14
Wanger, Walter 37, 63
Warner, Jack 79
The Warrior's Husband 95
Waters, John 125
Waxman, Franz 27
Way Down East (1920) 11
Wayne, John 43, 72, 110, 167, 193, 194, 202, 203
A Wedding (1978) 19
Wedding Present 148
Wedekind, Franz 35, 38
Welles, Orson 65, 165
Wellman, William 36, 37, 43, 138
West, Mae 69, 147, 148, 149
West Point (1927) 114
Wexley, John 177
Whale, James 159
The Whales of August (1987) 5, 19, 91
What Ever Happened to Baby Jane? (1962) 88, 124
Wheel of Fortune 57
When a Man Loves (1927) 31
When You're in Love (1937) 43
White, Christine 221
White Heat (1949) 141
White Mama (1980) 91
Wild River (1960) 206

The White Sister (1923) 12
The White Sister (1933) 172
White Woman (1933) 161, 164
Whitewater 110
Wicked Stepmother (1989) 91
Widmark, Richard 19
The Wild Duck 76
The Wild One (1953) 196, 197
Wild Orchids (1929) 50
Wilder, Billy 21, 26, 72, 73, 142, 155, 165, 190
Wilder, Thornton 200
Williams, Hope 95
Williams, Tennessee 106, 206, 212, 214
The Wind (1928) 13, 16, 20
Windust, Bretaigne 86
Windy Reilly Goes Hollywood (1931) 43
Winners of the Wilderness (1927) 114
Winters, Shelley 166, 205, 218
Witness for the Prosecution (1957) 73, 165
The Wizard of Beverly Grove (2006) 146
The Woman Accused (1933) 148
A Woman Called Golda (1982) 136
A Woman of Affairs (1928) 50, 56

Woman of the Year (1942) 103, 181
The Woman One Longs For (1929) 59, 60
A Woman Rebels (1936) 100
A Woman's Face (1941) 119
The Women (1939) 119
Wood, Natalie 216, 219
Wood, Sam 23, 129
Wyler, William 76, 77, 81, 82, 83, 84, 92, 203, 204
Wyman, Jane 72

Yankee Doodle Dandy (1942) 141, 177
You Only Live Once (1937) 193
Young, Loretta 174, 179, 207
Young, Roland 17
Young, Stark 29
Young Bess (1953) 164
The Young Lions (1958)

Zaza (1923) 24
Zinnemann, Fred 210
Zukor, Adolph 3